THERE IS A GUNMAN
ON CAMPUS

TRAGEDY
AND TERROR AT
VIRGINIA TECH

THERE IS A GUNMAN ON CAMPUS

BEN AGGER and TIMOTHY W. LUKE

ROWMAN & LITTLEFIELD PUBLISHERS, INC.
Lanham • Boulder • New York • Toronto • Plymouth, UK

ROWMAN & LITTLEFIELD PUBLISHERS, INC.

Published in the United States of America
by Rowman & Littlefield Publishers, Inc.
A wholly owned subsidiary of The Rowman & Littlefield Publishing Group, Inc.
4501 Forbes Boulevard, Suite 200, Lanham, Maryland 20706
www.rowmanlittlefield.com

Estover Road
Plymouth PL6 7PY
United Kingdom

Copyright © 2008 by Rowman & Littlefield Publishers, Inc.

All rights reserved. No part of this publication may be reproduced, stored in a retrieval system, or transmitted in any form or by any means, electronic, mechanical, photocopying, recording, or otherwise, without the prior permission of the publisher.

British Library Cataloguing in Publication Information Available

Library of Congress Cataloging-in-Publication Data:

There is a gunman on campus : tragedy and terror at Virginia Tech / [edited by] Ben Agger and Timothy W. Luke.
   p. cm.
   Includes bibliographical references and index.
   ISBN-13: 978-0-7425-6129-8 (cloth : alk. paper)
   ISBN-10: 0-7425-6129-1 (cloth : alk. paper)
   ISBN-13: 978-0-7425-6130-4 (pbk. : alk. paper)
   ISBN-10: 0-7425-6130-5 (pbk. : alk. paper)
   1. Virginia Tech Shootings, Blacksburg, Va., 2007. 2. School shootings—Virginia—Blacksburg. 3. Campus violence—Virginia—Blacksburg. 4. Cho, Seung-Hui, 1984–2007. 5. Virginia Polytechnic Institute and State University—Students. I. Agger, Ben. II. Luke, Timothy W.
   HV6534.B53T44 2008
   364.152'309755785—dc22   2007050907

Printed in the United States of America

∞™ The paper used in this publication meets the minimum requirements of American National Standard for Information Sciences—Permanence of Paper for Printed Library Materials, ANSI/NISO Z39.48-1992.

CONTENTS

Preface		vii
CHAPTER 1	April 16, 2007, at Virginia Tech—To: Multiple Recipients: "A Gunman Is Loose on Campus . . ." *Timothy W. Luke*	1
CHAPTER 2	Media Spectacle and the "Massacre at Virginia Tech" *Douglas Kellner*	29
CHAPTER 3	Mediated Ritual on Academic Ground *Neal King*	55
CHAPTER 4	Profiling School Shooters and Shooters' Schools: The Cultural Contexts of Aggrieved Entitlement and Restorative Masculinity *Michael Kimmel*	65
CHAPTER 5	"Victims Sought in Next Week's Shooting" *William Ayers*	79
CHAPTER 6	"We Are All Seung-Hui Cho!": American Social Psychosis and the Virginia Tech Killings *Stephen Pfohl*	93

CHAPTER 7	Satire, Guns, and Humans: Lessons from the Nacirema *Steve Kroll-Smith and Gwen Hunnicutt*	105
CHAPTER 8	S/he's Lost Control?: Damaging a Body of Knowledge. *Tara Brabazon*	119
CHAPTER 9	When Rhetoric Fails: The Heroic Teacher and the Basic Communications Course *Matthew Levy*	141
CHAPTER 10	There Is an Unknown on Campus: From Normative to Performative Violence in Academia *Patricia Mooney Nickel*	159
CHAPTER 11	The April 16 Archive: Collecting and Preserving Memories of the Virginia Tech Tragedy *Brent K. Jesiek and Jeremy Hunsinger*	185
CHAPTER 12	Colonization and Massacres: Virginia Tech, Jamestown, Korea, and Iraq *Roxanne Dunbar-Ortiz*	207
CHAPTER 13	All The Rage: Digital Bodies and Deadly Play in the Age of the Suicide Bomber *Carolyn Guertin*	213
CHAPTER 14	Is Virginia Tech an Exception? *Stanley Aronowitz*	229
CHAPTER 15	Baudrillard (1929–2007) & Mao: A History of Normal Violence *Charles Lemert*	235
CHAPTER 16	Cho, Not Che?: Positioning Blacksburg in the Political *Ben Agger*	243

About the Contributors 251
Index 255

| PREFACE

On the morning of April 16, 2007, one of us was in the Dallas area, watching the Boston Marathon on television. The other was on the Virginia Tech campus, working in his office. One building over and down the street, a troubled undergraduate student, Seung-Hui Cho, had just entered a classroom in Norris Hall after chaining the building's doors shut so that students and staff could not escape. In various engineering and foreign language courses, the students and their professors were meeting for their regular classes. Cho then entered several second-floor classrooms, one after another, and proceeded to kill with two semiautomatic handguns nearly three dozen people, including himself. Ultimately, thirty-three students and faculty members died in the onslaught, although some victims barricaded the doors of their classrooms and survived. Most notably, a seventy-six-year-old engineering professor, Liviu Librescu, a Romanian Jew who survived the Holocaust, blocked the door into his classroom. He stood against the door long enough for most of his fifteen students to escape through second-story windows, but then he was killed as Cho shot through the door. Twenty-six others were wounded by gunfire or injured during their escape, but most have recovered from these bodily wounds.

Both of us found out almost immediately about these events. One of us was far removed from the scene, while the other, although quite close, did not know much more than what was being reported on CNN and the national television networks. Only later could we begin to piece together what actually happened on that cold April day. We are all still learning about these events, and we may never know everything, especially because the shooter took his own life.

The shooter, a troubled Korean American student, was a mysterious figure surviving at the margins of student life on the Virginia Tech campus.

Some of his classmates and teachers feared him. A few tried to help, albeit to no avail. Bigger questions arise. Was he insane? Was he evil? Was he more like us than we care to admit? Could he have been stopped and perhaps redirected? Are universities responsible for finding and dealing with such figures before they erupt? Is a gun culture the problem here? Are Columbines and now Virginia Techs inevitable? Did the media fuel the frenzy? Should students and their instructors arm themselves or at least prepare for effective self-defense? Did the shooter's troubles begin in, or even before, high school? Did he have difficulty assimilating to American culture and then to the familiar "Big State U" football/fraternity culture of Virginia Tech? Was that April day in Blacksburg a metaphor about global modernity, contemporary higher education, or the United States of America in the twenty-first century? And, if so, then a metaphor of what?

In this collection of essays, our authors address these and many other questions. Some of our contributors are leading intellectuals who frequently offer their wisdom about issues of the day. Others are fresh new voices, just out of graduate school. Our perspectives are diverse. There is disagreement as well as consensus on certain issues. Some of the authors have worked at Virginia Tech for many years or just were passing through last year. Some are from other American universities. We also have international perspectives, and the clarity that such distance sometimes brings.

Several of these essays were first published online in a special issue of the journal *Fast Capitalism*, which can be found at www.fastcapitalism.com. These essays have been revised, and new ones added, to form this longer volume. The immediate theoretical interventions from late last spring in *Fast Capitalism*'s online electronic format with its hypertextual links and layered illustrations now come together here with much more new material as a print document. Both works are meant to record a wide range of reflections about an event that many public intellectuals and social scientists will explore for years to come.

Whether it was experienced "onsite" in Blacksburg or elsewhere "live on CNN," the April 16 shootings were very much a real-time media spectacle whose framing, narrative, perspective, and tone soon became almost at one with the crime itself. In turn, a continuing miniseries of forensic investigations, official inquiries, and popular commemorations about what exactly happened in West Ambler Johnston and Norris Halls that wintry spring day in Blacksburg has continued throughout the ensuing year. Like the Columbine attacks, this event will remain in the limelight for years to come. In one way or another, each of the authors in this volume is aware of the importance of reconsidering these complex events in the spirit of C. Wright Mills's "sociological imagination" (1959). The psychosocial anomie of Seung-

Hui Cho, his journey through the Virginia mental health system, the workings of higher education in the United States, and the mass media's coverage of brutal violence all bring together what Mills (1959:8) regarded as the turbulent confluence of contradictions running along within human thought and action as one peers "between 'the personal troubles of milieu' and 'the public issues of social structure'" in the United States.

Although he wrote his critique fifty years ago, C. Wright Mills speaks to the trying condition of many individuals, like Cho and so many others who had dealt with him across Virginia in his hometown and in Blacksburg, today in the 2000s. Indeed, Mills's call for sociological imagination recognizes that too many people today, as they did during the 1950s, "often feel their private lives are a series of traps," and that "within their everyday worlds, they cannot overcome their troubles" (1959:3). Often never sensing, whether it is inchoately or perhaps insightfully, that larger historical changes, institutional contradictions, and public threats somehow are usually at the deepest roots of their troubled awareness, "the more aware they become ... the more trapped they seem to feel" (Mills 1959:3).

As case studies of how the sociological imagination can work, these essays return to the April 16 Virginia Tech shootings to say something significant about the structure of American society, its shifting place in global history, and the characteristics of its people as they live and work today. And, in taking up the critical categories of sociological imagination, it clearly is the case that "an orientation to the present as history is sought" (Mills 1959:15) by all of the authors here. It is also their common resolve "to pay closer, and yet more imaginative, attention to the social routines and catastrophes which reveal (and which shape) man's nature in this time of civil unrest and ideological conflict" (Mills 1959:15). The range of opinion expressed is, therefore, intense, contestable, and wide. No matter how painful or critical, each account nonetheless needs to be listened to very attentively if we are to begin to hear what is now afoot in changes unfolding all around us. Like Virginia Governor Tim Kaine, each author here "knew it was critical to seek answers to the many questions" (2007:iii) rising from this tragic crime; and, like the members of the Commonwealth's Virginia Tech Review Panel, the authors ask the reader, again as Governor Kaine suggests about the review panel report, "to study" this collection of responses "carefully" to begin to assay key troubles and critical issues now challenging this society.

Above all, we agree that something important happened at Virginia Tech, something that discloses disturbing truths about America today. We also agree that the trouble started before the shooter entered the university, and we concur that the troubles are not over. These thoughts and reactions are entirely each author's own views; they do not constitute an official statement or offer any final words. Instead, we all want to help prevent future massacres. In order to help, however, we must name the problem. This book represents our efforts to do so. As such, we merely hope to first open a sustained discussion.

As we were preparing this book for publication, "Virginia Tech" happened all over again, on Valentine's Day, February 14, 2008. Steven Kazmierczak reportedly shot and killed five students, and then turned a weapon on himself at Northern Illinois University in DeKalb, Illinois. At least twenty other students were wounded in the rapid-fire shootings in a large NIU lecture hall during class. We have few certain details about the shooter, except that he used four weapons, two of which were purchased legally within the previous week—a shotgun and a 9mm Glock semi-automatic handgun. Ironically, he purchased two magazines and a holster for the Glock from the same online vendor that sold Cho, the Virginia Tech shooter, one of his guns through a dealer transfer last spring.

How are we to understand the sequencing and connections among Columbine, Virginia Tech, Tuusula, Finland, and now Northern Illinois? It is unimaginable that the Valentine Day's Massacre in DeKalb would have occurred in the way that it did, at least in part, without Virginia Tech having occurred, as the December school shootings in Finland also demonstrated. The April 2007 attack in Blacksburg is imbedded in DeKalb as its prototype and possibility. Kazmierczak might have found other ways to kill and to die without the example of Tech (and Columbine or Tuusula before it), but he surely framed his actions on Valentine's Day within the scenario of last spring at Virginia Tech.

What did the various shooters Klebold, Harris, Cho, Auvinen, and Kazmierczak have in common that led them to enact these epic killings and suicides, on school grounds? It seems they were alone in a crowd; they were alienated, lacking social ties. Whether they were mentally ill or not is somewhat beside the point. They might have been stopped, helped, redirected—yes, even medicated. We are intensely interested in the experience of being so alone in a crowd, in Cho's case as an Asian-American outsider on a big-time college/fraternity campus, which considers itself the homeland for a 'Hokie Nation,' —the illusion of tight community achieved through the gridiron *Gemeinschaft* shared by many on the Virginia Tech campus. And in the hours after the NIU attack, the response in DeKalb, Illinois, and around the nation was to appeal to the school's athletic mascot, the Huskie, and tout "Huskie Spirit." Perhaps we know only this: people more on the inside do not tend to commit mass murder and then take their own lives.

Were the killers evil madmen predestined to wreck havoc? Were they beyond social influence and redirection? They committed mad acts, to be sure. But there is a thin boundary between those who keep their demons within, and at bay, and those who erupt. The answer to these acts of deliberate madness lies not in armoring our campuses but in acknowledging people's interior turmoil and trying to help, where possible. This is difficult amid a sea of faces in large college lecture halls. But can we afford to reduce such acts merely to irreversible psychopathology? Columbine and Virginia Tech have now become a set piece—a media spectacle—with a certain inexorable momentum. Campus killings have become viral. Thus, we need to dig deeply into what happened at Virginia Tech in order to short-circuit these seemingly self-reproducing horrors.

Ben Agger
Tim Luke
March 1, 2008

References

Kaine, Governor Timothy M. 2007. "Foreword," *Mass Shootings at Virginia Tech: Report of the Review Panel, August 2007*. www.governor.virginia.gov/tempContent/techPanelReport.cfm

Mills, C. Wright. 1959. *The Sociological Imagination*. New York: Oxford University Press.

CHAPTER One

APRIL 16, 2007 AT VIRGINIA TECH—TO: MULTIPLE RECIPIENTS:
"A Gunman Is Loose on Campus..."

Timothy W. Luke

Monday, April 16, 2007, dawned coldly in Blacksburg, Virginia. This reflection about that terrible day for Virginia Tech is difficult to write, but something must be written. Universities work best when they are free, open, and untrammeled sites for intellectual growth, constant learning, and scholarly inquiry. This has been true at this university, and it remains the case in many places around the world. Because of April 16, there will be constant, strong, and understandable calls to abridge, if not, constrain these conditions, through expanded policing and constant surveillance.

To admit they are understandable, however, is not to agree that they are acceptable. Indeed, they could lead to overcompensating police measures that no outstanding university should tolerate as well as create a far more restrictive academic setting for teaching and learning that I would not wish to experience. Careful consideration of the violent events of that day, therefore, must defend, fully and forthrightly, the place of every university to serve as a free and open site for scholarship and study. Here is my effort to meet that task. While I have had many people at the university read through this account, my observations about April 16, and this analysis of what occurred here on that day, as well as many of the days since that event, represent only my personal perspective on many of the contradictory issues involved rather than an official statement of any sort. Many official statements already have been issued from the president of the United States to the governor of the Commonwealth to the president, Board of Visitors, and various faculty, staff, and student organizations here at the university. More official findings and statements will be forthcoming in the months to come; so this is just one study of the April 16 events and their aftermath.

The April 16 Events

After a night of intense blustery winds, the weather outlook from Roanoke television stations promised light snow and more gusts of high wind in Blacksburg. As usual, I drove to the office before 6:30 AM, crossing Washington Street (about a quarter mile east of where the West Ambler Johnston Residence Hall sits) on my way to campus; once there, I parked on Drillfield Drive, 120 yards or so down from Norris Hall. I had several sessions with graduate students and a long executive committee meeting for the School of Public and International Affairs down on my calendar for this date. It was to be a long hard day, but I did not know how long and hard it would be until after my first advising session about how to ready an M.A. thesis for its oral defense ended just at 9:30 AM.

Checking through my e-mail, which had been stacking up as my coworker and students got to campus after 8:00 AM, this message popped up:

> Date: Mon, 16 Apr 2007 09:26:24 -0400
> From: Unirel@vt.edu
> Subject: Shooting on campus.
> To: Multiple recipients <LISTSERV@LISTSERV.VT.EDU>
>
> A shooting incident occurred at West Ambler Johnston earlier this morning. Police are on the scene and are investigating.
>
> The university community is urged to be cautious and are asked to contact Virginia Tech Police if you observe anything suspicious or with information on the case. Contact Virginia Tech Police at 231-6411.
>
> Stay attuned to the www.vt.edu. We will post as soon as we have more information.
>
> http://april16archive.org/object/62.

This news was troubling. The bad grammar and misspellings all signaled haste, worry, even panic.

It also triggered memories of another bad morning months earlier. The first day of school in the 2006 Fall semester was disrupted terribly by a police man hunt; and, much of that effort came in an area of campus very close to West Ambler (not Amber) Johnston. Still, this area was over half-a-mile away, so I just waited for more news and e-mail alerts. Then many wailing sets of sirens—police cars, SWAT vans, EMS trucks—began converging outside my office as scores of officers ran up Old Turner Street, a dead-end, short side-street, across from my building on Stanger Street. Another far more disturbing e-mail popped up on the screen:

Date: Mon, 16 Apr 2007 09:50:07 -0400
From: Unirel@vt.edu
Subject: PLease stay put
To: Multiple recipients <LISTSERV@LISTSERV.VT.EDU>

A gunman is loose on campus. Stay in buildings until further notice. Stay away from all windows.
http://april16archive.org/object/62.

More strongly, this text soon became a voice message broadcast over the emergency alert system; the terse warning echoed off buildings in the wind for many minutes. Of course, then, many people then went to the windows, looking for the gunman. Others, who were eager to observe the flurry of police activity, or, who were hardy enough to brave the winds, then bundled up and left their offices to go see up close what was happening across Stanger Street. Within minutes, a more daunting e-mail came up in my in-box:

Date: Mon, 16 Apr 2007 10:16:40 -0400
From: Unirel@vt.edu
Subject: All Classes Canceled; Stay where you are
To: Multiple recipients <LISTSERV@LISTSERV.VT.EDU>

Virginia Tech has canceled all classes. Those on campus are asked to remain where there are, lock their doors, and stay away from windows.

Persons off campus are asked not to come to campus.
http://april16archive.org/object/62.

This message was quite ominous. Classes are rarely cancelled in Blacksburg, even on days with much rougher weather than April 16's. The note suggested a lockdown, quarantine, or hunkering down before some major lethal threat. Within the hour, we learned why that warning came as an e-mail relayed this news:

> Date: Mon, 16 Apr 2007 10:52:45 -0400
> From: Unirel@vt.edu
> Subject: Second Shooting Reported; Police have one gunman in custody
> To: Multiple recipients <LISTSERV@LISTSERV.VT.EDU>
>
> In addition to an earlier shooting today in West Ambler Johnston, there has been a multiple shooting with multiple victims in Norris Hall.
>
> Police and EMS are on the scene.
>
> Police have one shooter in custody and as part of routine police procedure, they continue to search for a second shooter.
>
> All people in university buildings are required to stay inside until further notice.
>
> All entrances to campus are closed.
> http://april16archive.org/object/62

Again, the poor diction, redundancies, and a terse tone were all fearsome. More ambulances, more police, more reporters kept arriving.[1] Then a single sentence came right during lunch:

> Date: Mon, 16 Apr 2007 12:15:57 -0400
> From: Unirel@vt.edu
> Subject: Counseling support available
> To: Multiple recipients <LISTSERV@LISTSERV.VT.EDU>
>
> Counseling is available in the Bowman Room in the Merriman Center (part of the athletic complex) for employees who seek assistance following today's events.
> http://april16archive.org/object/62

Coupled with fragmentary on-the-scene stand-ups being generated by local television stations from Roanoke, this announcement suggested an extremely severe incident was unfolding. Within a half hour, a brief statement was sent out by the university's president:

Date: Mon, 16 Apr 2007 12:41:44 -0400
From: Unirel@vt.edu
Subject: Statement by President Charles W. Steger
To: Multiple recipients <LISTSERV@LISTSERV.VT.EDU>

Shooting at Virginia Tech / Statement by President Charles W. Steger

The university was struck today with a tragedy of monumental proportions. There were two shootings on campus. In each case, there were fatalities. The university is shocked and horrified that this would befall our campus. I want to extend my deepest, sincerest and most profound sympathies to the families of these victims which include students There are 22 confirmed deaths.

We currently are in the process of notifying families of victims. The Virginia Tech Police are being assisted by numerous other jurisdictions. Crime scenes are being investigated by the FBI, University Police, and State Police. We continue to work to identify the victims impacted by this tragedy. I cannot begin to covey my own personal sense of loss over this senselessness of such an incomprehensible and heinous act The university will immediately set up counseling centers. So far centers have been identified in Ambler Johnson and the Cook Counseling Center to work with our campus community and families.

Here are some of the facts we know:

At about 7:15 a.m. this morning a 911 call came to the University Police Department concerning an event in West Amber Johnston Hall.
There were multiple shooting victims. While in the process of investigating, about two hours later the university received reports of a shooting in Norris Hall. The police immediately responded.
Victims have been transported to various hospitals in the immediate area in the region to receive emergency treatment.

We will proceed to contact the families of victims as identities are available.

All classes are cancelled and the university is closed for the remainder for the today. The university will open tomorrow at 8 a.m. but classes will be cancelled on Tuesday. The police are currently staging the release of people from campus buildings.

Families wishing to reunite with the students are suggested to meet at the Inn at Virginia Tech. We are making plans for a convocation tomorrow (Tuesday) at noon at Cassell Coliseum for the university community to come together to begin to deal with the tragedy.

http://april16archive.org/object/62

So within barely six hours of getting to work on April 16, we now knew this event was horrendous. I also feared its horrors would increase. They did.

With sharp bursts of high winds up to 50 MPH, and spinning flurries of snow with temperatures in the thirties skittered around our building, this April 16 morning was the sort of day that has earned Blacksburg one of its most common nicknames, "Bleaksburg." It rapidly became, however, its bleakest day after a silent solitary shooter—Seung-Hui Cho—allegedly slipped into West Ambler Johnston Residence Hall just past 7:00 AM and apparently shot a female student, Emily Hilscher, and Ryan Clark, a resident advisor in the dormitory. Running back to his room in nearby Harper Hall, he gathered up an overnight mail package that he sent to NBC News in New York from the downtown U.S. Post Office.

Then he made his way over to Norris Hall[2] on the north side of campus (where he was taking a sociology class, "Deviant Behavior," during Spring term). Once there, he chained the main exits shut, killed thirty more people, wounded dozens more, and then shot himself in the head as a police SWAT team closed their pursuit on him. Those who could ran outside, EMS units evacuated the wounded to three nearby hospital trauma centers, and swarms of police closed off and locked down all of Norris Hall as a crime scene.[3] For the rest of the day, and into the night, almost all of the thirty fallen lay where they were shot all around the building, awaiting identification and removal. Undoubtedly, for the officers on the scene, who were unable to touch the bodies (pending the visit by medical examiners), it was excruciating, since they had to listen helplessly as the cell phones of the dead rang incessantly as terrified relatives called their loved ones (Gangloff

2007:V1, 4). As many media reports noted, little could be bleaker than that frantic soundtrack floating over this scene of slaughter.

Violence, the Media, and America

On one level, events like the April 16 shootings are no longer a surprise (*Newsweek* 2007; *Time* 2007). Rampage shootings in America, whether they happen at a post office, cafeteria, office park, playground, high school, factory, college campus, stoplight, or commuter train, fascinate television audiences (Newman 2004). The fast capitalist media apparatus of 24/7 news, weather, sports, and other information has implicitly scripted attacks like these on its many screens of power for nearly four decades (Agger 1989; Luke 1989). The shock and horror of August 1, 1966, when Charles Whitman shot and killed sixteen and wounded thirty-one from the clock tower at the University of Texas set out the basic plot in black-and-white film at eleven for April 16, 2007, when Sueng-Hui Cho shot his way through West AJ Residence and Norris Halls at Virginia Tech in almost real-time cell phone video with CNN's high-definition color and stereo—only minor variations in the basic story-line occurred—not unlike stylized police dramas, sitcoms, game shows, and the news itself.

An English major, Cho first came to the university's attention in 2005 after a professor and students complained about him causing disturbances in a writing class. He was given special tutoring in the department, and then later he was referred to mental health professionals for treatment under a court order (*Time*, April 30, 2007:40–42). He had trouble with other professors and students in 2006, but he did not obtain his two handguns until February 9 and March 13, 2007 (*Newsweek*, April 30, 2007:27–29). After what was apparently a month of disciplined preparation and focused intention, he launched into his rampage on Monday, April 16. For the media, differences in the props (weapons, dress, vehicles, etc.), settings (K–12 schools, universities, professional academies, etc.), and criminals (troubled veteran, alienated teen-ager, angry immigrant, etc.) keep the viewers fascinated, the newscasters fixated, and the prior incidents freshened with each new example of such "programming."

While all of these themes and tropes turned as they do through the corporate media, it was interesting to see how many Blacksburg residents, university staff, and Virginia Tech students turned to nonprint, nonbroadcast, and noncorporate media in the hours after the attack. Beyond conventional radio or TV programming, cell phone videos, pictures, and calls often delivered the fastest breaking words and images of the event itself. To touch base with friends and families or colleagues and neighbors, many turned to the Internet, scanning blogs, official websites, Facebook, YouTube, or university news posts to capture the nature of the incident as it unfolded moment by moment. Virginia Tech and Blacksburg itself are heavily wired and wireless environments, so as Ralph Brauer notes on this point,[4] Cho's rampage quickly became an immense web of endless hypertexts, web scans, and video posts for millions on campus and off, especially during the first seventy-two hours of the shootings and their aftermath.

Still, for the corporate established media, school shootings in fast capitalist conditions of production have become a very valuable commodity to be delivered in a time-urgent "live" and "on-the-scene" manner; hence, they are hot sellers with long legs for the ratings regime. Any mention of Columbine school shootings still draws immediate attention nine years later, so it was no accident that ABC, CBS, NBC, CNN—as well as numerous other foreign TV networks and American local TV stations—sent their anchors to Blacksburg for their joint roll-out of a new raw reality show: "the Virginia Tech Massacre."[5] As former all-pro New York Giants running back, University of Virginia football star, one-time Montgomery County, Virginia, resident, and now *Today Show* personality with NBC, Tiki Barber observed about his few days in Blacksburg, the April 16 shootings media coverage was frenzied: "Anybody who was anybody in the industry was here, and for the most part I got to watch. I talked to the cameramen and the people who run those big trucks, and they said they'd never seen a staging ground like that" (Doughty 2007:A6).

On another hand, the events of April 16 in Blacksburg were quite a surprise. While it is not unknown, one cannot say Virginia Tech is well known. The largest university in the Commonwealth, Virginia Tech has 153 major buildings on 2,600 acres of land with nineteen miles of roads and many more miles of paved bike paths and sidewalks.[6] Up to 35,000 people are on campus every day, so it is very much like a small city in its own right. The university once was a small military engineering school, founded in 1872 (paired with Virginia Military Institute right after the War Between the States, in part, perhaps, for when the South might need to rise again). Its mission was to teach "the agricultural, mechanical, and other useful arts" in accord with the Civil War–era Morrill Act, but for only white students rather than blacks who, in turn, attended Hampton Institute or Virginia State University. Like many Southern colleges and universities, Virginia Tech did not admit its first African American students until the late 1950s. The university more than quintupled in student enrollment from the mid-1960s to mid-2000s in response to the Baby Boom and Baby Boomer Echo generations, and it has a respectable portfolio of academic strengths in many areas of study in addition to being a Big East, and more recently an ACC, college football powerhouse. Consequently, as an academic center, Virginia Tech tends to float uncomfortably in a gray zone between the Commonwealth's much lesser-known quick and dirty academic building projects from the frantic flurry of 1960s, like Old Dominion University in Norfolk, George Mason University in Fairfax, Virginia Commonwealth University in Richmond or James Madison University in Harrisonburg, and more venerable academic establishments in the state like the College of William and Mary or the University of Virginia. Unlike the crime-ridden areas of Norfolk, Northern Virginia, or Richmond, however, Blacksburg is a relatively small, out-of-the-way settlement with few big city social ills, a low crime rate, and many small town qualities.[7] Violent criminal acts do happen on and around the Virginia Tech campus, but they tend to occur once a decade, rather than as daily events.

Seung-Hui Cho's murderous rampage on April 16, 2007, therefore seemed more hideous, because it took place in this basically peaceful, rural college town with very little crime, few murders, and no sense of everyday violence.[8] Yet, the larger expanse of Montgomery County and the New River Valley, which surrounds Blacksburg and Virginia Tech, does have a higher crime rate—much of it tied to oxycodone and other illicit drug infractions all across Southwest Virginia. In fact, during 2006, there were two very high-profile shootings—now known as "the Morva incident"—that also affected the university after an escaped county jail prisoner shot and killed a security guard at the nearby Montgomery County Regional Hospital and then fled on foot into the woods.

K-9 units, SWAT teams, and helicopter patrols were called out through the night and into the next day when the suspect—allegedly armed and dangerous—was supposedly spotted on campus after shooting a county sheriff who had been searching for this escapee on a popular bicycle path near campus. At the university, there were rumors of a hostage-taking in Squires Student Center. In the confusion, some buildings closed, students stampeded; but, in the end, the criminal was caught some distance away from the central campus out in a patch of high brambles and thick weeds. Coming on the first day of class during Virginia Tech's Fall 2006 semester, this odd event startled many among the student body, faculty, and community into rethinking their sense of security, but it did not lead to many pleas for more policing.

To spurn greater policing on campus after the Morva incident might appear odd, especially to those who remembered one of Blacksburg's more infamous criminal distinctions, which its quiet, small college town atmosphere usually occludes, namely, the "local boy goes very bad" story of Henry

Lee Lucas, one of America's most wanted and vicious serial killers. Born in 1936 in sorry circumstances outside of Blacksburg, Lucas allegedly was subjected to considerable mental and physical abuse. His first murder was committed in 1953 during a rape, and his second murder victim was his own mother. A professed practitioner of bestiality and necrophilia, he claimed credit for killing over three thousand people with accomplices or by himself, but many now believe these confessions are fabrications. Some attribute only around five murders to him, but a Texas-based investigative team ultimately credited him with only around three hundred and fifty murders—using different weapons and methods—from 1953 to 1985 when he was taken into custody by Texan law enforcement authorities (for some online documentation of varying utility about Lucas, one can begin with Wikipedia, en.wikipedia.org/wiki/Henry_Lee_Lucas).

Convicted of murder, and sentenced to death, Lucas's execution order was commuted, ironically, by then-Texas Governor, George W. Bush, during 1998 after the evidence behind one of his confessed crimes was thrown into doubt. He died in prison in March 2001, but he remains one of the twentieth century's most notorious serial killers. Since the long vicious crime sprees of Henry Lee Lucas mostly took place outside of Blacksburg, the intense murder frenzy of Seung-Hui Cho will probably eclipse those of Lucas for their intensity and publicity forever. The major media spin placed on "the bucolic Blacksburg environs" must not be believed in toto. It is true, in some part, as much as it is just as false in another part.

Like the Columbine High School massacre, in which Dylan Klebold used a Tec-9 semi-automatic 9 mm weapon, the Virginia Tech April 16 massacre featured a 9 mm handgun—a Glock 19 semiautomatic—in many of the murders committed by Seung-Hui Cho. Indeed, he also used a Walther .22 semiautomatic pistol, and he apparently was also found with several combat-style knives on his body. Cho could have killed this many people, or even more, with some other weapons, but it was his 9 mm pistol that has become a pretext for pushing the popular technofix of additional gun control measures.[9] This rhetorical ball and bat—tied to "the ideology of gunism"—was swung and swatted around yet again all week in the five-ring media circus staged for the April 16 events (Lifton 2007:B 11).

Here, again, things are not clear as the *Newsweek* issue about the massacre strangely documented in its own coverage (April 30, 2007:22–47). Among industrial countries, the United States does have the highest level of gun ownership with 270 million for over 300 million people (90 per 100 persons) vs. 2.9 million guns in Finland (56 per 100 persons), 3.4 million guns in Switzerland (46 per 100 persons), 19 million in France (32 per 100 persons), or 25 million in Germany (31 per 100 persons). The United States also has 10.08 gun deaths per 100,000 people, while Switzerland has 6.40, France 4.93, Finland 4.51, and Germany much less than 1.00 (*Newsweek*, April 30, 2007:44–45). Of course, the media pundits who sat around town for weeks failed to focus on the Virginia Tech Corps of Cadets (VTCC), whose ranks now number several hundred. Cadets are frequently seen on campus carrying drill rifles, sabers, and assault weapons as part of their military training and/or tradition. Except for perhaps Texas A&M University, the Citadel in South Carolina, Virginia Military Institute, or the U.S. National Military Academies, Virginia Tech probably has more guns on campus out in the open every day than any other American university, because it also is a national senior military academy. Most of these weapons are just training pieces, but a few others are not. However, such guns and swords are always handled responsibly, and few object very strenuously on campus to seeing them.

Despite the uproar over high gun ownership and high gun deaths in the United States (about 10 deaths per 100,000 people) after April 16, other countries, like Brazil, Algeria, Russia, Jamaica, South Africa, Nepal, Venezuela, Kenya, and Ecuador (all more than 11 deaths per 100,000 people), have considerably higher rates of gun-related violence and death. There was little talk of their "gun culture" after April 16, 2007, or the fact that places like Mexico, Argentina, Uruguay, Estonia, Thailand, or Croatia equal America's firearm death rates per 100,000 people with far fewer guns per person in these countries (*Newsweek*, April 30, 2007:44–45). Perhaps television or video games are as much to blame in these other nations as the United States, but it seems quite unlikely. Still, as one might expect, the evergreen gun control debate plainly has been revitalized by the April 16 shootings. The debate blossoms a bit each time high-profile murders occur, but it is clear that clever killers, like Cho, always have been able to conform to, or successfully defy, existing gun control laws in the United States (Newman 2007:B20). Gun violence, however, is an exciting lead for the global news media. In a global marketplace where the various *Law and Order* and *CSI* television franchises run all day in many cities, ugly shootings have very rich forward and backward product links to titillating crime dramas on all the world's TV networks and cable systems. So an event of this magnitude quickly can be mobilized to fuel a fresh feeding frenzy among print, radio, television, and Internet journalists as if nothing else in the world mattered.

Even though these violent events took place on campus, and the Norris Hall attack happened nearby, the ensuing police swarm and campus lockdown rendered most individuals' understanding, including my own, of this criminal attack into a layered media event, which was experienced mostly on television, radio, and/or the Internet. While yards away, most of what I knew came from the local TV broadcasts, phone calls, Internet updates, or campus e-mail. On the first day, local reporters keep talking about what they saw some yards away from Norris Hall or repeating official news pool hand-outs from University Relations. Within hours, the murder scenes were marked with police tape and blockaded under a close twenty-four-hour guard, sealing them off from all but a few crime investigators. As national anchors arrived the next day, most television coverage was staged at a comfortable on-campus hotel where the scores of satellite trucks could park, anchors could do picturesque stand-ups and comfortable interviews, and the crowded news conferences in the Alumni Center could be rapidly organized. As this international media cavalcade trailed into town, the entire event acquired an even more layered juxtaposition of lived experience as seen on TV, as print documents were ripped from today's headlines, and as a huge blog fest occurred on the Web, which all were interwoven into one's daily routine on campus. I did not personally know any of the killed or wounded, although the highest number of dead and injured undergraduate students, or nine killed and five wounded, was racked up in my department's two major academic areas of study—International Studies and Political Science—which together now number more than one thousand students. Their identities for me are now almost totally print, broadcast, and televisual artifacts, but these young people also had walked our hallways, dealt with some of my colleagues, talked to all of our administrative support staff, and sat outside many of our offices. And, I have personally witnessed their families and friends on May 12, 2007, accept posthumous degrees and other academic recognitions for these students—it is obvious that those surviving loved ones share a pain as profound as these lost students' promise was vast.

It is difficult to write about any event as extraordinary and horrendous as April 16, because I know that the atrocity itself could make anyone reading of these written words easy to overinterpret, take wrongly, or see negatively when neither insult nor injury were meant by the analysis. Still, in this atrocious moment, and despite an inherent bias toward privileging a "readerly" over the "writerly" text, it must be noted that "extraordinary" does not mean unprecedented and "horrendous" cannot suggest unfamiliar when it comes to tragic violence. Indeed, Nikki Giovanni made clear mention of how endemic institutionalized violence is all across the world during her convocation address of April 17, 2007.[10]

Americans today live with violence on this scale every day as news from Iraq, for example, recounts tales of tens, dozens, or hundreds dying daily, but those losses also are highly mediated through electronic communication over a considerable distance in space, time, and social situation. Happening on the Monday of the week marking the eighth anniversary of the Columbine High School massacre, and standing out only for being the most recent, and most deadly, incident of school related violence, even this ugly crime was not purely a bolt from the blue. As Goss notes, a U.S. Secret Service analysis has found thirty-seven incidents of violence at American schools with forty-one shooters from 1979 to 2000 (2007:B10). Whether it is the Columbine incident in 1999, the August 1, 1966, shootings at the University of Texas, or even that very strange, and now almost forgotten, May 18, 1927, dynamite bombing of the Consolidated School in Bath, Michigan, four decades earlier by a custodian who killed his wife, himself, thirty-eight students, and seven teachers, while wounding sixty-one people,[11] April 16 should not come as a surprise, even if it was quite clearly a shock.

In a much longer view at the same time, April 16, 2007, strangely enough was not the first "historic massacre" or "brutal event" in Blacksburg. An earlier settlement, called Draper's Meadow, once lay on what are now the grounds of Blacksburg and Virginia Tech. Indeed, much of it is believed to have sat on land, quite ironically, in the background behind where Wolf Blitzer, Katie Couric, Matt Lauer, and Bryan Williams did their first national broadcasts from Blacksburg each day.[12] This tiny frontier outpost experienced a vicious assault by Shawnee warriors on a small group of settlers in which four Europeans were killed, five were abducted, and an unknown number of Indians perished in July 1755. This incident was one of many leading up to the French and Indian Wars, but it is regarded as one of the defining moments in the history of the town, the region, and the Commonwealth.

As a base for other brutal events, the lands around Draper's Meadow were resettled in 1772 by Colonel William B. Preston as the seat of Smithfield Plantation, which was one of the western-most slaveholding estates in the Commonwealth for many years. Built in part as a fort, the oldest surviving section of the still standing plantation house was erected in 1790. Again, quite ironically, some its fields and woods also were out in the background as the media filmed their accounts of the April 16 shootings from their own little media outposts on the Drillfield or from the Inn at Virginia Tech. Many Blacksburg natives see their small town, first founded in 1798, as an exceptional place far removed from the antebellum slave-based latifundia of the Shenandoah Valley, Piedmont, and Tidewater areas, and, in some sense, it is. Still, close studies of slaveholding in Blacksburg up into the 1850s show that enslaved and freed African Americans had made up much of the town's population prior to the Civil War.

An unnerving racial undertone in April 16 also must not be overlooked. The initial characterization of the shooter, first, as an "Asian male," and, then, as "a Korean" was, on one level, factually correct. On a second level, however, the label of "Korean" was fixed by many to Cho until his name was lost, and only the label "disturbed Asian and/or Korean student" remained hovering dangerously in the air for days. It challenged many of the psycho-babbling TV experts' stereotypes about the Columbine shooters, but it also sparked considerable anxiety among Virginia Tech Asian students after April 16. For some citizens, this racialized description of the shooter enabled them to explain away Cho's behavior as a case of difficult assimilation, failed acculturation, or personal anomie. Ironically, a few of Cho's own family members in reaction to his martyr video from April eased the possibility for making this interpretation when they reported that he talked more on camera than they ever heard him speak in real life at face-to-face family gatherings or occasional personal visits. For others, however, it has also affected the degrees of "whiteness" attached to prior cases of angry, anomic or alienated white middle-class kids who became school shooters, allowing police profilers more leeway to multiculturalize any next potential case of a likely school shooter. Either way, there is now a new "race factor" in the policing protocols for such crimes in the future.

Meanwhile, during the first few days following April 16 in Blacksburg, Chinese, Japanese, Thai, Indonesian, and Indian students reported random incidents of name-calling, threat-making, and even occasional fist-throwing against them; but, to their credit, the students and administrators, who were guiding the Hokies United memorialization campaign, moved the collective narrative about April 16 past this easily-circulated "cop perp talk" about "an Asian male" and into a more complex register of communal grief over the loss of so many individuals of different races, nationalities, classes, and majors in an extraordinary act of unforeseeable violence. The racial dimensions, like many affairs in Virginia, will never disappear, but it is no longer as intensely front and center as it was the first week.

None of this darker side in the area's history is hidden or secret. One easily can begin tracking it down from the VT "Where We Are" web pages.[13] One of the older established neighborhoods next to the university, where I have lived for almost twenty years, is called Draper-Preston; every local grade-schooler learns of Mary Draper Ingles's abduction in the Draper's Meadow massacre along with her captivity and return on her "long way home;" and, Smithfield Plantation now operates as a historic trust on the Virginia Tech campus surrounded by university property. In this regard, Blacksburg is no different from any American town: they all rest uneasily upon once contested, and then conquered, ground taken by force or guile from their original Native American occupants. And, like many southern towns, and almost any Virginia town, Blacksburg has a sorry past linked, in part, to the Commonwealth's practices of slavery, legally sanctioned from 1667 until after Appomattox. Violence and brutality are as American as apple pie, and Blacksburg has been as much one of their bakeries as any place in the country.

Consequently, the media circus ringmasters' barking about "the Massacre at Virginia Tech" or "the Virginia Tech Tragedy" must be taken cautiously as cynical hyperbole meant to hook viewers into staying with their networks' coverage. Yes, in one register, April 16, 2007, was the single worst instance of gun violence of a certain type in American history. Yet, there are many different types of "gun violence" in the United States, and those other types were ignored completely by the April 16 coverage. Numerous massacres committed by people of many races against other races mar the nation's history back into the seventeenth century's first conquests, and then since that time in wars, race riots, nativist panics, and labor revolts all across America. There were more trigger men, more victims, more resistant acts, and more witnesses in those violent incidents, so the mass media blather about April 16 tends to ignore these other types of gun violence. Still, this media coverage cannot be taken too seriously, as April 16 was not even the single worst day of school related violence. That distinction goes, once again, to the Bath, Michigan school dynamiting and murder rampage in 1927—eight decades ago.

Still, Kristin A. Goss repeats this gun-fixated myth-making about "mass shootings" over two weeks later in *The Chronicle of Higher Education*, as the opening line of an editorial calling for better gun control policies in the United States, when she asserts "when news broke April 16 of the worst mass shooting in U.S. history, the question many horrified Americans most wanted to answer was, 'Who was the shooter?'" (Goss 2007:B10). Her sense of the situation, however, begs too many questions. What a mass shooting actually is, that one must always assume there is only one, or a few, shooters(s), how the record of what counts as the worst is counted up, and who is given the task of making that measure are complex questions that are totally oversimplified by the very narrative itself. The Goss storyline about contemporary rampage shootings is already set: it always ends up being about deranged individuals who should be prevented, through better public policy, from getting access to guns. While she calls for collective policy solutions, she sees the individual shooter narrative as what audiences expect, and the media deliver it.

If one bites on such leading analytical questions, then "mass shootings" can only be these more recently observed pathological acts, like the murder rampage with thirty-two victims at Virginia Tech on April 16, 2007. However, is it that simple when it comes to "mass shootings"? There have been so many other massacres on a larger scale, which also can be tied together through "the guns," but few Americans wish to ask or remember, "who were those shooters?" Often a rampage also would be involved, but it typically is recategorized by exculpatory histories as a civic response, military battle, police action, or state-sanctioned strike that lets too many American citizens excuse, accept, or just forget those mass shootings and the massed shooters. Hence, Goss perpetuates such myth-making with a self-fulfilling prophecy in which she asserts, "if history is any guide, the nation is about to embark on a collective search for a narrative to explain what happened at Virginia Tech. And if history is any guide, those narratives will revolve around the private story of the killer, Seung-Hui Cho; his mental health status; his parents; and his upbringing" (Goss 2007:B10). Here, Goss is correct inasmuch as this guidance from history has shaped the current federal government's anodyne administrative analysis of the Virginia Tech shootings, which calls for more vigilant gun control and mental health interventions everywhere in the future as its main "official" response from Washington.[14]

Other messy narratives about nonsolitary shooters, more victims, and organized rampages, then, do not fit into either Goss's tidy moralizing fables about gun control or America's most wanted scripts about psycho-killers on the loose. Whether it is Wounded Knee, Sand Creek, Bear River, or Gnadenhutten, or it is Haymarket, Ludlow, Watts, or Kent State, April 16 effectively screens off other "mass shooting" atrocities by serving as a polemically correct form of "hideous murder" that mass media audiences now wish to watch in the United States. Cho's ugly martyr video came to light on April 18, 2007, but that day also saw five carefully planned car and suicide bombing missions in Baghdad, which targeted Shi'ite gatherings, killed 171 people and wounded scores of others (Semple 2007:A1, 10). Seung-Hui Cho and his bizarre information bomb from Blacksburg, delivered through the U.S. Post Office to NBC News, overshadowed this massive cluster of killings in Baghdad completely in the United States. Page one of *The New York Times* on Thursday, April 19, 2007, visually depicted this imbalance of attention with a still frame color photo of Cho brandishing his two hand guns in his camo ammo vest and backward baseball cap at the layout's top left column with two stories about his troubled mental state and the inability of colleges to do much in response, while the Baghdad bombing butchery sat on and below the front-page fold.

Strategies of Response to April 16

The Old Dominion, as its four-hundred-year anniversary celebration of Jamestown this year shows quite clearly for all to see, prides itself on "being first." So "Virginia Leading the Way"[15] has been advanced as the motto of the Kaine Administration in Richmond to bring distinction to Virginia: a place and people "constantly striving to surpass previous achievements." Governor Kaine clearly did not mean to include occurrences like the April 16 shootings at Virginia Tech when making this claim. Nonetheless, neither he nor the Commonwealth can deny the sinister effectiveness of Seung-Hui Cho in his spectacular strike to surpass the horrors of the Columbine High School shootings in 1999. Virginia has, in a sad sense, now "led the way" in setting a new benchmark for brutality. This attack must be set into the market-driven context of such fast capitalist-celebrating accolades by which the Commonwealth now judges its "national leadership": in August 2006, Forbes.com put Virginia first of all fifty states in a ranking of "Best States for Business"; in March 2006, corporate relocators Pollina Real Estate, Inc., ranked Virginia as the second friendliest state in the nation to business; in May 2006, *Forbes* magazine ranked Northern Virginia as 17 among the nation's top 165 "Best Places for Business" among metropolitan areas and Blacksburg was ranked 65 out of 105 "Best Small Places for Business"; and, in August 2006 Entrepreneur.com ranked Virginia as the second best state for entrepreneurs and Fairfax County as the second friendliest county for entrepreneurial activity.

Likewise, *Newsweek* ranked eighteen Virginia High Schools, including Cho's Westfield High School in Chantilly, Virginia, at forty-sixth in 2002 among the one hundred fifty best in the country; Virginia Tech was ranked seventy-seventh out of three hundred Best National Universities and thirty-fourth out the top fifty public universities by *U.S. News and World Report*; and, *Education Week* in 2007 reported that the typical Virginia K–12 student "enjoys higher achievement and is more likely to finish high school and continue on to college than in other states."[16] Amidst this ranking-crazed corporate consciousness for defining and then gaining "the Number 1 Spot," and in this business-friendly environment, Seung-Hui Cho and his family settled in the Northern Virginia suburbs as his parents set up shop in the dry cleaning business in 1992.

Cho did attend success-obsessed Westfield High School in Chantilly, Virginia, and then matriculated at Virginia Tech—a big state university eagerly restructuring itself after 2001 in an effort to rise as rapidly as it could on key national academic ranking scales. He was fifteen years old in 1999 when Columbine happened, seventeen years old when al Qaeda terrorists flew an airliner into the Pentagon not far from his home, nineteen years old when President Bush invaded Iraq, he died his last semester in college by his own hand at twenty-three. Nonetheless, Seung-Hui Cho in many ways, was a cipher. His web page presented him in these terms as he superimposed a "?" over his face, anticipating his final act of suicide in which the gunshots blew away his visage. The Virginia Tech 2006–2007 University

Directory on page 43 "Virginia Tech Student Listings" just records "Cho, Seung-Hui (ENGL)"—no phone number, no campus address, no home address, no home telephone—very unlike most other student entries. He was "Mr. Question Mark."[17]

A senior who was to graduate in May 2007, Cho had no friends, refused conversation with his dormitory suite mates, and worked at maintaining this near invisibility. Unable or unwilling to participate in the contrived communities of today's collegiate living, he idolized the Columbine killers, frightened his teachers and classmates in the English department, endured psychiatric observation by local mental health professionals, and then went ballistic on April 16, 2007. Of course, becoming first a Hokie fan, perhaps then a Virginia Tech student, and maybe then a university graduate is, in large part, a continually unfolding consumer relationship—rooted most deeply in big-name college athletics as it is at many other major American universities. One buys maroon-and-orange VT flags, sports VT baseball caps, finishes VT classes, writes VT tuition checks, and then supports the VT Alumni Association. Contriving such community from this mode of sports-driven consumption under fast capitalism appears to work for many individuals, but Cho did, or could, not buy it.

While many accept the embrace of "Hokie Nationhood," a few others cannot find a place within its community. Despite years of "orange and/or maroon effect" days, as the Hokies won football games and garnered postseason bowl bids, Seung-Hui Cho never seemed to connect to his classmates, academic major, or university life. Instead he believed, rightly or wrongly, that the Virginia Tech community had its own dark side as he excoriated his school mates for allegedly being alcoholic hedonists, rich kids, and arrogant protoprofessionals. In the pressure cooker of persecution he seemed to experience, in fantasy or reality, Cho declared to the Hokie Nation and America at large in his own martyr video: "You have vandalized my heart, raped my soul, and torched my conscience," and so, "Thanks to you, I die like Jesus Christ to inspire generations of the weak and defenseless people" (cited in Dewan and Santora 2007:A1).

April 16, 2007, strangely now has vaulted Virginia Tech to the heights of some ignominious first-place rankings for Virginia: site of the worst single incident of gun violence by one shooter in U.S. history, site of the highest number of on-campus deaths and woundings at an academic institution, and site of the worst single murder of students and faculty by a student. Knowing how the university is very keen to jump into the ranks of Top 30 in the NSF rankings of research expenditures, a few enterprising university faculty members recognized within twenty-four to thirty-six hours that they had gained a remarkable place of comparative advantage for their research. Of course, no one sought this position, but some now do hope to leverage this cluster of number one records in collegiate murder and mayhem for their varied research programs. In this vein, the Virginia Tech faculty received a fascinating e-mail (redacted below) on May 10, 2007, from the University's Provost, because April 16, 2007, is now a major new "external funding" and "research initiative" opportunity:

> Date: Thu, 10 May 2007 09:38:31 -0400
> From: "McNamee, Mark" <mmcnamee@vt.edu>
> Subject: Committee Formation Announced
> To: Deans, Department Heads, and University Center Directors
> From: Mark McNamee (mmcnamee@vt.edu), University Provost and Vice President for Academic Affairs
>
> (PLEASE SHARE)
>
> Dear Colleagues:
>
> As we move forward from the events of April 16, our university community is flooded with offers of assistance and support. We are getting requests from multiple faculty members and groups about research and response initiatives for which external funding may be available. Many of these projects require IRB approval and most will involve working closely with the Office of Sponsored Programs.
>
> We run the risk of overloading our students, faculty, and staff with surveys, interviews, and other forms of data collection. It is important that we be strategic in managing processes related to conducting research and assessment in which our community is asked to be involved. Our own faculty members would like to be key players and it is important for us to be coordinated in our efforts.
>
> I am appointing a small committee reporting to the Research Division to provide me and other senior administrators with high-level advice on projects and strategy. The added review is in addition to requests to the IRB for technical review and approval. The purpose of this committee is to ensure coordination with faculty members and university units in order to be responsive to the needs of the university community.

> Thank you for your support of this important work. Anyone planning to submit a research proposal related to the April 16th events should contact Robert Walters at rwalters@vt.edu.
>
> Mark

Intent mostly upon protecting wounded psyches from rapid bombardment by waves of upsetting questionnaires, this provost also now has a gatekeeping body to monitor the players pursuing any externally funded research on April 16. The provost's immediate goal is to protect and preserve everyone's emotional state; yet, this intervention also organizes the rush for research dollars as well as controls access to the populations to be surveyed. Both goals necessitate being "strategic" about managing the collective processes of research and assessment. Having become number one nationally in campus violence, if only for a moment before a worse incident yet to occur in the future, Virginia Tech is now intent upon being number one in studying how it happened, coping with its aftermath, and managing its assessment. Under fast capitalist conditions of knowledge production and consumption, any study of mass murder—as it transpired both on and off the screens of power—is a very fundable research undertaking (Luke 2005:13–32).

Since that day, like 9/11 with its diverse global contingent of victims, the thirty-three dead individuals from April 16, 2007, also have been since transformed into lost "Americans" posthumously, even if they were perhaps Korean, Canadian, Israeli/Romanian, Peruvian, Indian, Egyptian, or Indonesian beforehand.[18] Another memorial on Main Street on the grounds of a local Baptist church had the other nations' flags flying amidst an array of American flags along with the Puerto Rican and Lebanese flags to underscore the murders' transnational impact, but the effect is still one of "the red, white, and blue."[19] Violent death on Virginia as well as American soil, coupled with 24/7 media coverage for almost ten days across the globe on so many screens of power, earned each victim (and the alleged murderer, too) an American flag billowing by their individual Hokie Stone markers for the campus' makeshift memorials within two weeks, although Cho's stone tends to disappear a lot. Here, in its cultural practices of coping with violence, prejudice or injustice, Virginia, again, strangely leads the way, and often in a uniquely unanticipated fashion. While it legalized slavery in 1667, and kept it in force for nearly two centuries, Virginia also elected the nation's first African American governor in 1989 as well as expressed the nation's first "deep regret" for slavery by official legislative action in 2006.

Similarly, in 1958, Charlie L. Yates graduated from Virginia Tech with an honors mechanical engineering degree as the university's first black graduate. This landmark event preceded the graduation of any other African American from any state university as well as all other white land-grant schools in the eleven former breakaway Confederate states. On the one hand, it was this strange culture that seemed to enrage Cho to commit mass murder; but, on the other hand, the culture also carries a strong enough sense of care to accept a thirty-third Hokie Stone for Cho at the memorial semicircle of thirty-two markers for the fallen.[20]

Regardless of their national origin, cultural background, current passports, or ethnic diversity, the dead now all are "American" characters set into several long-running scripts of national shame and pride, economic division and unity, political cohesion and fragmentation. Thanks to the memorializing efforts of Virginia Tech students, and coupled with the mythos of Virginia Tech's Hokie Nationhood for all of its intense fusion of athletic boosterism and academic community, the fallen students and faculty now serve as a rallying point to further advance the maroon and orange consciousness of this single university within the universal state of emergency hovering over the United States in general. Not everyone left dead on April 16 was "all-American" or "all-Hokie," but this gradual naturalization ritual has transformed each of them into individuals worthy of the stars-and-stripes. And, in an act of memorialization by the university, the students, regardless of prior progress toward completion of their degrees prior to April 16, became posthumous degree winners on May 11 and 12, 2007, to comfort friends, family, and the community.

Memorials, like these stone markers, as they have risen after April 16 also have become a strange exercise of healing in which the university community is intent upon finding proof its new "We Will Prevail" slogan, which was put forth in the poem by Nikki Giovanni on April 17, 2007, at a memorial service with President Bush, Governor Kaine, the Virginia Congressional delegation, and thousands of students, faculty, and townspeople in Blacksburg actually has meaning.[21] From one perspective, it has worked with candlelight vigils, vernacular memorials, and mass rallies.[22] The imagined community of the Hokie Nation is proving to be a tangibly active society. Its maroon and orange wearing fans, alumni, graduates, and faculty whose fascination with both the dead and wounded students are all walking and talking more and more each day toward their reconciliation with the April 16 events. Undeniably, their passions are frequently quite moving. However tenuous, there is a tangible *Gemeinschaft* of sorts here that one cannot simply reduce to ACC football, frat parties, engineering culture, Southern traditions, or rural Appalachia. Hence, the university has now planned to semifinalize this shrine by turning its vernacular origins into an "intermediate official memorial."[23] With thirty-two permanent new stone markers, a paved arcing pathway, and an evergreen hedge to the site, construction on it has already begun. And, it is meant to maintain many of the meaningful traces of what the community first created so spontaneously during that first week.[24] A permanent memorial might be built one day elsewhere on campus—further away from Norris Hall and West AJ—but still on the Drillfield closer to more visitor parking and better road access.

As these efforts were unfolding on campus to create a physical memorial, thousands of people sent donations of support to Blacksburg from the first day of the attacks. In turn, the Hokie Spirit Memorial Fund, which quickly was established right after the shootings to do something to aid those harmed or killed in the April 16 attack, pooled these millions of dollars of donations from all over the world. In addition to meeting some initial expenses incurred by many on April 16, the fund disbursed payments of nearly $7 million to the most affected families and individuals. Those families who had students or faculty killed were given $208,000, while payments to injured students or faculty were tied to the severity of their injuries in a range from $11,500 to $104,000. At the time of the fund's transfers, the payments were treated as taxable events; but, special legislation was introduced in Washington to make the payments tax-exempt in accord with several historical precedents.

After six months, and despite thousands of hours devoted to rebuilding plans, public commemorations, and private memorials, the university often seems trapped in a vortex of melancholia rather than moving ahead in mourning. Partly the result of the April 16 incident's extraordinary violence, partly the outcome of numerous local, statewide, and national review panels, and partly the backwash from a string of impending law suits, there still seems to be, as Žižek (2000) might observe, an inability to regain effective social agency. Žižek regards mourning as a path to reconciliation, reorientation, and reactivation after traumatic events, while melancholia tends to freeze effective thought and action by compelling subjects to march in place, if not in circles, within an institutional and individual void in a strange fealty to the objects of loss. So much was lost on April 16 that this reaction could have been anticipated, but those losses are not yet sublated. Even now, many discussions about "what must be done" all too often are tied—melancholically to what occurred, for what happened, and how it transpired—back to April 16, 2007. This state of being is full of activity, but it also appears to lack efficacy as regenerative historical agency.

One sign of this recursive fixation upon April 16, which is caught between the twin towers of Hokie football spirit and high-technology innovation, was the "Hokies Thank the World" happening staged on November 17, 2007, seven months to the day after the memorial convocation at Cassell

Coliseum. On the morning prior to the last 2007 football season home game, thousands of students, faculty, staff, and fans were invited to the Drillfield to spell out a message of thanks with their massed bodies that was captured by ground, aerial, and even satellite cameras (using imagery from the IKONOS earth imaging satellite operated by GeoEye in Dulles, Virginia). Drawn to Blacksburg to watch Virginia Tech play the University of Miami, this contingent assemblage of bodies explicitly paid tribute to the thirty-two murdered students of April 16; but, the Hokie Nation implicitly also reaffirmed its own spectacular self-representations as produced so often for so many other national television events before, during, and after other ACC gridiron showdowns. While it could have some idiosyncratic reconciliatory qualities, this event typifies how much of the Hokie Nation continues to march in place to mark one more recognition of the April 16 event's loss—especially if it can be recast as extraordinary remote sensing imagery from outer space in another new televisual spectacle.

Aptly, and yet still bizarrely, these November 17 images are arrayed such that the three thousand to five thousand massed celebrants, mostly clad in orange and maroon, stand in front of Burruss and Norris Halls on the Drillfield directly in front of the new memorial to those killed on April 16, 2007 (Adams 2007:V1, 10). Signaling with their bodies the words "VT THANKS YOU" in that "VT" which is the University logo and the "THANKS YOU" all in capital letter as in e-mail/text message shouting, the huge outline letters all stood with vast empty centers, leaving the message's declarative quality quite contestable. Manifestly, this was an effort by the university aimed at "thanking the world." In assembling bodies at a game day happening to be documented from 423 miles out in space, however, the ambiguities are deep and varied. With both Burruss Hall and Norris Hall sitting squarely above message, is Virginia Tech thanking all who have cared? Are the fallen victims and their survivors speaking somehow through another tangle of bodies? Is the Hokie Nation materializing in school colors through an outline sports logo as a transitory greeting? Or, at the end of the day, is anyone ready to stand in formation for a media event anonymously garnering his or her fifteen minutes of fame?

Strangely enough, like April 16, 2007, murders themselves, this gesture of gratitude was made for the media, mobilized through the media, and rendered readable/recordable/recognizable completely only from aloft through a camera. Not unlike the full sweep of the shootings in the media on April 16, this happening seven months after was basically just one more machine-readable event of televisual production/consumption/accumulation/circulation, only brimming with melancholy. Ironically, "the university" was the focus of the image by presenting itself as/of the Drillfield, and then the

Hokie Nation drew the outlines of its sports logo and words of thanks at the base of the broken monumental circle of stones memorializing the dead now positioned in front of the long-standing old Reviewing Stand (also made of Hokie Stone).

With regard to student life at Virginia Tech, the media spotlight on the mass murder in Blacksburg seems to have proven, once again, that there is no such thing as bad publicity. Each articulate student, engaged townsperson, and every faculty member interviewed on television seemed to project something to the outside world that appears serious, solid, and supportive. There is no student exodus out of Blacksburg. Freshmen enrollment with paid deposits at Virginia Tech for Fall 2007 is 5,215, up from 5,185 in 2006; average SAT score for this new 2011 class is 1,205, up from 1,201 for 2010; and, the average GPA for the 2007 entering freshman class is 3.77, up from 3.74 in 2006. Application levels for 2008 entry will not be known until December 2007, but all indications are that interest in Virginia Tech remains very strong and will increase. Indeed, there were 1,441 students on the 2007 admissions waiting list who have been told there is no space for them, and only seven students offered admission turned the offer down because of the shooting (Esposito 2007b:8A).

College years are now such a part of so many individuals' personalities, and the life of any large university anchors the economy and society of quite a few localities. The atrocity that rose out of restless anomie in both the D.C. suburbs and dorm life in Blacksburg poses uncomfortable questions; and, the strange solidarity that athletics and academics cogenerate pulls many admixtures of mixed meaning in America from many dark recesses of today's global economy, transnational society, and world culture. Cho may have been deeply disturbed when he arrived at Virginia Tech, but his painful isolation never eased while he was in residence on campus. Not all loners are mass murders, but the multitude has before, is now, and will again in the future bring others here and elsewhere who need better, bigger, and broader community than that given by gridiron *Gemeinschaft*. These kinds of mass shootings have happened in many places, from Scotland to Tasmania, Canada to Japan, California to Virginia. Empire brings forth multitudes (Hardt and Negri 2000; 2004), but too many members of the multitude are angry, isolated, and powerless in this age of endless war and fitful democracy, which the ethos of endless emergency is only aggravating post-9/11.

Access to camcorders and guns, in turn, enables a few to shoot, and reshoot, their way into infamy, which works well for Empire's televisual economy of celebrity even for those who were ciphers in life and criminals in death. While many were aware of Virginia Tech on April 15, 2007, few will forget April 16, 2007, at this university for decades. April 16 is already on its way to serving as a salient teletradition as the media networks carry the endless replays of images from the attacks of that Monday, and then replay the bizarrely banal death manifesto from Cho released on video that Wednesday, April 18, 2007. These pixels will be played, printed, and pounded on the screens of power innumerable times all around the planet again and again in the years to come. Likewise, this day's events in and around the "Blacksburg Electronic Village" will spin up though blogs, Facebook, YouTube, and their successor media for just as long.

The reach of this televisual phenomenon was reconfirmed on November 7, 2007, eerily on the other side of the Atlantic in Finland at the town of Tuusula's Jokela High School. A day after posting a YouTube video with the title "Jokela High School Massacre—11/7/2007" scored with the song "Stray Bullet" by KMFDM (a song much admired by Eric Harris of the 1999 Columbine School shooting), an eighteen-year old student, Pekka-Eric Auvinen, killed five of his male school mates, and three female adults (a school nurse, the school principal, and a twenty-five-year-old student). He then killed himself with a .22 semiautomatic Sig Sauer Mosquito pistol after firing at least sixty-nine shots and leaving 320 unfired rounds in a bag (Whitlock 2007:A17). Auvinen's Cho-like video on the Internet was accompanied by a posting which read: "I, as a natural selector, will eliminate all who I see unfit, disgraces of human race and failure of natural selection" (*New York Times*, November 8, 2007:A20). After going public online, Auvinen, like Cho, then randomly strode through his school's corridors, shouting into various classrooms, and shot people—five boys, three adults, and himself. While Cho sent his manifesto off to NBC News in New York, Auvinen posted hundreds of messages on the Internet along with his YouTube attack video that foretold the attack by a day with antisocial declarations, like: "Hate, I'm so full of it and I love it. It is the one thing I really love" (Whitlock 2007:A17).

In this violence-soaked media environment, however, one must be cautious. Despite all that has happened, we need to question greater policing, additional security, and more intrusive surveillance. The Commonwealth launched a special investigative commission to examine the events of April 16, which was headed by former State Police Superintendent Col. Gerald Massengill; and, part of its charge is how to improve campus safety.[25] The November 2007 Board of Visitors meeting at Virginia Tech reviewed scores of recommendations made by three internal review panels as well as the state-appointed Massengill Commission. There is an emerging consensus about the need to replenish funds for the overstretched mental health system in the state, but no one has made any solid guarantees that it will be enough to repair decades of neglect. Even though no definite actions have been decided upon by the Board of Visitors for the university at this juncture, the range of responses seem to be pointing toward more and more security. Universities are open, free, and unfettered sites by their very nature, and reacting to the violent act of a disturbed individual by abridging these freedoms is a serious mistake. Of course, everyone at Virginia Tech will be more vigilant and cautious in the future, and they need to be. Nevertheless, "a gunman loose on campus" can be a gunman in the mall, at the stadium, on the beach, at the race, in the factory or on the plaza.

Living is risky, and having freedoms is riskier, but those benefits are well worth running the risks. The costs of reducing risk, especially at a university, are far greater than their potential benefits, particularly if the campus is made—through densely embedded security measures—more like a prison, a command center, a casino, a major airport, or a bank with metal detectors, swipe card locks, biometric scans, or ubiquitous video sweeps. After all, Cho killed his first two victims on April 16 after getting past a swipe card door locking system on a dormitory that he was actually cleared to enter for mail service. None of these other allegedly more "high-security" sites prevent all acts of violence, and turning college campuses into such restrictive zones of control and surveillance will surely ruin the university's bigger, greater, and deeper purposes.

Norris Hall is being quickly renovated and redecorated to keep it in service for the College of Engineering; but, after being brought back into service during June 2007, its use only as a laboratory and office building (Esposito 2007a:A1, 6) now is being once again vaguely debated in another cloud of melancholy. Even though it once provided about 5 percent of all classroom space on campus, no formal academic classes probably will ever be taught there again. There are two new plans, however, for either a violence prevention and peace studies center coupled with a student engagement and community learning space or a site to re-create a student-centered community for engineering students.[26] In any event, future access for all will be very highly controlled through a single guarded entry point by security guards. While understandable, this new practice sets a dangerous precedent for future policing of the campus' academic and nonacademic space everywhere else.

Because one disturbed individual committed heinous acts of murder, it makes little sense to spend millions disrupting the everyday routines and basic freedoms of thousands at the university with videocams everywhere, building access restrictions anywhere, and routine body scans somewhere on campus until the end of time. Further reflections on those contradictory realities—when some new mass murderer, lone gunman, or twisted gang tries to best the toll at Virginia Tech or Columbine at some newly hardened site or still soft target—must wait for another day. I hope, of course, that such violence will not occur again, but we should fully expect at the same time that it will. Responding to those incidents to come with additional thoughts shall be an assignment that we could accept at that time; however, we can consider that task only when they come, since they undoubtedly will. By the same token, anticipating such acts of violence on America's college campuses inevitably will direct some of our attention to personal safety in the present and collective protection in the future. Meanwhile, these security measures must neither determine everything we in the university community always have resolved to be nor define anything less than what we already as scholars hope to become.

Notes

1. See www.april16archive.org/object/279.
2. See www.april16archive.org/object/333.
3. See www.april16archive.org/object/419.
4. See www.april16archive.org/object/455.
5. See www.april16archive.org/object/248.
6. See www.vt.edu/about/vtsnaps/aerials/2.html#Anchor-604709-46919.
7. See www.april16archive.org/object/303.
8. See www.ee.unirel.vt.edu/index.php/vt/flip_book/C11/P5/.
9. See www.april16archive.org/object/315.
10. See www.april16archive.org/object/19.
11. See www.nytimes.com/2007/04/us/17virginia.html?ex=1178164800&en=9457250afccd.gced&ei=5070.
12. See www.april16archive.org/object/384.
13. See www.vt.edu/where_we_are/blacksburg/area.php.
14. See www.april16archive.org/object/523.
15. See www.governor.virginia.gov/intiatives/caleads/index.cfm.
16. See www.governor.virginia.gov/initiatives/valeads/index.cfm.
17. See www.april16archive.org/object/230.
18. See www.april16archive.org/object/343.
19. See www.april16archive.org/object/43/.
20. See www.april16archive.org/object/551.
21. See www.april16archive.org/object/416.
22. See www.april16archive.org/object/390.
23. See www.vtnews.vt.edu/story.php?relyear=2007&itemno=333.
24. See www.april16archive.org/object/546.
25. See www.vtreviewpanel.org/index.html.
26. See www.vtnews.vt.edu/story.php?relyear=2007&itemno=680.

References

Adams, Duncan. 2007. "Words of Gratitude," *Roanoke Times* (November 18): V1, 10.
Agger, Ben. 1989. *Fast Capitalism*. Urbana: University of Illinois Press.
Dewan, Shaila, and Marc Santora. 2007. "Officials Knew Troubled State of Killer in '05." *New York Times* (April 19): A1, 18.
Doughty, Doug. 2007. "Tech Story Hit Close to Home for Barber," *Roanoke Times* (May 17): A1, 6.
Esposito, Greg. 2007a. "Going Back Inside: Norris Hall to Reopen," *Roanoke Times* (June 6): A1, 6.
———. 2007b. "Enrollment at Tech Stays Robust for '07," *Roanoke Times* (May 17): A8.
Gangloff, Mike. 2007. "From War Zone to Campus Disaster: Longing for Home," *Roanoke Times* (May 17): V1, 4.
Goss, Kristin A. 2007. "Aftermath of a Tragedy: Good Policy, Not Stories, Can Reduce Violence," *The Chronicle Review: The Chronicle of Higher Education*, Vol. LIII, no. 35 (May 4): B10. www.chronicle.com/weekly/v53/i35/35601001/htm.
Hardt, Michael, and Tony Negri. 2004. *Multitude: War and Democracy in the Age of Empire*. New York: Penguin Press.
———. 2000. *Empire*. Cambridge, MA: Harvard University Press.
Lifton, Robert Jay. 2007. "An Ideology of 'Gunism,'" *The Chronicle Review: The Chronicle of Higher Education*, Vol. LIII, no. 35 (May 4): B11.
Luke, Timothy W. 2005. "From Pedagogy to Performativity: The Crisis of Research Universities, Intellectuals, and Scholarly Communication," *Telos* 131 (Summer): 13–32.
———. 1989. *Screens of Power: Ideology, Domination, and Resistance in Informational Society*. Urbana: University of Illinois Press.
Newman, Katherine S. 2004. *Rampage: The Social Roots of School Shootings*. New York: Basic Books.
———. 2007. "Before the Rampage: What Can Be Done?" *The Chronicle Review: The Chronicle of Higher Education*, Vol. LIII, no. 35 (May 4): B20.
Newsweek. 2007. "Morning of Terror." April 30: 22–47.
New York Times. 2007. "Student Kills 8, and Himself, at Finnish High School," *New York Times* (November 8): A20.
Semple, Kirk. 2007. "Bombs Rip Through Baghdad in Wave of Attacks, Killing 171," *New York Times* (April 19): A1, 10.
Time. 2007. "Trying to Make Sense of a Massacre." *Time*, 169, no. 18, April 30: 36–59.
Whitlock, Craig. 2007. "Finland's Gun Culture Facing New Questions: Details of Deadly School Shooting Revealed," *Washington Post* (November 9): A17.
Zizek, Slavoj. 2000. "Melancholy and the Act," *Critical Inquiry* 26 (Summer): 657–81.

CHAPTER TWO

MEDIA SPECTACLE AND THE "MASSACRE AT VIRGINIA TECH"[1]

Douglas Kellner

The mainstream corporate media today process events, news, and information in the form of media spectacle.[2] In an arena of intense competition with 24/7 cable TV networks, talk radio, Internet sites, and blogs, and ever proliferating new media like Facebook, MySpace, and YouTube, competition for attention is ever more intense leading the media to go to sensationalistic tabloidized stories which they construct in the forms of media spectacle that attempt to attract maximum audiences for as much time as possible.

The 1990s saw the emergence and proliferation of cable news networks, talk radio, and the Internet, and megaspectacles of the era included the O. J. Simpson murder trials, the Clinton sex scandals and impeachment, and on a global level the life and death of princess Diana. The era also saw an intensification of celebrity news and scandals, with Michael Jackson perhaps the most sensational case (see Kellner 2003a).

The new millennium opened with a hung 2001 presidential election between Al Gore and George W. Bush, and a thirty-six-day Battle for the White House and frenzied media spectacle, resulting in a 5-4 Supreme Court decision for Bush that blocked the counting of votes in Florida and generated one of the most momentous political crimes in history that I describe in my book *Grand Theft 2000* (Kellner 2001). This spectacle was soon followed by the 9/11 terror attacks on New York and Washington, the deadliest attack on U.S. soil in its history, and perhaps the most extensive global media spectacle ever, inaugurating an era of Terror War (Kellner 2003b).

Following the model of his father's 1991 war with Iraq, the second Bush administration's Iraq War was also orchestrated as a media spectacle, although after declaring victory in May 2003, events flipped out of control and the spectacle in Iraq has often been a negative and highly contested one, leading to a collapse of Bush's approval ratings and unraveling of his administration (Kellner 2005).

The Bush years have been a series of spectacles from 9/11 and Iraq to the abject failure of the Bush administration during Hurricane Katrina,[3] scandals involving criminal trials of its highest officials and top Republican congressional supporters, and in Spring 2007 a scandal that involves its Attorney General and Bush loyalist Alberto Gonzales. The spectacle of "Gonzogate" involves one of the most systematically political attempts to establish partisan control of the justice system in U.S. history, whereby federally appointed Attorney Generals who failed to carry out Bush policies were fired, however competent, while those who carried out Bush administration politics were kept on or promoted, however corrupt or incompetent.

In addition to making a spectacle out of major political events, the media produce spectacles around events and controversies of social and everyday life, often providing forums through which major political issues and social struggles are negotiated and debated. In April 2007 alone, revelations that three Duke lacrosse players accused of gang rape were innocent raised issues of a rogue prosecutor and prosecutorial media flying out of control. During the same week, racist and sexist comments by radio and television personality Don Imus, who called the Rutgers University women's basketball team a "bunch of nappy-headed hoes," generated a media firestorm and debate over appropriate language in regard to race and gender, the limits of free speech, and corporate media responsibility. The resultant media spectacle and focus on the event and issues led to the disruption of Imus's long radio career and a subsequent heated debate over the incident.

The shooting rampage at Virginia Tech on April 16, 2007, generated a media spectacle with local, national, and even global media following every twist of a shooting that was represented in the media as producing the highest death toll of any gun-related mass murder in recent U.S. history.[4] Such a claim was irresponsible and false and is setting the stage for someone to try to break the record. Yet the event has also generated debates over gun laws and control, school safety, mental health care, and what causes teenagers and young students to kill their classmates and teachers. There was also a racial dimension to the shooting as the assassin was revealed to be Korean American Seung-Hui Cho.[5]

Reading the Spectacle with Critical Social Theory and Cultural Studies

In my studies of media spectacle, I deploy cultural studies as *diagnostic critique*, reading and interpreting various spectacles to see what they tell us about the present age, using media spectacles to illuminate contemporary social developments, trends, and struggles.[6] The "popular" often puts on display major emotions, ideas, experiences, and conflicts of the era, as well as indicating what corporations are marketing. A critical cultural studies can thus help decipher dominant trends, social and political conflicts, and fears and aspirations of the period and thus contribute to developing critical theories of the contemporary era (see Kellner and Ryan 1988; Kellner 1995, 2003a, 2003b, 2005).

I therefore see the spectacle as a *contested terrain* in which different forces use the spectacle to push their interests. Against Debord's more monolithic and overpowering totalitarian spectacle, I see the spectacle as highly contested, subject to reversal and flip-flops, and thus extremely ambiguous and contradictory. For instance, the media spectacle of the U.S./UK invasion of Iraq was used by the Bush administration to promote their war policy and the so-called Bush doctrine of preemptive war. While the spectacle went through several stages from the opening triumphant "shock and awe" bombing of Iraq through Bush's May 2003 "Mission Accomplished" spectacle, later horrific events in Iraq caused a reversal of the spectacle, and it is now hotly and bitterly contested.

Since the rise of the Centre for Contemporary Cultural Studies in Birmingham, England, in the 1960s, as well as in subsequent versions of cultural studies throughout the world, there has been a long-standing tradition of taking on the big issues of the era. The Birmingham School critically analyzed the assaults against working class culture by American mass media and consumer culture. In this conjuncture, British cultural studies stressed the need for media literacy and critique, learning to read newspapers, television news, advertisements, television shows and the like just as one learns to read books (see Kellner 1995). The project helped generate a media literacy movement, expanded the concept of literacy, and introduced a new, powerful dimension of pedagogy into cultural studies.

Later, in the 1980s, British cultural studies took on the rise of Thatcherism and the emergence of a new right-wing conservative hegemony in

Britain, by explaining how British culture, media, politics, and various economic factors led to the emergence of a new conservative hegemony (see Hall and Jacques 1983). Larry Grossberg (1992), Stanley Aronowitz (1993), myself (Kellner and Ryan 1988; Kellner 1990, 1995), and others engaged in similar work within the United States during the Reagan era of the 1980s, applying cultural studies to analyze the big issues of the time.

Indeed, one of my major focuses of the past two decades has been the use of cultural studies and critical social theory to interrogate the big events of the time: *The Persian Gulf TV War* (Kellner 1992), *Grand Theft 2000: Media Spectacle and a Stolen Election* (Kellner 2001), *From 9/11 to Terror War* on the September 11 terrorist attacks and their exploitation by the Bush administration to push through right-wing militarism, interventionism, unilateralism and a hard-right domestic agenda, including the Patriot Act (Kellner 2003b), and *Media Spectacle and the Crisis of Democracy* (Kellner 2005), which demonstrated how the Bush administration consistently manipulated media spectacle during its first term and in the highly contested and controversial 2004 election. In my books *Media Culture* (Kellner 1995) and *Media Spectacle* (Kellner 2003a), I use cultural studies to critically interrogate major phenomena of the day like Reagan and Rambo, Madonna and pop feminism, rap and hip hop, cyberpunk and the Internet, McDonald's and globalization, Michael Jordan and the Nike spectacle, and other defining cultural phenomena of the era.

Cultural studies is an interdisciplinary, transdisciplinary, and counterdisciplinary approach that can be used to address a wide range of cultural phenomena from advertising to political narratives (see Kellner 1995, 2003). A multiperspectival and interdisciplinary enterprise, it draws on a number of disciplines to engage production and political economy of culture, critical engagement with texts, and audience research into effects. As a transdisciplinary enterprise, it has its own integrity as defined by the practices, methods, and work developing in its ever-expanding tradition. And it is counterdisciplinary, by refusing assimilation into standard academic disciplines, being open to a variety of methods and theoretical positions, and assuming a critical-oppositional stance to the current organization of the university, media, and society.

In the following study, I will illustrate my approach to merging cultural studies with critical social theory by providing a diagnostic reading of the tragic shootings at Virginia Tech in April 2007. First, I analyze the construction of the media spectacle of the Virginia Tech shooting, and how old and new media together helped produce the spectacle. Examining how the spectacle was constructed by various individuals and social groups, I analyze how the text of

"The Virginia Tech Massacre" was interpreted and deployed by different individuals and groups to use the spectacle to promote their own agendas.

The Shooting and the Politics of Race

Initial media reports indicated that there was a shooting in a dorm on the Virginia Tech campus shortly after 7:00 AM on April 16. The first word was that it apparently involved a romantic clash in which a young woman and her resident dorm adviser were shot and the boyfriend was under suspicion. At the initial news conference after the first shooting, the Virginia Tech president, Charles Steger, stated that authorities initially believed the murder in the West Ambler Johnston dormitory was a domestic dispute and that the gunman had left campus.[7] Apparently, police who arrived at the dormitory questioned the roommate of the young woman, Emily Hilscher, who was the first victim of the day, and she said that her boyfriend had just dropped her off, and that he was a well-known gun enthusiast. This led the Virginia Tech police and administrators to believe that it was a lovers' quarrel gone awry, thus falling prey to a stereotype of media culture.

Approximately, two hours after the West Ambler Johnston shootings reports broke out that a shooter had entered Norris Hall, which houses the Engineering Science and Mechanics program, and was at the time also the site of many language courses, and began a killing rampage. Suddenly, it was clear that a major media event was underway and representatives from all the major U.S. broadcasting networks and print publications rushed crews to the scene, as did many foreign media.

Throughout the United States, and indeed the world, websites like www.nytimes.com highlighted reports indicating that over thirty students and faculty were killed and that the gunman had shot himself, setting off a media frenzy that involved old and new media. Virginia Tech information websites like www.Planetblacksburg.com and the student newspaper site www.collegiatetimes.com were loaded with hits and many student observers of the horror posted on these or other Internet sites, or on their Facebook or MySpace pages. One enterprising young student, Jamal Albarghouti, used his mobile phone to capture the gunshots coming out of Norris Hall and police breaking in. After filming the events, Albarghouti sent it to CNN, which placed it on its online I-reports site where it was watched by millions. CNN quickly broadcast it on air, where it was replayed repeatedly and then shown by other networks. Jamal was described by CNN as our "I-reporter," interviewed throughout the day, and featured in an interview with Larry King on his *Larry King Live* show.

Dan Gilmor, author of the popular citizen journalism text *We the Media*, noted: "We used to say that journalists write the first draft of history. Not so, not any longer. The people on the ground at these events write the first draft."[8] Gilmore perhaps exaggerates, but it is true that old and new media now work in tandem to piece together breaking stories with "citizen journalists" supplementing regular journalists and bloggers supplementing corporate media pundits.

As people throughout the world accessed mainstream media sources and new media, so too did mainstream reporters check out MySpace and YouTube and used material drawn for these and other new media sources. As young people from Virginia Tech disseminated cell phone video images, as well as first person written reports put up on their own new media spaces, it was clear that new media were now playing an important role in the time of the spectacle in constructing representations of contemporary events. Old media had lost its monopoly and was forced to rely on new media, while a variety of voices and images previously omitted from the mainstream corporate media found their own sites of dissemination, discussion, and debate for, as we will see, better and worse.

Every major news corporation rushed crews and top network broadcasting people to Blacksburg in one of the most highly-saturated media sites of all time. There were estimates that at the peak of the coverage, there were more than six hundred reporters on the scene and four or five acres of satellite television trucks.[9]

The shooter was at first described as an "Asian male," leading to a flurry of speculation. Often initial racialized attributions of the killer in a mass murder spectacle plays on deeply rooted racism. In the Oklahoma City bombings of 1994, initial allegations targeted Arab, Middle Eastern perpetrators, setting off a paroxysm of racism. Soon after, when it was discovered that the villain was a white American Timothy McVeigh, who had fought in the Gulf War, there was shock and disbelief (see chapter 3.12).

Likewise, on the day of the Virginia Tech shooting, as *Media Matters* reports:

> right-wing pundit Debbie Schlussel "speculat[ed]" in an April 16 weblog post that the shooter, who had been identified at that point only as a man of Asian descent, might be a "Paki" Muslim and part of "a coordinated terrorist attack." "Paki" is a disparaging term for a person of Pakistani descent.

Schlussel wrote, "The murderer has been identified by law enforcement and media reports as a young Asian male," adding, "The Virginia Tech campus has a very large Muslim community, many of which are from Pakistan." Schlussel continued: "Pakis are considered 'Asian,'" and asked, "Were there two [shooters] and was this a coordinated terrorist attack?" Schlussel asserted that the reason she was "speculating that the 'Asian' gunman is a Pakistani Muslim" was "[b]ecause law enforcement and the media strangely won't tell us more specifically who the gunman is." Schlussel claimed that "[e]ven if it does not turn out that the shooter is Muslim, this is a demonstration to Muslim jihadists all over that it is extremely easy to shoot and kill multiple American college students."[10]

Soon after, the media began reporting that the murderer was "a Chinese national here on a student visa,"[11] which led Schlussel and right-wing bloggers to find "[y]et another reason to stop letting in so many foreign students." Some conservative bloggers talked of how young Chinese receive military training and that this could account for the mayhem, while other right-wing websites and commentators argued that the Virginia Tech event showed the need for tougher immigration law.[12]

When the killer was identified as a "South Korean national," Seung-Hui Cho, and "a South Korean who was a resident alien in the United States," racist comments emerged about the violent authoritarianism of Koreans.[13] Frightened Korean students began leaving the Virginia Tech campus, Korean communities everywhere grieved, and the president of South Korea made a formal apology.[14]

This apology was not enough for the likes of Fox TV's Bill O'Reilly who argued that "the Virginia Tech killer was Korean, not American."[15] When Jam Sardar, an Iranian American and correspondent for Comcast Network, went on Fox News Channel's "O'Reilly Factor" on April 20, 2007, to discuss the question of whether representation of Cho's ethnicity was overplayed, O'Reilly did most of the talking, argued that Cho's ethnicity deserved top billing and denied that Arab Americans were victims of any significant backlash after September 11, leading Sardar to comment: "Thanks for letting me listen."

There were also speculations throughout the first day that Cho had not acted alone and that there was a second shooter. On the 8:00 PM CNN *Paula Zahn Now*, Zahn and her CNN correspondent Brianna Keilar repeatedly speculated about a second suspect, confusing what officials described as "a person of interest," probably the boyfriend of the young woman shot in the first dorm murder, with a possible second suspect. Zahn, Keilar, and others on the show spoke, however, of intense anger of Virginia Tech students that there was not an alert by the administration after the first shooting, a theme that disappeared from the mainstream corporate media soon thereafter.

Early revelations about the shooter profiled Cho as a loner who seemed to have few if any friends and who generally avoided contact with other students and teachers. There were reports that he had left a rambling note directed against "rich kids," "deceitful charlatans," and "debauchery," which police found in his dorm room and which commentators used to narrativize the event as unspecific revenge killings.

The first representation of Cho portrayed a static photo of an unsmiling, shy, sad, and rather ordinary young man in glasses, that replicated a certain stereotype of Asian American males as nerdy, awkward, and self-effacing, but also nonthreatening. Classmates interviewed on television indicated that he rarely spoke and that few knew him. Other reports recount his extreme alienation, starting in high school. There were reports that in high school Cho was mocked in school for the way that he spoke. According to a student at Virginia Tech, Chris Davids, who went to high school with Cho:

> Once, in English class, the teacher had the students read aloud, and when it was Cho's turn, he just looked down in silence, Davids recalled. Finally, after the teacher threatened him with an F for participation, Cho started to read in a strange, deep voice that sounded "like he had something in his mouth," Davids said.
>
> "As soon as he started reading, the whole class started laughing and pointing and saying, 'Go back to China,'" Davids said.[16]

While there were reports of bullying at middle and high school, and in a Christian youth group that Cho participated in,[17] there was no evidence that he was bullied at Virginia Tech where it appears he initially tried to fit in. Yet he was obviously haunted by demons and insecurities evident in his writings, two of which from a play-writing class were posted on the Internet.[18] These texts, and previous work in his writing classes, had deeply disturbed other students who had access to them, leading one of his teachers to confront the English Department chairperson about Cho. Professor Lucinda Roy, a distinguished English professor and then Chair of the Department, agreed to work with him personally, but Cho was unresponsive, leading Roy and others to advise him to seek campus counseling in 2005, an event that I will return to later in the narrative.

As the media spectacle unfolded during the first days, it was generally overlooked that the Virginia Tech Massacre could be seen as an attempt to act out some of his violent fantasies and create a media spectacle in which Cho appears as the director and star. Just as al Qaeda has been orchestrating terror events to promote their Jihadist agenda, and the Bush administration orchestrated a war in Iraq to promote its geopolitical agenda, so too have individuals carried through spectacles of terror to seek attention, revenge, or to realize violent fantasies.

In 1994, Timothy McVeigh participated in the bombing of the federal building in Oklahoma City, killing hundreds and unleashing a major media spectacle of the era—linked to the deadly U.S. government attack on a religious compound in Waco a year before (see *Guys and Guns Amok*, chapter 3.12).[19]

Almost exactly eight years to the day after the Oklahoma City bombing, two teenage middle-class white boys, Eric Harris and Dylan Klebold, went on a shooting rampage in Columbine, Colorado before taking their own lives (see *Guys and Guns Amok*, chapter 3). Hence, perhaps not by accident the Columbine High shootings took place on April 20, while the Oklahoma City bombings took place on April 19, 1995, on the anniversary of the government siege of Waco that killed members of a religious community some years before. While Cho's April madness preceded the April 19–20 nexus by a couple of days, he joined a constellation of American domestic male terrorists that call attention to a constellation of serious social problems in the United States today.

Cho's Multimedia Dossier

The cable news networks were covering the "Virginia Tech Massacre," as it quickly became designated, in wall to wall coverage and when George W. Bush agreed to speak at a convocation at Virginia Tech along with the Virginia governor on April 17, the two state Senators, and a congressional delegation, the major broadcasting networks put aside their soap operas and daytime programming and covered the convocation live, making it a major media event.

Although George W. Bush had avoided for years going to funerals for victims of his Iraq War, he arrived with his wife Laura ready to make a speech and then do interviews with the network broadcasting news anchors who had assembled in Blacksburg for the event. Bush was at a critical time in his presidency. His Iraq policy was opposed by the majority of the public and the Democrats appeared ready to fight Bush on his costly and contested intervention in Iraq. In November 2006 Congressional elections, Republicans lost control of the House and the Senate and committees in both chambers were investigating a series of scandals in the Bush administration. Bush's Attorney General, one of his closest operatives Alberto Gonzalez, was caught up in a major scandal and there were calls for his resignation. Questions concerning Bush's competency were intensifying and it appeared that his last months in office would be conflicted ones.

Yet, in 1995 it appeared that Bill Clinton's presidency had failed and was collapsing after Republicans won control of Congress in the 1994 off-term elections, and when Talk Radio was fiercely savaging the Clintons and inventing scandals like the so-called Whitewater Affair (see Lyons and Conason 2001). It is believed that after the tragedy of the Oklahoma City bombings Clinton reconnected with the public and his ratings went up steadily from that time, taking him handily through the 1996 presidential elections and enabling him to survive a major sex and impeachment scandal (see Kellner 2003a).

Could Bush also establish himself as Mourner-in-Chief and would publics rally around him as they did after 9/11? Bush's speech, live on all the major U.S. television networks, followed Virginia governor Timothy Kaine. Kaine took an Old Testament approach, speaking of Job and his sufferings and the mysteries of faith. Bush, by contrast, took a New Testament line speaking of the love and care of God for his people, suggesting that belief in God and the power of prayer would get them through their ordeal. His carefully crafted sound byte read: "Today our nation grieves with those who have lost loved ones at Virginia Tech. We hold the victims in our hearts. We lift them up in our prayers. And we ask a loving God to comfort those who are suffering." After a few further clichés and generalities from Bush, members of the local Christian, Moslem, Judaic, and even Buddhist faith got a few minutes of national airtime to pitch their religions, before the convocation turned inward to Virginia Tech concerns and the major broadcasting networks cut off their coverage.

Bush and his wife Laura were interviewed for the major news networks that night and it was clear that he was not even going to consider stricter gun control laws and by the weekend the buzz word for his administration was "mental health," a safe topic that could replace gun control for national debate and political action. It is unlikely that Bush's performance as Consoler-in-Chief would help him much as the following day there were some of the most deadly bombings in the Iraq War and by the end of the week hundreds of Shi'ites were dead from terrorist bombings, Shia politicians were pulling out of the government, and it appeared the Iraq debacle was worsening. And on Thursday, April 19, 2007, a congressional grilling of Bush's attorney general Alberto Gonzalez produced such an inept and embarrassingly incompetent performance that even conservative Republicans were calling for his resignation, which eventually occurred on September 17, 2007.

Meanwhile, intense media focus continued to unravel facts about the assassin Cho, about his victims and acts of heroism, and about failures of the Virginia Tech administration to deal with Cho and the resultant crisis. A multimedia package that Cho mailed to NBC News on April 16, apparently after the first murder in the dorm, and widely shown on April 18, revealed that Cho indeed was planning a media spectacle in the tradition of the Columbine shooters who he celebrated as "martyrs."

A picture and video gallery in the multimedia dossier sent to NBC is said to have contained a DVD that held twenty-seven video clips, forty-three captioned still photos, and a 1,800-word document that could reproduce the rant that was reported on the first day.[20] The material made it clear that Cho was planning to carry out himself a plan that he had constructed as "Massacre at Virginia Tech." One of the photos in which Cho posed with a hammer in his hand reprises the Korean "Asian Extreme" film *Oldboy*,[21] which itself is a revenge fantasy in which a young Korean inexplicably imprisoned in a room goes on a rampage of revenge against his captors. Another pose shows Cho pointing a gun at his own head, another iconic image of *Oldboy*, which in turn is quoting Robert de Niro's famous scene in *Taxi Driver*, in which he follows a slaughter of perceived villains with a suicidal blowing of his head apart, just as Cho did. Further, as Stephen Hunter argues, much of the iconography in the photo gallery quotes poses in films by Hong Kong action director John Woo, as in the images where Cho holds two guns in his hands, and points a gun at a camera. Further, Cho brandishes the same weapons featured in Woo's movies, that include *The Killer* where a professional assassin goes down a corridor, enters a room, and systematically mows down its occupants.[22]

The transformation of Cho's image was striking. The shy nerdy student was suddenly aggressively staring in the camera with cold and calculating eyes, tightly holding guns, wearing a backwards black baseball cap, fingerless black gloves, and a black T-shirt under a khaki photographer-style vest. When he spoke in a mocking monotone, he spit out belligerent taunts and verbal assaults at all and sundry, laced with obscenities. Cho's construction of a violent masculinity is apparent in the gap between the first still photo and his multimedia dossier when he assumes the guises and paraphernalia of an alpha dog, ultra-macho man. The very exaggeration and hyberbole of the dossier, hardly a "manifesto" as Brian Williams of NBC described it when he introduced it to a shocked nation, calls attention to the constructedness and artificiality of hypermaleness in U.S. society. Further, his extreme actions call attention to the potential destructiveness and devastation in assuming an ultramacho identity. Since Cho was apparently not able to construct a normal student and male identity, he obviously resorted to extremism and exaggeration.

Cho's literary expressions in his dossier and personal symbols also point to an aesthetic of excess. Earlier reports indicated that Cho had written in ink "Ismail Ax" on his arm. The "Ismail Ax" reference led some conservatives to conclude that Cho was Islamic inspired. Jonah Goldberg, for instance, speculated that:

First it was Johnny Muhammad, now it was Cho Sueng Hui aka Ismail Ax. Precisely how many mass shooters have to turn out to have adopted Muslim names before we get it? Islam has become the tribe of choice of those who hate American society . . . I'm talking about the angry, malignant, narcissist loners who want to reject their community utterly, to throw off their "slave name" and represent the downtrodden of the earth by shooting their friends and neighbors.

This morning I read that the Virginia Tech shooter died with the name Ismail Ax written in red ink on his arm. The mainstream press doesn't seem to have a clue as to what this might mean. To quote Indiana Jones, "Didn't any of you guys go to Sunday School?"[23]

But on the evening of April 18, NBC reported that the package with the multimedia dossier was addressed as sent from "A. Ishmael." The latter literary spelling of the Old Testament and Koranic "Ismail" could refer to the opening of Herman Melville's classic *Moby Dick*, where the narrator begins with "Call me Ishmael." This reading would position the shooter as on a revenge quest, as was Captain Ahab against the White Whale, Moby Dick. But it also positions Cho himself within the great tradition of American literature, as Ishmael is the narrator of one of the United States's great novels. Another Internet search noted that the literary character Ishmael is also "tied to James Fenimore Cooper's novel *The Prairie*, Ishmael Bush is known as an outcast and outlawed warrior, according to an essay written in 1969 by William H. Goetzmann, a University of Texas History professor. In Cooper's book, 'Bush carries the prime symbol of evil—the spoiler's axe,' the professor wrote."[24]

Perhaps the Ishmael Ax moniker positions Cho as well in the tradition of Hollywood and Asian Extreme gore films featuring Ax(e) murderers, as other photos in his dossier show him with knives and hammer in hand, iconography familiar from horror and gore films, which he had apparently studied.[25]

Yet, Ismail/Ishmael is also a Biblical name, prominent in both the Judaic and Islamic religions. As Richard Engel points out: "Ismail is the Koranic name of Abraham's first-born son. In one of the central stories of the *Koran*, God orders Abraham (called Ibrahim) to sacrifice Ismail as a test of faith, but then intervenes and replaces him with a sheep. Muslims reenact this story by sacrificing a sheep on Eid al-Adha (feast of the sacrifice) during the Hajj, the annual pilgrimage to Mecca."[26]

Cho's references in his text thus span high and low culture and various religious and literary traditions in a postmodern pastiche. The references to Christ in his rambling "manifesto" position Cho himself as sacrificial and redemptive, although he also blames Jesus for his rampage, writing: "You have vandalized my heart, raped my soul and torched my conscience. You thought it was one pathetic boy's life you were extinguishing. Thanks to you, I die like Jesus Christ, to inspire generations of the weak and the defenseless people." But then: "Jesus loved crucifying me. He loved inducing cancer in my head, terrorizing my heart and ripping my soul all this time."

Another excerpt from his text positions Cho as a domestic terrorist carrying out a revenge fantasy when he writes: "you had a hundred billion chances and ways to have avoided today. . . . But you decided to spill my blood. You forced me into a corner and gave me only one option. The decision was yours. Now you have blood on your hands that will never wash off."

The "you" in the message seems to refer to all the fellow students and teachers who failed to grasp his creative genius and who ridiculed his writings and behavior. "You" also could refer to you and I more generally as part of a culture that Cho had come to violently and psychotically reject, although "You" could also refer to the media itself as his inspiration, for his sick murder rampage was clearly based on media culture and its vehicle was media spectacle.

Cho thus can be seen as a domestic terrorist assassin in the tradition of Timothy McVeigh, the Unabomber, and the two Columbine shooters (see *Guys and Guns Amok,* chapter 3), the latter of whom he mentions in the text as "martyrs." Richard Engel, NBC's Middle East Bureau chief noted in his blog that Cho's "testimony" videos were grimly reminiscent of suicide bombers who left videos explaining their actions and trying to justify themselves with grievances and higher purposes.[27] But Cho also positions himself as a vehicle of class revenge:

> You had everything you wanted. Your Mercedes wasn't enough, you brats. Your golden necklaces weren't enough, you snobs. Your trust fund wasn't enough. Your vodka and Cognac weren't enough. All your debaucheries weren't enough. Those weren't enough to fulfill your hedonistic needs. You had everything.

The ensuing media spectacle apparently achieved what the crazed Cho had in mind, a spectacle of terror a la the 9/11 terror attacks which attracted scores of media from all over the world to Blacksburg in saturation coverage of the event. His carefully assembled multimedia package revealed to the world who Cho was, and won for him a kind of sick and perverted immortality, or at least tremendous notoriety in the contemporary moment.

There was a fierce, albeit partially hypocritical, backlash against NBC for releasing the media dossier and making a potential hero and martyr out of Cho. No doubt, any network getting such a scoop would broadcast it in the current frenetic competition for media ratings, and all of the networks gave saturation coverage to the dossier, each image of which was burned with the NBC logo, just as earlier video camera footage of the gunshots echoing from Norris Hall all contained the CNN logo.

Cho was media savy enough to know that NBC (or any television network) would broadcast his material, while it is well-known that the police in the Columbine shootings only later released small portions of the killers' videos and writings. It should also be pointed out that Cho's videography and picture posing replicated the form of young people's posting on sites like MySpace or Facebook, while his video is similar to the kinds of postings young people put on YouTube. Previously, Cho's Facebook nom de plume was QuestionMark?, a phrase he also used in text-messaging. Now the world had at least some idea who Seung-Hui Cho really was, although many question marks remain.

Guns and Political Scapegoating

Every time that there is a significant school, university, or workplace shooting, there is discussion of the need for stricter gun laws, but after some brief discussion the issue falls away. After Virginia governor Timothy Kaine returned to Blacksburg from a Tokyo trade conference on April 17 of the Virginia Tech Convocation, he announced that he would appoint a panel at the university's request to review the authorities' handling of the disaster. But, in a widely quoted statement, he warned against making snap judgments and said he had "nothing but loathing" for those who take the tragedy and "make it their political hobby horse to ride."[28]

The pro-gun lobby, however, and right-wing pundits, was ready with its ammunition and took an offensive role. Right-wing Internet sites began immediately claiming that the fact that Virginia had banned guns from state universities meant that there were no student shooters able to take down the assailant. I saw this position articulated on MSNBC the day of the shooting itself by a Denver law school professor with the MSNBC Live anchor Amy Robach agreeing that the scale of murder might have been reduced if students were allowed to carry guns. A sane gun authority on the show reacted with horror to the idea of having unrestricted guns on campus, but was cut off by the anchor and not able to articulate his position. Indeed, consider having a classroom, dorm, or public university space full of armed students, faculty, or staff, who might go off on a sudden whim, and one can easily imagine a daily massacre in a gun-saturated America.

While both sides on the gun controversy tried to get out their points of view, the pro-gun control side was quickly marginalized, as I will show. Initially, however, in Sacha Zimmerman's summary:

> Before the blood had even dried at Tech, the gun-control debate erupted. Both sides of the issue seemed to be in a race for the first word, for the best spin. "It is irresponsibly dangerous to tell citizens that they may not have guns at schools," said Larry Pratt, executive director of Gun Owners of America. Meanwhile, White House spokeswoman Dana Perino was quick to awkwardly assure the world that the president still believes in the right to bear arms. And Suzanna Hupp, a former Texas state representative and concealed-weapons advocate, appeared on CBS's *The Early Show* not twenty-four hours after the shootings for a debate: "Why are we removing my teachers' right to protect themselves and the children that are in their care?" Her opposition, Paul Helmke, president of the Brady Center to Prevent Gun Violence, swiftly sprung into action: "Let's prevent these folks from getting these guns in the first place.... If they can't get that gun with a high-powered clip that's shooting off that many rounds that quickly, then we're making our community safer."[29]

The corporate broadcasting media, however, allowed few pro-gun control voices to be heard. Representative Carolyn McCarthy (D-NY), whose husband was killed and son seriously injured in a Long Island Rail Road shooting, was on several networks. She urged House leaders to move quickly to push forward stalled legislation that would improve databases that could be used in conducting criminal background checks on potential gun purchasers, an issue she had been pushing for years. While Philip Van Cleave, president of the Virginia Citizens Defense League conceded that allowing faculty and students to carry guns might not have prevented the rampage, he claimed that at least "they wouldn't die like sheep, ... but more like a wolf with some fangs, able to fight back."[30] The macho Right, in fact, attacked the Virginia Tech students for not fighting back more ferociously against the assassin. As *Media Matters* compiled the story:

> In the April 18 edition of his daily program notes, called Nealz Nuze and posted on his website, nationally syndicated radio host Neal Boortz asked: "How far have we advanced in the wussification of America?" Boortz was responding to criticism of comments he made on the April 17 broadcast of his radio show regarding the mass shooting at

Virginia Tech. During that broadcast, Boortz asked: "How the hell do twenty-five students allow themselves to be lined up against the wall in a classroom and picked off one by one? How does that happen, when they could have rushed the gunman, the shooter, and most of them would have survived?" In his April 18 program notes, Boortz added: "It seems that standing in terror waiting for your turn to be executed was the right thing to do, and any questions as to why twenty-five students didn't try to rush and overpower Cho Seung-Hui are just examples of right wing maniacal bias. Surrender-comply-adjust. The doctrine of the left.... Even the suggestion that young adults should actually engage in an act of self defense brings howls of protest."

In the April 17 edition of his program notes, Boortz had similarly asked: "Why didn't some of these students fight back? How in the hell do you line students up against a wall (if that's the way it played out) and start picking them off one by one without the students turning on you? You have a choice. Try to rush the killer and get his gun, or stand there and wait to be shot. I would love to hear from some of you who have insight into situations such as this. Was there just not enough time to react? Were they paralyzed with fear? Were they waiting for someone else to take action? Sorry.... I just don't understand."[31]

Boortz and other right-wing macho Rambos dishonor the heroism of professors and students who blocked classroom doors, with one elderly seventy-six-year old professor, Holocaust survivor Liviu Librescu, getting killed trying to block the door shut so students could escape out the window. Another professor and his students were able to block the door of their classroom and prevent Cho from entering. Further, there could well be untold tales of heroism, as well as many documented ones.[32]

Right-wing response to the Virginia Tech tragedy was both appalling and revealing. Some prominent rightist commentators took the occasion of the tragedy and intense media spectacle to bash liberals or their favorite targets. *Media Matters* reported that "(o)n the April 19 broadcast of his nationally syndicated radio show, host Rush Limbaugh declared that the perpetrator of the April 16 Virginia Tech shootings 'had to be a liberal,' adding: 'You start railing against the rich, and all this other—this guy's a liberal. He was turned into a liberal somewhere along the line. So it's a liberal that committed this act.'"[33] But it is doubtful Cho had a coherent political ideology, and he clearly inserted himself in the tradition of domestic terrorists including the Columbine shooters and Timothy McVeigh, hardly "liberal."

Professional 1960s-basher Thomas Sowell blamed the Virginia Tech and Columbine shootings on 1960s culture and its alleged "collective guilt" that supposedly blamed 1960s urban violence on society and somehow sent out the message that it was okay to kill people because it's all society's fault.[34] Sowell's failure in argument and reasoning is stunning, as no one makes the arguments about the 1960s he claims, and puts on display the simple-minded tendency of right wing ideologues to blame everything on their own pet peeves and ideological obsessions.

But the most extreme example of rank hypocrisy and political exploitation of the Virginia Tech tragedy was a dual intervention by *Washington Post* columnist Charles Krauthammer. Krauthammer, one of the most enthusiastic advocates to this day of the Iraq War, reasonably wrote in his April 19 *Washington Post* column that it is terribly inappropriate to exploit tragedies like the Virginia Tech shootings to make ideological arguments. But later in the day and less than forty-eight hours after the shooting, Krauthammer was on Fox News exploiting the shootings to promote one of his personal hobby horses. As Glen Greenwood notes in his *Salon* blog, Krauthammer just couldn't help running to Fox News "to explain why the Virginia Tech shootings and the killer's 'manifesto' are connected to Al Jazeera, the Palestinians and other Muslim Enemies who dominate Krauthammer's political agenda":

> KRAUTHAMMER: What you can say, just—not as a psychiatrist, but as somebody who's lived through the a past seven or eight years, is that if you look at that picture, it draws its inspiration from the manifestos, the iconic photographs of the Islamic suicide bombers over the last half decade in Palestine, in Iraq and elsewhere.
>
> That's what they end up leaving behind, either on al Jazeera or Palestinian TV. And he, it seems, as if his inspiration for leaving the message behind in that way, might have been this kind of suicide attack, which, of course, his was. And he did leave the return address return "Ismail Ax." "Ismail Ax." I suspect it has some more to do with Islamic terror and the inspiration than it does with the opening line of *Moby Dick*.[35]

In fact, the "Ismail" and "Ishmael" references in Cho's testimony could refer to the Ishmail character in either the Old Testament or the *Koran*, or it could refer to *Moby Dick*'s narrator Ishmael, or a hybridized fantasy of Cho's deranged and disordered mind. Krauthammer's blaming the massacre on "Al Jazeera, the Palestinians and other Muslim Enemies" gives us insight into Krauthammer's deranged and disordered mind that sees his Muslim enemies at work everywhere from Iraq to Blacksburg, Virginia.

Never missing an opportunity to attack pharmaceuticals, the "church" of Scientology cited Cho's reported use of antidepressants and sent twenty of its "ministers" to Blacksburg to help with the "healing" process. A Scientologist spokesperson Sylvia Stannard claimed that the killings demonstrate "these mind-altering drugs" make "you numb to other people's suffering. You really have to be drugged up to coldly kill people like that." Indeed, according to a report by George Rush and Joanna Rush Molloy: "Even before Cho's name was released, the Citizens Commission on Human Rights, a group founded by the church [of Scientology], said in a press release that 'media and law enforcement must move quickly to investigate the Virginia shooter's psychiatric drug history—a common factor amongst school shooters.'"[36]

Obviously, Cho had major mental health issues, and serious psychiatrists saw clinical evidence in Cho's dossier, writings, and behavior of classical paranoid schizophrenia,[37] that itself could be genetically generated or the product of some terrible brain disorder, while others saw evidence of depression, acute autism, or various forms of psychosis, or claimed that there was no evidence he suffered from any specific mental illness.[38] Yet such disease is itself overdetermined and often impossible to pinpoint the exact casual etiology, just as shootings like the Columbine rampage are socially overdetermined. Medical reductions cover over the social problems to which school shootings and societal violence call attention, just as do the repeated evocations by pundits that Cho was simply "insane," and that this explains everything, or that he was an exemplar of "radical evil," another popular conservative (mis)explanation.

After school or workplace shootings or similar events that become media spectacles, there are demands for simple explanation, scapegoats, and actions. After the Columbine shootings, certain pundits attacked the Internet, Marilyn Manson, and various forms of goth or punk music and culture, violent films and television, video games, and just about every form of youth culture except bowling. In Cho's case, his alleged earlier interest in video games, his deep Internet fascination, and his seeming affinity for violent movies could lead some to scapegoat these forms of youth culture. This would be, I believe, a serious mistake. Rather than ban media culture from the lives of youth and its study from schools, I would advocate critical media literacy as an essential part of education from early grade schools through the university level (see Kellner 1995 and *Guys and Guns Amok,* chapter 4).

In addition, however, I want to argue for multiperspectivist interpretations of events like the Virginia Tech Massacre or the Columbine Shootings (or for that matter for political events like the Iraq War). We still do not know exactly why the Columbine shootings took place and there are no doubt a multiplicity of factors ranging from the experiences at school of the extremely alienated teenage boys, to any number of cultural influences, including the culture of violence and violent gun culture in the United States, or specific familial or individual experiences. As Michael Moore and a father of one of the teenagers shot at Columbine concluded in the film *Bowling for Columbine,* there's no one simple answer to why there is so much gun violence in the United States, but rather a variety of interacting causes, requiring multicausal explanation (*Guys and Guns Amok,* chapter 3.32).

Likewise, we may never know why Cho choose to engineer and orchestrate the Virginia Tech Massacre and from his multimedia dossier it is clear that there were a range of influences spanning violent Korean and Asian films, the Columbine shooters who he referred to as "martyrs," religious texts and references ranging from the Koran to the both the Old and New Testaments of the Bible, to possible literary influences. Reports of his life indicate that earlier he was devoted to basketball and video games and his dormmates note that he spent hours on the computer, often listening repeatedly to certain songs. Such reports were used to attack Internet games,[39] but few criticized his basketball obsession as fuelling murderous fantasies. Moreover, one report indicated that he wrote the lyrics to his favorite Collective Soul song "Shine," that he reportedly repeatedly listened to, on the walls of his dorm room:

> Teach me how to speak
> Teach me how to share
> Teach me where to go
> Tell me will love be there[40]

While the disappointment of such yearning could inspire rage, it is ludicrous to blame the music, or any one of Cho's media cultural influences, for the Virginia Tech Massacre, and pundits who pick out any single influence, usually one of their favorite targets, are irresponsible. Complex events always have a multiplicity of causes and to attempt to produce a single-factor explanation or solution is simplistic and reductive. As noted, Cho also had creative ambitions, understood the workings of the media and media spectacle, and carefully planned his moments of infamy. No doubt more facts and information may emerge concerning Cho's influences, motivations, and warped actions, but it would be wrong at this time to try to provide a one-sided interpretation or explanation.

There is no doubt that Cho became obsessed with guns and violent gun culture during his last days. There are reports that he had thoroughly immersed himself in the culture of gun violence, buying one gun from a local store and another over the Internet, where the seller indicated he appeared a highly knowledgeable gun consumer. Cho bought ammunition from the Internet, went to a gym to buff himself up, went to a shooting range to engage in target practice, and thoroughly immersed himself in ultramasculinist gun culture.[41]

Yet a constellation of influences helped construct Cho and we may probably never know the precise influences of media culture, models of masculinity, gun culture, and the specific environmental influences of family, school, and social life. The overdetermined nature of events like school shootings requires multiperspectivist analysis and contextualizing the event in the life-situation of those involved. I have criticized certain one-sided interpretations of Cho's rampage and shown how the media spectacle of the "Virginia Tech Massacre" has been a contested event. In my forthcoming book *Guys and Guns Amok* (Kellner 2008), I put the Virginia Tech shootings in the context of analyses of alienation of youth, domestic terrorism, the construction of masculinist male identities in media culture and gun culture, and situate Cho in a constellation that includes Timothy McVeigh and the Oklahoma City bombings, the Unabomber, and the Columbine school shootings to provide examples of individuals who construct their identities and produce media spectacles to advance their politics in a context of guns and men running amok. Hence, the sketch here of the "Virginia Tech Massacre" is provisional and requires a broader context to fully engage.

Notes

1. I am using the term "The Virginia Tech Massacre" because this was the phrase that the major broadcasting networks used from the beginning and continued to use through the opening days of the spectacle. This text is part of a larger project where I engage the spectacle of the Virginia Tech Massacre and put it in the context of the domestic terrorism of the Oklahoma City bombings, the Unabomber, and the Columbine High School shootings. The book, *Guys and Guns Amok: Domestic Terrorism and School Shootings from the Oklahoma City Bombings to the Virginia Tech Massacre*, will be published by Paradigm Press in 2008. Thanks to Jennifer Knerr and Henry Giroux for facilitating a fast contract and for helpful comments on the text. Finally, I am putting all articles referenced in footnotes, most of which have hypertext links, while am referencing books in standard form.

2. My notion of media spectacle builds on French theorist Guy Debord's society of spectacle (1967), but differs significantly from Debord's concept (see Kellner 2003a and 2005). Debord's *The Society of the Spectacle* (1967) was published in translation in a pirate edition by Black and Red (Detroit) in 1970 and reprinted many times; another edition appeared in 1983 and a new translation in 1994. The key texts of Debord and his group, the Situationist International, are found on various websites, producing a curious afterlife for Situationist ideas and practices. For further discussion of Debord and the Situationists, see Best and Kellner 2001, Chapter 3; see also the discussions of spectacle culture in Best and Kellner 2001 and Kellner 2003a.

3. See Douglas Kellner, "The Katrina Hurricane Spectacle and the Crisis of the Bush Presidency," *Cultural Studies, Critical Methodologies*, Vol. 7, no. 2 (May 2007): 222–34, and Giroux (2006).

4. Thanks to Christine Kelly for e-mailing me (April 23, 2007) that: What also has to be challenged is the media's assertion that the VT tragedy is the "deadliest mass shooting in U.S. history." This isn't true. According to Peter Hart on FAIR's (Fairness and Accuracy in Reporting) "CounterSpin" radio program this week, "The 1873 massacre of Black militia soldiers during Reconstruction left an estimated 105 dead, the Sand Creek Massacre of Cheyenne left a comparable death toll, Wounded Knee was a massacre of around three hundred, the 1921 killings in Tulsa, Oalahoma ... killings of African Americans in what is often referred to as "The Black Wall Street" left dozens dead." I would add to that the 1871 killing of nineteen Chinese men and boys in Los Angeles and the 1885 massacre of twenty-eight Chinese killed and fifteen wounded, some of whom later died, in Rock Springs, Wyoming. This is not to diminish what happened at VT but if the media wants to make statements regarding an incident's historical context they should take the time to make sure they do the research. Or, perhaps, the killings of Native Americans, Asians, and African Americans by white mobs don't really matter.

5. Following Korean conventions of listing the family name first, the Virginia Tech shooter was first referred to as Cho Seung-Hui in the U.S. media, but the family intervened and requested the more Americanized designation Seung-Hui Cho, and I will follow this convention here.

6. On diagnostic critique, see Kellner and Ryan 1988 and Kellner, 1995, 116–17.

7. Hank Kurz, Jr., "Questions Raised on Va. Tech Security," *Washington Post*, Associated Press report, April 16, 2006, retrieved on April 16, 2007. See also Michael D. Shear, "Campus Shutdown never Considered," *Washington Post*, April 22, 2007:A01, which indicates that when Virginia Tech president Charles W. Steger and his top lieutenants gathered to assess the first shooting, they were called from the dorm by Campus Police Chief Wendell Flinchum who informed them that the police were on top of the case and were on the trail of the dead student's boyfriend, the suspect in the killing. Obviously, this assumption was wrong and a debate has unfolded concerning what the proper response should have been after the initial shooting.

8. Gilmore was quoted in Bobbie Johnson and Conor Clarke, "America's first user-generated confession. The U.S. college shooting marked a watershed moment for old and new media." *The Guardian*, April 23, 2007, at media.guardian.co.uk/site/story/0,,2063112,00.html.

9. Michael Bush, "Virginia Tech creates comms team in wake of tragedy," *PRWeek*, April 23, 2007 at www.prweek.com/us/sectors/crisiscommunications/article/651936/Virginia-Tech-creates-comms-team-wake-tragedy/.

10. Quoted from mediamatters.org/items/200704170006.

11. This story was first reported by Michael Steed in the *Chicago Sun-Times* who claimed that the suspect was "a Chinese national who arrived in the United States last year on a student visa ... [who] ... reportedly arrived in San Francisco on a United Airlines flight on Aug. 7, 2006, on a visa issued in Shanghai" at www.SunTimes.com (no longer accessible). The story quickly disappeared from the

paper's website but not before it circulated through mainstream broadcasting media networks and the Internet.

12. For instance, see the posting by Peter Brimlow, "Virginia Tech Massacre: Gun Control—Or Immigration Control?," April 18, 2007, at the right-wing blog www.vdare.com/pb/070418_vt.htm.

13. On the fringes, there was speculation by Mae Brussell on whether Cho had CIA or Moonie connections given South Korea's close connections with the CIA and whether Cho was a Manchurian candidate whose programming ran amok, or was intended to divert attention from Bush administration scandals; see Brussells, "The Conspiracy Theory Blog" which continues to probe Cho/CIA/Moonie connections at theconspiratorsnest.blogspot.com/search/label/VaTech%20Massacre (accessed May 13, 2007). See also, Paul Joseph Watson, "Seung-Hui Cho Was a Mind Controlled Assassin," Prison Planet, April 19, 2007, at www.prisonplanet.com/print.php (accessed June 2, 2007).

14. See Sandy Banks, "Ethnicity brings an unwelcome focus," *Los Angeles Times*, April 19, 2007:A01.

14. Bill O'Reilly, "Politics and Mass Murder," April 18, 2007, at www.foxnews.com/story/0,2933,266711,00.html.

16. See Matt Apuzzo, "Former high school classmates say Va. Tech gunman was picked on in school," Associated Press, April 19, 2007, at www.thetimesnews.com/onset?id=903&template=article.html.

17. Evan Thomas, "Quiet and disturbed, Cho Seung-Hui seethed, then exploded. His odyssey." *Newsweek*, April 30, 2007, at www.msnbc.msn.com/id/18248298/site/newsweek/.

18. Two of Cho's plays were available online on April 21, 2007 at news.aol.com/virginia-tech-shootings/cho-seung-hui/_a/richard-mcbeef-cover-page/20070417134109990001. In its inimitable fashion, when these artifacts emerged on the Internet, a *New York Post* headline read "PSYCHO PENNED POISON PLAYS," by Leela de Kretser and Kate Sheehy, April 18, 2007, at www.nypost.com/seven/04182007/news/nationalnews/psycho_penned_poison_plays_nationalnews_leela_de_kretser_and_kate_sheehy.htm.

19. We still do not know exactly who participated in the Oklahoma City bombings (see chapter 3 of *Guns Amok*, forthcoming, for discussion of various theories).

20. Cho's multimedia dossier was archived at boingboing.net/2007_04_01_archive.html (accessed May 8, 2007).

21. The phrase "Extreme Asia" was a marketing slogan used to highlight an extreme form of horror and violence film emerging in Asia over the last decade, and the Sundance Channel regularly features "Asian Extreme" films. *Oldboy* (2004) is one of the most praised of this genre; made by Korean director Chanwook Park, it is part of his "vengeance triology." Curiously, Park directed the second segment of *Three Extremes* (2005), an Asian Extreme Horror fest by major Hong Kong, Korean, and Japanese directors. Park's segment features a successful director terrorized by one of the extras from his films who kidnaps his family, cuts off fingers of his piano-playing wife, induces the director to tell of his infidelity, and to kill a young girl in

the house. The crazed extra wants to demonstrate that although the director is rich, successful, famous, and thinks he is "good," he is no better than the pathetic extra. Bizarrely, the extra who torments the director looks quite similar to Cho.

22. Stephen Hunter, "Cinematic Clues to Understand the Slaughter: Did Asian Thrillers Like 'Oldboy' Influence the Va. Tech Shooter?" *Washington Post*, April 20, 2007; Page C01 at www.washingtonpost.com/wp-dyn/content/article/2007/04/19/AR2007041901817.html?hpid=topnews. A. O. Scott attacked Hunter's article, putting it in the context of attempts to blame media culture for shootings or acts of terror, but, in fact, Hunter does not overstep his claims on influence and was the first to call the attention to the uncanny resemblance between Cho's dossier and images in Asian Extreme films. See A. O. Scott, "Drawing a Line from Movie to Murder," *New York Times*, April 23, 2007 at www.nytimes.com/2007/04/23/movies/23movi.html?ex=1180843200&en=9bb670a872403172&ei=5070. I take the mediated position that media culture may have significant impact on behavior but should not be stigmatized or demonized as it is at most one factor among many in influencing violent behavior (see Kellner 1995).

23. Jonah Goldberg, *National Review* blog at corner.nationalreview.com/post/?q=MWJlNDUxODE4NjQ5NGY3NjlmMGY4MWI0OGRkNjJhODE=.

24. See "No Answers," *Tampa Bay Times*, April 18, 2007, at www.tbt.com/america/ataglance/article38944.ece.

25. It was reported that Cho had taken courses in contemporary horror films and literature, a fact that enabled conservatives to attack the study of popular culture and literature. See Marc Santora and Christine Hauser, "Anger of Killer Was on Exhibit in His Writing," *New York Times*, April 20, 2007, at www.nytimes.com/2007/04/19/us/19gunman.html.

26. Richard Engel, "Cho's 'religious' martyrdom video," at worldblog.msnbc.msn.com/archive/2007/04/19/157577.aspx. Another reading was offered by the *New York Post* cited by the *New York Times*' blog "the Lede" at thelede.blogs.nytimes.com/tag/virginia/:

The reference may be to the Islamic account of the Biblical sacrifice of Abraham, where God commands the patriarch to sacrifice his own son. Abraham begins to comply, but God intervenes at the last moment to save the boy. . . . Abraham uses a knife in most versions of the story, but some accounts have him wielding an ax.

A more obscure reference may be to a passage in the Koran referring to Abraham's destruction of pagan idols; in some accounts, he uses an ax to do so.

I should emphasize that these readings are all hermeneutical constructions and we will probably never know what meanings Cho was assigning to his text.

27. Richard Engel, op. cit.

28. Matt Apuzzo, "Va. Tech gunman writings raised concerns," Associated Press Writer, Tuesday, Apr 17, 2007, at news.yahoo.com/s/ap/20070417/ap_on_re_us/virginia_tech_shooting.

29. Sacha Zimmerman, "The true roots of the Virginia Tech massacre. Generation Columbine, TNR Online, April 19m 2007 at www.tnr.com/doc.mhtml?i=w070416&s=zimmerman041907.

30. Leslie Eaton and Michael Luo, "Shooting Rekindles Issues of Gun Rights and Restrictions," *New York Times*, April 18, 2007 at www.nytimes.com/2007/04/18/us/18pistols.html?ref=us.

31. "Boortz, others blame VA Tech victims for not fighting back,"at mediamatters .org/items/200704180007. *Media Matters* further notes that:

> In questioning the actions of Virginia Tech students involved in the April 16 incident, Boortz joined the ranks of various commentators, including *National Review Online* contributor John Derbyshire, *Chicago Sun-Times* columnist Mark Steyn, who also writes for the *National Review*, and right-wing pundit and Fox News analyst Michelle Malkin.

In an April 17 weblog post on *National Review Online's* The Corner, Derbyshire asked: "Where was the spirit of self-defense here? Setting aside the ludicrous campus ban on licensed conceals, why didn't anyone rush the guy? It's not like this was Rambo, hosing the place down with automatic weapons. He had two handguns for goodness' sake-one of them reportedly a .22." Time.com Washington editor Ana Marie Cox criticized Derbyshire in an April 17 post on *Time* magazine's political weblog, Swampland.

Steyn and Malkin have made similar statements, as the weblog Think Progress noted. In her April 18 syndicated column, Malkin wrote: "Instead of encouraging autonomy, our higher institutions of learning stoke passivity and conflict-avoidance. And as the erosion of intellectual self-defense goes, so goes the erosion of physical self-defense." In his April 18 *National Review* column, Steyn suggested that Virginia Tech students were guilty of an "awful corrosive passivity" that is "an existential threat to a functioning society." (op. cit.)

32. For a detailed account of the shooting, see David Maraniss, "'That Was the Desk I chose to Die Under," *Washington Post*, April 19, 2007: A01. See also Raymond Hernandez, "Inside Room 207, Students Panicked at Rampage and Then held Off Gunman's Return," *New York Times*, April 18, 2007. And for a full account of the events, see *Report of the Review Panel* (2007).

33. "Limbaugh said Virginia Tech shooter 'had to be a liberal'" at http://mediamatters.org/items/200704190008.

34. Thomas Sowell, "Are Today's Mass Shootings a Consequence of '60s Collective Guilt?" *Baltimore Sun*, April 26, 2007: 19A.

35. Glen Greenwood, "Charles Krauthammer takes rank hypocrisy to new lows," *Salon*, April 20, 2007 at www.salon.com/opinion/greenwald/2007/04/20/krauthammer/print.html.

36. George Rush and Joanna Rush Molloy, "Critics: Scientologists' Va. Trip: A Time to Prey," *Daily News* (New York), April 18, 2007: 24. Unfortunately, for the Scientologists' crusade against prescriptive drugs, a toxicology report indicated that there was no evidence of prescriptive drugs or toxic substances found in Cho. See "Cho's toxicology report released, Tech announces changes," *Collegiate Times*,

June 21, 2007 at collegiatetimes.com/news/1/ARTICLE/9130/2007-06-21.html (accessed June 23, 2007). While I think it is a mistake a la the Scientologists to blame school shootings on prescriptive drugs tout court, there are serious concerns about overprescription and misprescription of dangerous drugs that I do not want to ignore.

37. See, for example, Michael Welner, "Cho Likely Schizophrenic, Evidence Suggests," ABC News, April 17, 2007 at abcnews.go.com/Health/VATech/story?id=3050483.

38. For wide-ranging discussion of the psychiatric debates concerning Cho's condition, that no one can obviously definitively resolve at this point, see the open-minded and -ended discussions on Robert Lindsay's blog at robertlindsay.blogspot.com/2007/04/did-cho-have-prodromal-paranoid.html.

39. Antivideo game activist Jack Thompson appeared on Fox News the day of the shooting to point the finger of blame at video games, and Dr. Phil appeared on Larry King Live to attack video games; see Winda Benedetti, "Were Video games to blame for massacre? Pundits rushed to judge industry, gamers in the wake of shooting," MSNBC Commentary, April 20, 2007 at www.msnbc.msn.com/id/18220228/. The commentary notes that the *Washington Post* had just pulled a paragraph from a story that claimed Cho was an avid fan of the game "Counter-Strike," and then indicated that no video games were found in his room and that his suitemates had never seen him play video games.

40. Cited in Nancy Gibbs, "Darkness Falls," *Time*, April 19, 2007 at www.time.com/time/magazine/article/0,9171,1612715,00.html.

41. For a detailed account of Cho's Life, the shooting, and the aftermath, see *Report of the Review Panel* (2007).

References

Aronowitz, Stanley. 1993. *Roll Over Beethoven*. Hanover, NH: University Press of New England.
Best, Steven, and Douglas Kellner. 2001. *The Postmodern Adventure: Science, Technology, and Cultural Studies at the Third Millennium*. New York: Guilford.
Giroux, Henry. 2006. *Stormy Weather: Katrina and the Politics of Disposability*. Boulder, CO: Westview Press.
Grossberg, Lawrence. 1992. *We Gotta Get Out of this Place*. New York and London: Routledge.
Hall, Stuart, and Jacques Martin, eds. 1983. *The Politics of Thatcherism*. London: Lawrence and Wishart.
Kellner, Douglas. 1990. *Television and the Crisis of Democracy*. Boulder, CO: Westview Press.
———. 1995. *Media Culture*. London and New York: Routledge.
———. 2001. *Grand Theft 2000*. Lanham, MD: Rowman & Littlefield.
———. 2003a. *Media Spectacle*. London and New York: Routledge.

———. 2003b. *From 9/11 to Terror War: Dangers of the Bush Legacy.* Lanham, MD: Rowman & Littlefield.
———. 2005. *Media Spectacle and the Crisis of Democracy.* Boulder, CO: Paradigm Press.
———. 2008. *Guys and Guns Amok: Terrorism and School Shootings from the Oklahoma City Bombings to the Virginia Tech Massacre.* Boulder, CO: Paradigm.
Kellner, Douglas, and Michael Ryan. 1988. *Camera Politica: The Politics and Ideologies of Contemporary Hollywood Film.* Bloomington: Indiana University Press.

CHAPTER Three

MEDIATED RITUAL ON ACADEMIC GROUND

Neal King

Invasion of Sacred Space

In the days following a gunman's rampage in April 2007, departments at Virginia Tech convened to discuss the losses of students and colleagues, the upcoming resumption of school, and requests from journalists to bring cameras to class. This last choice evoked a ceremonial language among faculty who usually discuss their work in more instrumental terms. Some dismissed journalists as parasitic intruders and demanded that classrooms be treated as "healing," "sacred space" free of their taint. This short essay ponders the souring of a collegial relationship among storytelling professions in the aftermath of an event that drew wide coverage.

The eruption of violence left university members scrambling for news, first about the nature of the incident, and then about the fates of people they knew. Broadcast, cable, and Internet outlets assumed more central places in our lives than they usually enjoy. Though the campus newspaper provided a clearinghouse for announcements, its server crashed under the pressure of global demand, leaving private news companies, with their greater resources, to supply news even to those who worked where shots were fired. The speed at which commercial reporting conveys images and relays statements made it useful to locals as events unfolded. The incident was mass mediated for those nearby because fast capitalism trumped state channels and friendship networks.

But the reporters who respond to these demands compete for advertisers' dollars, which dangle before them in such huge numbers that journalists approach survivors en masse. Virginia Tech sprouted forests of satellite dishes; cameras surrounded survivors; and reporters swamped relatives with requests for their time. Many locals developed a siege frame of mind; so that by the time national politicians gathered for a local memorial, ambivalence about exposure had begun to rise. Handwritten signs told camera crews to leave ("Hokie Nation needs to heal. Media stay away," said one version); and the administration followed suit with requests that reporters stay out of campus buildings.

Though the ceremonial language of "sacred space" inspires speculation at the end of the essay, much of the offense taken by educators to journalists seems easy to explain. In the aftermath of group death, professional norms require reporters to swarm the living and shoot footage of anyone choked with emotion. The rapid progress of events impels them to gain access quickly, via entreaty and intrusion. Famed anchors left phone mail for grieving kin and sent flowers (and lackeys) to homes at all hours. Many locals spoke in grim humor of the cameras and boom mikes that hovered when mourners neared tears. Reporters grew aware of this reaction to their work and made enquiries in the hushed tones of undertakers.[1]

In search of footage not facts, would-be interviewers were easily dismissed by agreements to talk *off* camera; but the courting of kin of the fallen was harder to avoid. Some surviving families had friends run interference, standing watch over houses to intercept callers. Others abandoned their homes.

Such coverage of disaster can outrage those who feel their grief made spectacle for distant masses, even if they value the more caring attention that the exposure makes possible. During the reporters' visit to campus, group boundaries clarified and many faculty began to express an oppositional logic:

Education	Journalism
Enculturation	Exploitation
Sacredness	Profanity
Belonging	Intrusion

With these polarities, teachers could scorn the journalists whose profit-seeking work threatened to prolong the trauma. We who had seen our students and teachers victimized at the start of the week could at least rise against this new imposition. Nevertheless, faculty and journalists came to share at least a few goals in this aftermath, in that reporters not only spread news and provide attention but also mediate civil religion. I next discuss the ways in which professional norms combined with communal impulses to shift faculty responses to journalists from reliance and solidarity to outrage within days.

Civil Religion through Mass Media

Shortly after the shooting, faculty were drawn to civic rituals—the public gatherings in which crowds focus on objects of totemic significance (mass death and killers prominent among them) and engage in activities that communicate emotion.[2] By such ritual means they generated solidarity; and media broadcast allowed for people far away to share in the contagious mood. Those people in turn expressed support back to those at the ritual center. Because faculty at Virginia Tech took comfort at having been contacted in this way by people around the world, and because journalists on the scene could share in the infectious mood, members of these professions found themselves aligned in their activities and goals for a short time, despite the disparities in their professional and communal needs.

Marvin (2002) notes that rituals of civil religion tell stories that celebrate the sacred and untouchable, and thus constitute the totems that symbolize groups (204–205). The most potent rituals include stories that celebrate sacrifices made for those groups, featuring such figures as the innocent young (whose deaths states avenge if they can), the confessed guilty who suffer punishment, and the willing soldiers sent to battle. Virginia Tech's violence produced some of these elements—blameless victims and fallen heroes—though no criminal left alive to punish. Thus, university officials and journalists worked together to foster civic bonding.

Marvin (2002) outlines the criteria of successful rituals, most of which reporters met by their framing of the violence at Virginia Tech (207). By approaching the story from these angles, journalists aligned themselves with locals in their veneration of the slain.

1. *Sacrifices must declare themselves willing.* Reporters focused upon stories of engineering faculty who waded into danger and died protecting students, but paid less attention to the nearby class that barred its door and escaped unscathed.

2. *Group members must agree on the propriety of the sacrifice.* The killer at Virginia Tech took his own life, usurping the right of the state to do it for him. He failed to affirm state killing power and thus sapped the strength of

this media event as civil ritual. Still, the appropriateness of that death went unquestioned in public; and pundits' commentary on the killer's background and apparent mind-state suggested that he ought to have been punished with incarceration before.[3]

3. *The outcome of the ritual must be genuinely uncertain.* Though the violence was over before the public knew of it, audiences waited days to learn the names of the deceased, the motive of the killer, and whether an accomplice remained—delays that drew rapt attention and maintained uncertainty.

4. *The ritual must have a definite end and beginning.* The announcements of answers to questions mentioned above, and the resumption of classes the following week, marked the end of most coverage. Final ceremonies took place with assurance that the event was drawing to a close. Those rituals were reprised briefly during graduation the next month, after which the university cleared most memorial sites and reopened parts of Norris Hall.

5. *The sacrifice must be valuable.* Most rituals named the deceased; and the displays and reportage reproduced their smiling photos, recounted their personal attributes, and listed contributions that they had or would have made.

Because news companies benefit from coverage of drama, they tend to frame events in a manner that fosters ritual. Reporters found many ways to emphasize such aspects of the event; and though the attention paid to Virginia Tech did not make for the fullest ritual veneration of civil sacrifice, it came close enough to have generated regional solidarity. People donned school colors, cheered politicians, and planted U.S. flags at memorial spots—pairing the red stripes that recall the blood of fallen soldiers with the turkeys that stand for the university. In these ways, the rituals magnified by the media attention helped to boost solidarity on campus. As a result of that attention, faculty found themselves, improbably, central to a national event. At their most comic, tales of this bright spot in a sickening week blurred lines between gratitude and pride. (Hallway chatter: I heard from people I haven't seen in years. Well, I have an e-mail from colleagues in Europe. Why, I got a note from Hong Kong!)

I do not mean that faculty acted as one. Reportage of large gatherings can suggest greater attendance than occurs. Many faculty likely restricted their roles in mediated events to leaving the TV news on longer or checking Internet outlets more often than they otherwise might. Indeed, university faculty tend to remain aloof from national ceremony and display, distancing themselves from the more passionate (and trusting) mass at times of national crisis (Collins 2004b:63–64). But Hokie spirit (no easy sell to status conscious professionals at most times, with its folksy name, garish colors, and muscle-bound fowl as mascot) suffused this group that week, mixing with grief. The killer had made it easy to assemble under the rubric by restricting his attacks to school buildings; but Virginia Tech also controls the best resources for local assembly: public spaces, established symbols, and e-mail networks that form the infrastructure of regional identity. The principal ceremony (a day after the shootings) that gathered national politicians in a basketball stadium drew tens of thousands, both from the surrounding community and from ranks of parents come to pick kids up from school. The larger point is that faculty were both given valuable information, and drawn into rituals of campus solidarity, in ways that corporate journalists augmented with the resources at their disposal.

With the encouragement of officials, faculty did much storytelling of our own, in op-ed pieces, interviews with reporters, and in classrooms the week after the shooting. Instructors across the nation were keen to use the event as a "teaching moment," in order that students might learn from the compelling event. Substantive discussions included analyses of the killer's motives and the school's response. University-sponsored guidelines for Tech faculty encouraged a counseling orientation once classes resumed, including validations of students' feelings and referrals to the health center. For the sake of encounters with reporters at graduation, officials made available such talking points as the following: "A terrible tragedy happened here of horrific proportions, and while we must live with this memory and knowledge, we will persevere," and "Hokie Spirit will enable us to prevail in the face of tragedy and grow stronger as we move forward together." Thus, like reporters, did faculty and university officials order events into narratives that served institutional purposes, including those of the rituals that foster solidarity.

For all of those means of alignment, though, faculty and journalists differed in their institutional loyalties, which led to the conflict deeper than that caused by camera crews alone.

Institutional Conflict

The most serious threats to faculty solidarity came from stories that emphasized loony bloodshed and police failure over and above noble sacrifice. On these points, journalists' and teachers' interests diverged. As workers for profit-seeking companies, journalists not only augment solidarity in times of crisis but also violate the ethics of community and security as they craft dramas that promote their enterprise.

The publication and broadcast of images of grief place reporters at the center of rituals and storytelling, as mediators of information, as interpreters of events, and as teachers of the rules of mourning (Walter, Littlewood, and Pickering 1995:585; Cottle 2006:427; Sumiala-Seppanen and Stocchetti 2007:340). During such media events, for instance, viewers observe how others handle grief; and the implicit moral instruction becomes part of a larger "invigilation" of emotion (Walter, et al. 1995), in which bystanders learn to "deploy the appropriate attitude, the right mindset, even the right emotions" (Sumiala-Seppanen and Stocchetti 2007). Disaster coverage tends to activate and shape proprietary feelings about how to handle grief in public. Thus can journalists assume teaching roles.

The role that reporters play in such interpretation and invigilation can draw fire from academics who might regard themselves as the more proper instructors. For example, Liebes (1998) argues that

> the shared collective space created by disaster time-out, zooming in on victims and their families, is the basis not for dignity and restraint but for the chaotic exploitation of the pain of participants on screen, and for the opportunistic fanning of establishment mismanagement, neglect, corruption, and so on. (75–76)

Thus did many faculty come to feel in the aftermath of the violence at Virginia Tech, as journalists first dramatized the possibility of neglect by the administration of security, and then broadcast aggrandizing images from the killer's press kit that could provide fodder for copycats. "The Virginia Tech Massacre" became a tagline on television, threatening to "brand" the university with the most stigmatized terms, at just the moment that coverage of the aftermath was teaching audiences to identify with endangered students.

In his analysis of disaster marathon, Liebes (1998) notes that professional norms lead journalists to feature opposition views rather than rally around national leaders as they do during most media events (73). The rush of concern and demand for details sends reporters in hasty search, which precludes the careful research that can shed light on social forces (Liebes 1998:75). Many outlets demand twenty-four-hour coverage in competition with others, in situations in which officials take days to share the most prized knowledge (Rohlinger 2007:139). While they wait for more information about the causes of disasters, reporters not only harass survivors and focus on grief, but also seize nearby prey in their search for people to blame, beginning with the authorities most directly in view. Thus did they tar the university with epithets related to bloodshed, calling its governance into question. This search for villains can frustrate locals by fulfilling the wishes of mass murderers, who usually meant either to shame authorities or to gain infamy (Liebes 1998:75).[4]

In the case of Virginia Tech, journalists gave airtime and column inches to those who blamed police for not stopping the gunman (by "locking down" campus or profiling and jailing the unstable).[5] Indeed, Liebes summarizes this tension in disaster marathons:

> Whereas the principle of broadcast ceremony is to highlight emotions and solidarity and to bracket analysis, a disaster marathon constitutes a communal public forum where tragedy is the emotional motor which sizzles with conflict, emphasizing anxiety, argument, and disagreement (Liebes 1998:76).

In this environment, group boundaries grow clear and opposition strengthens. Handgun enthusiasts demanded repeal of laws that ban firearms from campus, valorizing handguns as symbols of self-protective manhood and goodness against evil. The faculty who spoke up in public rejected these bids, demanding that classrooms remain pure of arms. Thus does a disaster marathon nurture opposition alongside the solidarity, and thus did journalists compete with and offend local storytellers.

Both journalists and scholars provide perspective and guide display of emotion. We can call those lessons enculturation or exploitation, the spread of knowledge, or the sale of sensation. Though some stories are more empirically grounded than others, and may spring from all manner of loyalties (to the analysis of capitalism as the exploitation of workers, for instance, versus service to a capitalist corporation), each of us can think of reasons to emphasize conflict, to criticize authority, and to speak to the victims of social forces. Journalists do this in profit-seeking corporations whereas Virginia Tech faculty do it in service to the state. Institutional loyalties divide us.

Haunted Rituals

Complaints about disaster marathons are easy to understand, in view of the crass intrusions of the press and the different allegiance felt by faculty. But how shall we explain the more ceremonial language with which some came to hallow our own venues as sacred and imbue them with healing power? Such a response draws a line between good and evil—a demarcation that often results from moral discomfort. For this reason, I wonder if some marathons attain intensities sufficient to haunt their viewers. Gordon (1997) describes hauntings as animated states in which people grow aware of social tensions. Societies could well feel a strain between the payoffs and the price of violence against their citizens—the solidarity that memorials provide versus the grief at our loss. What Marvin (2002) calls the "totem secret" bubbles beneath national awareness: the hidden knowledge that the group can gain from the killing of its members because it allows for celebration of their sacrifice (205). During times of contested warfare, opposition parties proclaim that secret, as an accusation against the state of sending its young to die and then spending the political capital. After cases of unauthorized murder, the secret is better kept; most of those who benefit by memorial veneration can do so with a sense of innocence. (After all, they didn't elect the killers, even if they can enjoy the communal warmth that follows.) Still, the tension remains and perhaps appears when rituals grow most intense.

I suggest that the intrusions and focus on conflict that allow journalists to do their work risk unearthing citizens' investments in the rituals that follow disaster. Our discomfort under the cameras' glare may have tarnished the memorials by association. There is nothing terribly rational about hallowing classrooms as healing space or shunning journalists as the unwashed. Perhaps such thoughts occurred as part of local citizens' attempts to exorcise what haunts us. We want our fallen friends restored, and an end brought to our grief, yet basked in the glow of the rituals that honored their memories. We would trade those rites for a chance to bring back the dead, but could not and thus remained haunted as we joined in school cheers. The ghoulish solidarity might offend when viewed from the right vantage. To blame crass sensation on reporters could help to banish what troubles us.

The dead animate civil religion, lifting survivors in solidarity. The role played by out-of-town, for-profit reporters in national rituals make them convenient targets of the scorn haunted by communal grief and guilt. This connection between rituals that foster solidarity and the storytelling that enhances conflict and drama came into focus in the days following this widely reported violence. The imperatives that drive professions differ enough that we can draw lines between us when so inspired; but where some faculty sought to resolve moral tension by posing classrooms as sacred, and repudiating journalists as infidels, I suggest a more dialectical relation of public education to private journalism.

Notes

1. Tactful reticence about their professional goals produced odd locutions among journalists. During a walk through the memorials on campus, my spouse and I were asked by a camera crew whether we were parents. After a pause, a reporter specified, "parents of children." As I wondered what other creatures we might have raised, it became clear that "children" had become code for those who had been shot, or at least for students at the university.

2. This focus on ritual may strike as odd those who either avoid language associated with sociological functionalists or share Benjamin's (1968) distrust of electronic reproduction. However, one need neither ignore social conflict nor be naïve about the force of media technology to note that groups employ rituals to mark their boundaries, affirm their rules, and generate solidarity (Collins 2004a:12; Marshall 2002)—even in a late capitalist era, and in ways that can challenge ruling blocs (Cottle 2006; Liebes 1998).

3. As this essay goes to press, a governor-appointed panel has complained of a breakdown in the killer's medical supervision, and families of the slain weigh the possibility of lawsuits.

4. Rohlinger (1998:139–40) also finds a journalistic taste for conflict in her study of abortion-debate coverage: the increased focus on profitable, rather than important, news has turned political and social coverage away from the deepest contexts toward the sharpest conflicts.

5. Spree killings might decline in frequency were news media to neglect them. In order for this to work, reporters would mostly ignore such killings (as with television editors' decisions to cease broadcasting news of local teen suicides decades ago after a series of copycat waves followed such reporting). But journalists exercise no such restraint once incidents gain national attention. People most often prevent spree killings when those who observe the antisocial behaviors of would-be killers share their information and intercede. Such peers and teachers must trust law enforcement in order for this to work, which is why draconian lock-downs and zero-tolerance policies fail. Lock-downs don't separate killers from their intended victims. And zero-tolerance policies alienate trivial offenders from law enforcement, reducing the rate of tips that could alert authorities to serious threats. Finally, profiling cannot distinguish between young men who are just creepy and those who are planning sprees. In short, the most popular responses to spree killings do little to solve the problem.

References

Benjamin, Walter. 1968. *Illuminations*. New York: Harcourt Brace and World.
Collins, Randall. 2004a. *Interaction Ritual Chains*. Princeton, NJ: Princeton University Press.
———. 2004b. "Rituals of Solidarity and Security in the Wake of Terrorist Attack." *Sociological Theory* 22: 53–87.
Cottle, Simon. 2006. "Mediatized Rituals: Beyond Manufacturing Consent." *Media, Culture and Society* 28: 411–32.
Gordon, Avery. 1997. *Ghostly Matters: Haunting and the Sociological Imagination*. Minneapolis: University of Minnesota Press.
Liebes, Tamar. 1998. "Television's Disaster Marathons: A Danger for Democratic Processes?" Pp. 71–84 in *Media, Ritual, and Identity*, edited by T. Liebes, J. Curran, and E. Katz. London: Routledge.
Marshall, Douglas A. 2002. "Behavior, Belonging, and Belief: A Theory of Ritual Practice." *Sociological Theory* 20: 360–80.

Marvin, Carolyn. 2002. "Scapegoating and Deterrence: Criminal Justice Rituals in American Civil Religion." Pp. 203–18 in *Practicing Religion in the Age of the Media: Explorations in Media, Religion, and Culture*, edited by S. M. Hoover and L. S. Clark. New York: Columbia University Press.

Rohlinger, Deana A. 2007. "American Media and Deliberative Democratic Processes." *Sociological Theory* 25: 122–48.

Sumiala-Seppanen, Johanna and Matteo Stocchetti. 2007. "Father of the Nation or Arch-Terrorist? Media Rituals and Images of the Death of Yasser Arafat." *Media, Culture and Society* 29: 336–43.

Walter, Tony, Jane Littlewood, and Michael Pickering. 1995. "Death in the News: The Public Invigilation of Private Emotion." *Sociology: The Journal of the British Sociological Association* 29: 579–96.

CHAPTER Four

PROFILING SCHOOL SHOOTERS AND SHOOTERS' SCHOOLS:
The Cultural Contexts of Aggrieved Entitlement and Restorative Masculinity

Michael Kimmel

In the aftermath of Seung-Hui Cho's horrific massacre of thirty-two of his classmates and professors at Virginia Tech on April 16, 2007, pundits from all over the political spectrum weighed into the national grief and confusion over what could have led this young man to commit such a vicious, murderous act.

When I watched the redacted portions of the enraged tirade that Cho left as his Last Will and Testament, I kept hearing the words of those other two, now infamous school shooters, Dyland Klebold and Eric Harris at Columbine High School in Littleton, Colorado. As they began their shooting spree, a group of girls asked Harris and Klebold "Why are you doing this?"

They replied: "We've always wanted to do this. This is payback. We've dreamed of doing this for years. This is for all the shit you put us through. This is what you deserve."[1]

How and why do these boys get to such a place where they could murder their classmates and take their own lives in a paroxysm of violence?

In the aftermath of Cho's rampage at Virginia Tech, three sorts of explanations were offered. Most frequently, we heard hyperindividualized psychological profiles of a certifiably mentally ill young man, diagnosed but largely untreated, with ready, legal, access to guns despite his diagnosis. To some it was mental illness, to others pure evil, but these explanations stopped short of any social analysis.

A second, pernicious, if predictable, response was entirely social, based on grandiose ethnic stereotyping. Finally, after two decades of school shootings by white kids in which race was never once mentioned as a variable, suddenly the entire explanation centered on the fact that Cho was Asian-American. "Whatever happened to the model minority?" some asked. Perhaps being an Asian American came with so much pressure to perform, to be that model minority that it was simply too much. Perhaps he simply cracked under the strain.

Such an explanation can, of course, either be antiracist—those poor Asians have such racialized expectations that it's a wonder they can perform at all—or racist, echoing the claims about the Chinese during the Cold War and or the Vietnamese during that war, claiming that Asians just don't have the respect for human life that "we enlightened Americans" have.

A third type of explanation tried to steer through middle range variables that might have prompted Cho to explode as he did. The usual suspects—violent video games, access to guns—were trotted out as the intervening variable that inspired a deranged young man to embark on such a deadly rampage.

Of course, in the past, we've heard, for example, that Columbine was caused by Goth music, Marilyn Manson, violent video games. Then-President Clinton argued that it might be the Internet; Newt Gingrich credited the hippie embrace of freedom of the 1960s, while Thomas Sowell argued that the 1960s exonerated individuals from responsibility ("it was 'society's' fault") that led to rampage violence. Tom DeLay just blamed daycare, the teaching of evolution, and "working mothers who take birth control pills."[2]

All of these pretty much missed the point. Or, better put, missed one point to make another. As with all rampage school shootings, the rush to develop a psychological profile of school shooters left us without a sociological profile of the "shooters' school."

It is surely the case that some "students" are more likely to explode in a murderous rage than others. But it is equally true that some schools are more susceptible to such rampages than others. If we are really going to understand "school shooters" we have to look at each word separately, and then look at the phrase as the synthesis of the two different elements. In this essay, I will consider these three levels of analysis—shooters, schools, and school shootings—suggesting that there is a profile of the type of school that is more likely to witness rampage school shootings, and that, in such schools, only some students are the likely perpetrators.

But first, a few caveats. Random school shootings are extremely rare. More than 99 percent of public high schools have never had a homicide—and never will. In the 1992–1993 school year there were fifty-four violent deaths on high school campuses; in 2000 there were sixteen. And yet students report that they are increasingly afraid to go to school; among young people ages twelve to twenty-four, three in ten say violence has increased in their schools in the past year and nearly two-fifths have worried that a classmate was potentially violent. Nearly two-thirds (63 percent) of parents believe a school shooting is somewhat or very likely to occur in their communities.[3]

That's just not true. School shootings are extremely rare, and will remain so. But that doesn't mean that some schools are not more prone than others. Or that some students are not more likely to open fire than others.

Profiling Shooters

Government-supported investigations—such as the FBI report, the Surgeon General's report on *Youth Violence*, and the Bureau of Justice Statistics "Indicators of School Crime and Safety 2000" as well as the major new study of bullying all concentrated on identifying potential antecedents of school violence—for example, media influence, drugs and alcohol behavior, Internet usage, father absence, parental neglect. Such models assume that these causal influences spread evenly over everyday life like the old advertisement for Sherman-Williams paints covering the globe.[4]

But these variables would apply equally to boys and to girls. And so it is that we worry about "teen violence," "youth violence," "gang violence," "suburban violence," "violence in the schools." Just who are these teens, youths, gangs—girls? Imagine if the killers in schools in Littleton, Pearl, Paducah, Springfield, and Jonesboro were all black girls from poor families who lived instead in New Haven, Newark, or Providence. We'd be having a national debate about inner-city poor black girls. The entire focus would be on race, class, and gender. The media would invent a new term for their behavior, as with "wilding" a decade ago. We'd hear about the culture of poverty; about how living in the city breeds crime and violence; about some putative natural tendency among blacks toward violence. Someone would even blame feminism for causing girls to become violent in vain imitation of boys.

Yet the obvious fact that nearly all the school shooters were middle class white boys barely broke a ripple in the torrent of public discussion. This uniformity cut across all other differences among the shooters: some came from intact families, others from single-parent homes; some boys had acted violently in the past, others were quiet and unsuspecting; some boys also expressed rage at their parents (two killed their parents the same morning), and others seemed to live in happy families.

It is no doubt true that several of the boys who committed these terrible acts did have serious psychological problems; but such framing also masks the way race and class play a significant role in school violence. Again, imagine if all the school shooters had been poor African-American *boys* in inner-city schools. It is unlikely that our search for causes would have pathologized the boys as much as the culture of poverty or the "normality" of violence among inner-city youth.

So, why is it that only boys open fire on their classmates? And why are the shooters almost exclusively white boys?

First, well, the obvious: it's not just any boys. It's boys who have been targeted, bullied, beat up, gay baited, and worse—virtually every single day of their lives. They were called every homophobic slur in the books, and then some. They were ridiculed, threatened, attacked and tortured. Nearly all have stories of being mercilessly and constantly teased, picked on, and threatened. And, most strikingly, it was *not* because they were gay (none of them was gay as far as I can tell), but because they were *different* from the other boys—shy, bookish, an honor student, artistic, musical, theatrical, nonathletic, a "geek," or weird. Theirs are stories of "cultural marginalization" based on criteria for adequate gender performance—specifically the enactment of codes of masculinity.

And so they did what *any* self-respecting man would do in a situation like that—or so they thought. They retaliated. In his insightful book on violence, James Gilligan suggests that violence has its origins in "the fear of shame and ridicule, and the overbearing need to prevent others from laughing at oneself by making them weep instead." Shame, inadequacy, vulnerability—all threaten the self. Violence is restorative, compensatory.[5]

Boys who are bullied are supposed to be real men, supposed to be able to embody independence, invulnerability, manly stoicism. (In fact, the very search for such collective rhetorics might be seen as an indication of weakness.) The cultural marginalization of the boys who committed school shootings extended to feelings that they had no other recourse: they felt they had no other friends to validate their fragile and threatened identities; they felt that school authorities and parents would be unresponsive to their plight; and they had no access to other methods of self-affirmation. It was not because they were deviants, but rather because they were overconformists to a particular normative construction of masculinity, a construction that defines violence as a legitimate response to a perceived humiliation.

Profiling Schools

Bullying and gay-baiting take place in every school. But rampages have taken place at only a small number. Is there something that distinguishes the schools as well as the shooters? What makes a violence-prone school different from a violence-free school? Let's first look at the distribution of school shootings (see figure 4.1).

Notice anything? Well, for one thing, it's clear that school shootings are *not* a national trend. Of twenty-eight school shootings between 1982 and 2001, all but one were in rural or suburban schools (one in Chicago). New York, Boston, Minneapolis, San Francisco, Los Angeles—nothing. All but two (Chicago again, and Virginia Beach) were committed by a white boy or boys. The Los Angeles school district has had no school shootings since 1984; in 1999, San Francisco, which has several programs to identify potentially violent students, had only two kids bring guns to school.

OK, here is that same map, modified slightly.

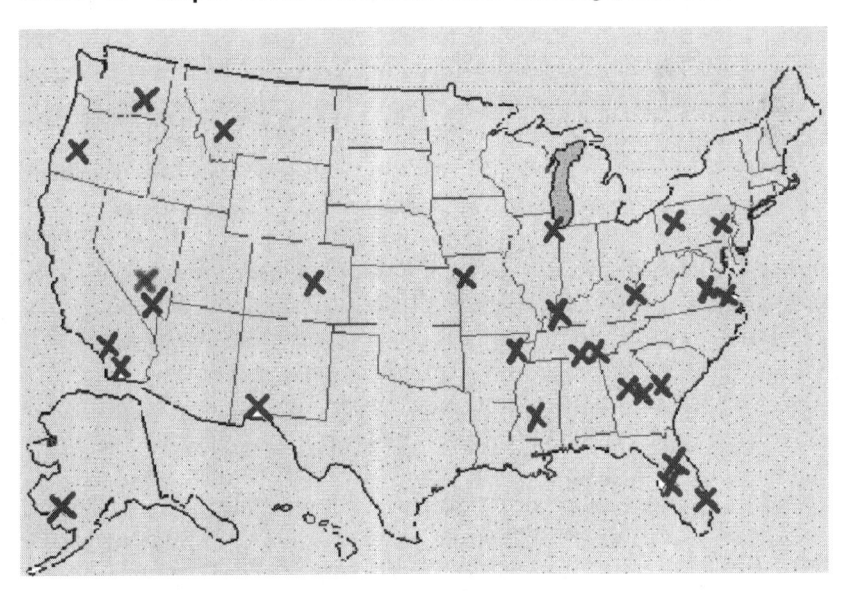

FIGURE 4.1 Map of United States with school shootings, 1982–2001

FIGURE 4.2 Map of United States with all school shootings, 1982–2001, superimposed on map of state-by-state voting for president, 2000

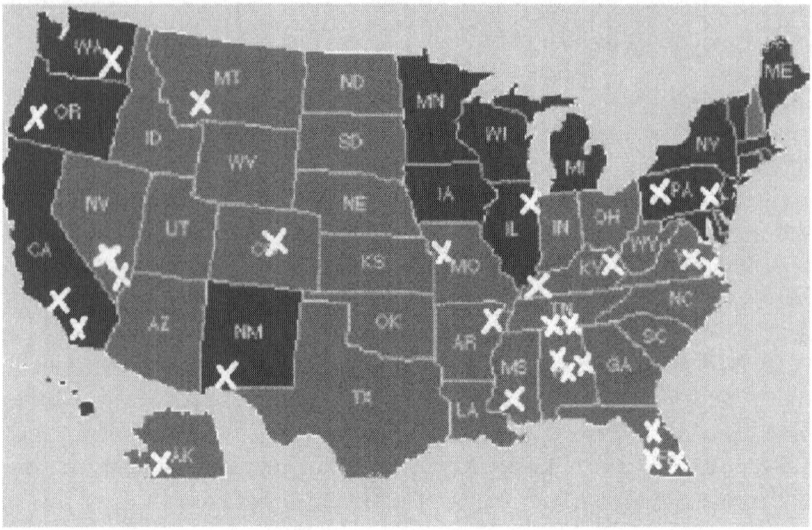

Figure 4.2 is the electoral map from the 2000 presidential election. Of the twenty-eight school shootings that took place prior to Virginia Tech, twenty took place in red states. Of those in the blue states, one was in suburban Oregon; one was in rural (eastern) Washington; two were in Southern California; one was in rural and another in suburban Pennsylvania; and one was in rural New Mexico. Of those eight from "blue states," half of the counties in those blue states (Santee, California; Red Hill, Pennsylvania; Moses Lake, Washington; and Deming, New Mexico) voted Republican in the last election.

What this suggests is that school violence is unevenly distributed. Of course, I'm not suggesting that Republicans are more prone than Democrats to random school shootings. But I am suggesting that different political cultures develop in different parts of the country, and that those political cultures have certain features in common. Some of those features are "gun culture" (what percentage of homes have firearms, gun registrations, NRA memberships), local gender culture, and local school cultures—attitudes about gender nonconformity, tolerance of bullying, teacher attitudes.

Here's one element of local cultures that directly affects whether or not the psychological profile would show up on anyone's radar. Since local school districts are funded by local property taxes, some "violence prone schools" may have been subject to a significant decline in school funding over the past two decades. Coupled with the curricular demands of the No Child Left Behind Act, which mandates performance outcomes that require increased attention to a set curriculum, schools have cut back significantly on after-school programs, sports, extracurricular activities, teacher training, remedial programs, and, most importantly, counseling.

One in five adolescents have serious behavioral and emotional problems and about two-thirds of these are getting no help at all. In the average school district in the United States, the school psychologist must see ten students each day just to see every student once a year. In California, there is one counselor (not to mention psychologist) for every one thousand students, and 50 percent of schools do not have guidance counselors at all. It is likely that this paucity of funding for psychological services enabled several very troubled students to pass undetected in a way they might not have in past years.

In his exemplary analysis of the shootings at Columbine High School, sociologist Ralph Larkin identified several variables that he believed provided the larger cultural context for the rampage. The larger context—the development of a culture of celebrity, the rise of paramilitary chic—spread unevenly across the United States; some regions are more gun-happy than others. (Larkin credits the west; Cho's rampage implicates the south.) But more than that, he profiles both the boys and the school, and suggests that the sociological and psychological variables created a lethal mixture.

First, he stresses that the school must be characterized by the presence and tolerance of intimidation, harassment, and bullying within the halls of the high school and on the streets of the larger community. One boy described what it was like to be so marginalized:

> Almost on a daily basis, finding death threats in my locker. . . . It was bad. People . . . who I never even met, never had a class with, don't know who they were to this day. I didn't drive at the time I was in high school; I always walked home. And every day when they'd drive by, they'd throw trash out their window at me, glass bottles. I'm sorry, you get hit with a glass bottle that's going forty miles and hour, that hurts pretty bad. Like I said, I never even knew these people, so didn't even know what their motivation was. But this is something I had to put up with nearly every day for four years.[6]

One friend said that "[e]very time someone slammed them against a locker and threw a bottle at them, I think they'd go back to Eric or Dylan's house and plot a little more—at first as a goof, but more and more seriously over time."[7]

It wasn't just that Harris and Klebold—and other eventual rampage shooters—were bullied and harassed and intimidated every day; it was that the administration, teachers, and community colluded with it. At Columbine, when one boy tried to tell teachers and administrators "the way those who were 'different' were crushed . . . what it was like to live in constant fear of other kids who'd gone out of control" the teachers and administrators invariably would turn a blind eye. "After all," he says, "those kids were their favorites. We were the troublemakers." Thus, Larkin concludes, that "[b]y allowing the predators free reign in the hallways and public spaces and by bending the rules so that bad behavior did not interfere too much with sports participation, the faculty and administration inadvertently created a climate that was rife with discrimination, intimidation and humiliation."[8]

And sanctimony. Larkin also argues that religious intolerance and chauvinism directly contributed to the cultural marginalization of the boys. Jefferson County, where Columbine High School is located, is more than 90 percent white, 97 percent native-born, and almost entirely Christian with nearly 40 percent evangelical Protestants. (Indeed, it has one of the largest concentrations of Christian evangelicals in the country.)[9] And while local preachers saw in Klebold and Harris the presence of the devil, Larkin believes that evangelical intolerance of others is more cause than consequence. "Evangelicals were characterized," he writes, "as arrogant and intolerant of the beliefs of others." Evangelical students were intolerantly holier than thou—they would "accost their peers and tell them that if they were not born-again, they would burn in hell."[10]

In most cases, Larkin writes, this would be "merely annoying." But "in combination with the brutalization and harassment dished out on a regular basis by the student athletes, it only added to the toxicity of the student climate at Columbine High School" (61).

That toxic climate combined brutal harassment, sanctimonious superiority, traditional gender norms and a belief in violence as restorative. It's a long-standing masculine trope. Cho and the others were, according to *New York Times* columnist Bob Herbert, "young men riddled with shame and humiliation, often bitterly misogynistic and homophobic, who have decided that the way to assert their faltering sense of manhood and get the respect they have been denied is to go out and shoot somebody."[11] In a 1994 study, Felson and his colleagues found that regardless of what a boy's personal values, boys are much more likely to engage in violence if the local cultural expectations are that boys retaliate when provoked. And their local gender culture certainly encouraged that.

Klebold and Harris, and Seung-Hui Cho, experienced what I call "aggrieved entitlement"—a gendered sense that they were entitled—indeed, even expected—to exact their revenge on all who had hurt them. It wasn't enough to have been harmed; they also had to believe that they were justified, that their murderous rampage was legitimate.

Once they did, they followed the time honored script of the American western: the lone gunman (or gang) retaliates far beyond the initial provocation and destroys others to restore the self. It's historian Richard Slotkin's thesis on American history—a "gunfighter nation" pursuing "regeneration through violence." It's Margaret Mead's indictment of the culture of revenge, *And Keep Your Powder Dry*. American men don't get mad; they get even. It's Grand Theft Auto and hundreds of other violent video games. It's not just some westerns or action movies—it's virtually *every* western or action movie.

The Aggrieved Entitlement of Seung-Hui Cho

The profile of Seung-Hui Cho suggests less overt bullying, but certainly some. He was teased and dismissed as a nonentity. Perhaps he was less overtly bullied, but he was no less marginalized. Awkward socially, Cho never seemed to feel that he fit in. He had no friends, rarely, if ever spoke with his dorm mates, and maintained a near-invisibility on campus. His web screen name was a question mark—he toyed with his invisibility. No one seems to have actually known him—although his teachers in the English department said they thought he was strange and possibly dangerous.

His marginalization also appeared cultural, and class-based, not entirely the result of his obvious overdetermining psychiatric problems. His videotape raged against the "brats," and "snobs" at Virginia Tech, who weren't even satisfied with their "gold necklaces" and "Mercedes." And, apparently, some of it had a racist component. The few times he had mustered the courage to actually speak in class, his tormentors told him to "go back to China." (Remember, Cho was Korean-American; his parents owned and operated a dry cleaner, and he felt his marginalization had a class and race basis.)

And his marginalization also seems to have been a deep alienation from campus culture as well. Few campuses are as awash in school spirit than Virginia Tech: the campus is festooned with maroon and orange everywhere, and the branding of the campus is a collegiate consumerist orgy of paraphernalia.

But what if one doesn't feel to be much of a citizen in "Hokie Nation"? What if one isn't much interested in football, or in sports-themed, beer-soaked weekend party extravaganzas? It's possible that to the marginalized, "Hokie Nation" doesn't feel inclusive and embracing, but alien and coercive. If one is not a citizen in Hokie Nation, one does not exist. And perhaps, for some, if *I* don't exist, then *you* have no right to exist either.

Of course, as Ben Agger notes, "[n]ot everyone who is bullied in school, or marginalized, picks up the gun."[12] There has to be something more. His videotaped testament shows a young man enthralled with fantasies of revenge, in full-bore aggrieved entitlement, externalizing his inner torment on everyone around him. "You have vandalized my heart, raped my soul, and torched my conscience," he declared on his videotape. "You thought it was one pathetic boy's life you were extinguishing. Thanks to you, I die like Jesus Christ to inspire generations of the weak and the defenseless people." He was a time-bomb, and he exploded.

But did he have to? Many have commented that no one in authority seemed to pay any attention to Cho, despite warnings from teachers and female students that they felt unsafe around him, that his fantasies expressed in class papers were disturbing enough to warrant attention. Nikki Giovanni, the celebrated feminist poet, refused to teach him because she said he was "mean." Diagnosed with mental problems, he was able to buy guns, attend classes, fantasize revenge, and eat in the dining halls—all, apparently, just like anyone else.

There are so many Seung-Hui Chos out there, so many victims of incessant bullying, of having their distress go unnoticed. So many teen suicides have this same profile: they turn their rage on themselves. So many teenagers who fit this profile self-medicate, taking drugs, drinking, cutting themselves. So many others revel in their marginalization as a coping strategy, the way Erving Goffman described "minstrelizing" in the face of experiencing the shock of a stigmatized identity. There are so many of them, and virtually all fly just beneath the radar of teachers, parents, administrators. (And, as I have suggested, the level of distress has to rise to heightened radar levels, since the paucity of funding has so raised that bar.)

But they don't all explode. Is it possible that the environment in which Cho lived had anything to do with it? Is it possible that the elements of a rampage school shooting include access to firepower, an explosive young man who is utterly marginalized, humiliated, and drenched in what he feels is righteous rage—as well as an environment that sees such treatment of its weakest and most marginalized as justified, as "reasonable."

A culture like Columbine, where one of the predators openly and proudly recalled the relentless torment he and his fellow wrestlers and football teammates unleashed on Klebold and Harris:

> Sure we teased them. But what do you expect with kids who come to school with weird hairdos and horns on their hats? It's not just jocks; the whole school's disgusted with them. They're a bunch of homos....

If you want to get rid of someone, usually you tease 'em. So the whole school would call them homos, and when they did something sick, we'd tell them "You're sick and that's wrong."[13]

Consider, for a moment, the case of a young woman named Christy Brzonkala. In the first semester of her freshman year in 1994, Christy was viciously gang raped by two football players at her school. Traumatized by the event, she sought assistance from the campus psychiatrist, who treated her with antidepressants. Neither the campus psychiatrist nor any other "employee or official made more than a cursory inquiry into the cause of [her] distress." Christy eventually recovered enough to bring charges against her attackers, and, to her surprise, was successful in prosecuting the case through campus judicial channels. The fact that everyone testified that she repeatedly said no seemed to count! One of the players was suspended for a year. However, the judicial board soon reversed her decision, largely, it appeared because the football coach pressured the administration to make the problem go away. The university restored his scholarship, and postponed his suspension until after he graduated.

Shocked, humiliated, and outraged, Christy never returned to school, but eventually brought a Title IX suit against the university for creating a hostile environment. The 4th Circuit Court found that the university had "permitted, indeed fostered, an environment in which male student athletes could gang rape a female student without any significant punishment to the male attackers, nor any real assistance to the female victim."[14]

What sort of university was so in thrall of its football players that it would trample over an innocent young woman, and create such a hostile environment, you might ask?[15]

Or take another example. I lecture about issues such as sexual assault, violence against women, date rape, and, more generally about why men should support gender equality. In fifteen years, lecturing at about twenty to twenty-five colleges and universities every year I have only been physically harassed once after a lecture. There, members of some on-campus fraternities had been required to attend, after reports of some potentially actionable incidents on campus. As I walked to my hotel room, in the hotel located on campus, a bunch of guys hanging off the back of a moving pick up truck threw a glass beer bottle at me, missing me by inches. The truck had decals from both the fraternity and the university on its rear window.

At what kind of university are the men so threatened by such a message, and so emboldened to assault a visiting lecturer?

Virginia Tech.

Let me be clear: I am not in any way saying that Virginia Tech was itself to blame for Cho's enraged madness, or even that one might have predicted his horrifying explosion by the callous indifference of the administration to a young first-year student a decade earlier. Indeed, Virginia Tech is in no way unique: it embodies, as Tim Luke explains in this volume, a heritage of violence: in the coercive coherence of the community of Hokie Nation, the nexus of campus and regional cultures with the jockocratic dominance of football (what Luke called "gridiron *Gemeinschaft*")—and the sanctimoniously sadistic exclusion of anyone who doesn't fit in to that narrowly circumscribed community. Community is always about membership and belonging—and about exclusion and isolation.

I am saying, however, that one of the things that seems to have bound all the school shooters together in their murderous madness was their perception that their school was a jockocracy, a place where difference was not valued, a place where, in fact, it was punished. There are students hovering on the precipice of murderous madness everywhere, young boys who "feel so weak [they] just want to explode . . . and tear this whole town apart," as Bruce Springsteen famously sang in a song that showed how he believed in a "Promised Land."

But as we learned with Klebold and Harris, the boys also had to feel that no one was paying attention, that no one in authority noticed, that no one gave a damn at all. No one tried to stop Cho—and he believed that was because everyone was part of the problem.

Social science is a tricky predictive science, and one would have to go way out on a limb to hypothesize that despite there being plenty of disturbed young men at other schools—say, for example, at Vassar or Princeton or NYU or Williams or UC Santa Barbara—those schools would be less likely to experience a rampage school shooting.

Such an argument would be tendentious: it's a virtual certainty that none of them will—but because such rampage school shootings are so unbelievably rare in the first place.

Yet, on the other hand, those schools also do not extract such universal allegiance to campus culture, nor are they ruled by one, impenetrable, entitled, jockocratic clique. Nor is the administration under relentless alumni pressure to maintain and build the sports programs at the expense of every other program—especially the campus counseling program that might identify and treat such deeply troubled, indeed maniacally insane, students, a bit sooner.

Rampage school shooters may be mad, but their madness must pass unseen, their marginalization be perceived as justified. And those dynamics have less to do with crazy individuals and more to do with campus cultures.

But. The emphasis on local school cultures must also be placed alongside the possibility that global media cultures exert such an important countervailing impact as to virtually overdetermine the possible globalization of rampage school shootings. When, for example, Pekka-Eric Auvinen opened fire at his Tuusula, Finland, high school in November 2007, he claimed access to the same global media culture as the Americans. His framing of his distress, his growing rage, drew from the same narrative repertoire as Harris and Klebold, and from Cho. And before his massacre of eight of his classmates and himself, Auvinen posted his intentions on YouTube.[16]

That narrative has become a globalized rhetoric of aggrieved entitlement, and teenagers all over the world have access to the same story. And yet it is still an utterly gendered story, and that suicidal explosion remains a distinctly masculine trope.

So, while it may be necessary to shift our frame slightly, to implicate the more local cultures of schools, regions, the political economy of psychological intervention, the institutional complicity with bullying and harassment (as long as it's "our guys" who are doing it). And yet alongside these local iterations lies the possibility of an overarching global master narrative to which an increasing number of young boys might find murderous solace.

At the local level, schools that want to prevent such rampage school shootings in the future might do well to profile the shooters—identify those students whose marginalization might become entangled with such aggrieved entitlement—as well as conduct a profile of their school, to mediate the effects of that marginalization on all its marginalized students (including those who are suicidal, self-medicating, and self-harming).

Local school culture and this globalized media culture form two of the three legs of a triangulated explanation of rampage school shootings; only placed in this "glocal" context will any psychological profiling make sense. Good wombs may have borne bad sons, as Dylan Klebold said, quoting *The Tempest*, "But there are bad seeds everywhere. They also need fertile ground in which their roots can take firm hold."

Notes

1. Ralph Larkin, *Comprehending Columbine* (Philadelphia, PA: Temple University Press, 2007), 6.

2. Thomas Sowell, "Are Today's Mass Shootings a Consequence of '60s Collective Guilt?" in *Baltimore Sun*, April 26, 2007, p. 19A; "News of the Weak in Review," in *The Nation*, November 15, 1999, 5.

3. J. Cloud, "The Legacy of Columbine," in *Time*, March 19, 2001, p. 32; "Fear of Classmates," in *USA Today*, April 22, 1999, A1; D. Carlson, and W. Simmons,

(March 6, 2001). Majority of parents think a school shooting could occur in their community. Gallup Poll Release, www.gallup.com/poll/releases/pr010306.asp.

4. Nansel, T., Overpeck, M., Pilla, R., Rune, J., Simmons-Morton, B., and Scheidt, P. (2001). "Bullying Behaviors among U.S. Youth: Prevalence and Association with Psychosocial Adjustment." *Journal of the American Medical Association, 285* (16), 2094–2100.

5. James Gilligan, *Violence* (New York: Vintage, 1998), 77.

6. Larkin, *Comprehending Columbine*, 91

7. Eric Pooley, "Portrait of a Deadly Bond," in *Time*, May 10, 1999, p. 26–27.

8. Larkin, *Comprehending Columbine*, 107, 121.

9. Larkin, *Comprehending Columbine*, 17, 119.

10. Larkin, *Comprehending Columbine*, 53, 61.

11. Bob Herbert, "A Volatile Young Man, Humiliation, and a Gun," in *New York Times*, April 19, 2007.

12. Ben Agger, "Cho, Not Che?: Positioning Blacksburg in the Political," in *Fast Capitalism*, 3.1; available at: www.uta.edu/huma/agger/fastcapitalism/3_1/agger.html.

13. Cited in *Time*, December 20, 1999, 50–51.

14. The case against the state of Virginia was eventually settled out of court, and the Supreme Court eventually ruled that Congress had overreached its authority by basing the Violence Against Women Act on the commerce clause of the U.S. Constitution, thus rendering moot Brzonkala's federal case against the university.

15. *Brzonkala v. VPI State University*, 4th Ct 96-1814, 1997.

16. I'm grateful to Tim Luke for raising this issue, which reframes these issues as truly "glocal."

CHAPTER Five

"VICTIMS SOUGHT IN NEXT WEEK'S SHOOTING"

William Ayers

Whenever the night is dark and I feel that I'm far from home, I turn to the *Onion* for perspective and consolation—maybe even insight. The *Onion*, the smart and biting satirical journal founded by a couple of irreverent University of Wisconsin students, like the *Daily Show* and the *Colbert Report* from Comedy Central, is absolutely essential for my mental health, providing a perfect antidote to the earnest credulousness of public radio and the *Times*—it opens up some imaginative breathing space as it exposes and ridicules the powerful and the current crop of controlling clichés shackling our minds.

As a longtime teacher, an article a couple of years ago knocked me out: the headline read "New Study Reveals 20 Million American Children Suffering from YTD" (Youthful Tendency Disorder). There was a boxed and bulleted section in the middle of the article describing the early warning signs of YTD: has an imaginary friend, for example, prefers playing outside to doing homework, is subject to spontaneous outbursts of laughter. The authors interviewed a fictional mother for the story: "We were devastated to learn that our daughter had YTD," she said soberly. "But relieved to know that we're not bad parents." Ridiculous, of course, but the spoof points to something real—this is the way we actually talk about youth, the way we categorize them and label them, the way we judge them and sort them. We never encounter a study of young people without the alphabet soup of scientific sounding gobbledy-gook.

Here's another *Onion* piece: "Nation Shocked by Prenatal Shooting," the story of an unborn child who fatally shot his twin with a .38 caliber revolver during an "altercation in their shared Albuquerque womb." And here's another, post-Columbine and pre-Virginia Tech: "Victims Sought in Next Week's Shooting." In this story a shooter asks for potential victims to contact him immediately, "if you can be a target for my insane outburst of rage, or if you know someone who might be." Others interviewed include a police officer—"It sounds like it will be like nothing I'll have ever seen in my twenty years in law enforcement;" and an eyewitness—"I'm sure I won't be able to believe the things I'll see, and I'll have to ask myself why did God allow this to happen." All the recyclable clichés trotted out and put on full display, the whole well-rehearsed litany—if it makes us laugh, we laugh uneasily, for these are exactly the comments that we'll hear in the next round of school or post office or mall assaults, comments that are entirely recognizable and that we ourselves could make. The accompanying person-in-the-street interviews about school shootings go over the top and add a layer of lunacy: "Kids shooting kids with rifles? What is this world coming to? A snub-nosed .45 offers much better stopping power;" and, "What fifteen-year-old doesn't dream of taking out his whole class? And who are we to tell a child not to pursue his dreams?"

In many ways talking about youth violence in the United States today couldn't be easier—the received wisdom is already in place and the script is already written as the *Onion* so clearly illustrates. All that's missing are a few authenticating details—name, place, date—and the story writes itself. It becomes a simple exercise of filling in the blanks and—BAM!—it's a front-page story ready for a Pulitzer: pundits will pontificate, experts will diagnose, politicians will posture. But still I feel obliged to take it up, if only for a moment—even though you already know what I'm about to stay:

- According to school principals, 71 percent of public elementary and secondary schools experienced at least one violent incident during the 1999–2000 school year. In all approximately 1,466,000 such incidents were reported in public schools. These incidents included rape, sexual battery other than rape, physical attacks or fights with or without a weapon, threats of physical attack, and robbery with or without a weapon.
- If you remove the category, "without a weapon," 20 percent of public schools experienced at least one serious violent incident. Elementary schools were least likely to report a violent incident.

- Secondary schools were more likely than elementary or middle schools to report serious violent crime.
- The size of a school's student enrollment was related to the prevalence of both violent and serious violent incidents. The bigger the school, the more likely such incidents would occur.
- City schools were much more likely than suburban or rural schools to report serious violent crime.
- Schools which reported a regular assigned police presence of thirty hours or more a week were much more likely to experience a serious violent incident.
- Schools with the highest proportion of minority students were more likely to report crime and serious crime than schools with the smallest proportion of minority enrollment.
- Schools located in neighborhoods with high levels of crime were more likely to experience a violent or serious violent incident.
- Schools with the largest percentage of students below the fifteenth percentile on standardized tests were more likely than those schools with the smallest percentage of students below the fiftieth percentile to experience at least one violent or seriously violent incident.
- The percentage of students who principals felt "considered academics to be very important" was inversely related to the prevalence of violent and serious violent incidents.
- Schools in which a greater number of serious discipline problems (three or more) occurred were more likely to experience a violent or serious violent incident than schools with fewer discipline problems.
- Schools that reported at least one disruption (such as a bomb threat or an anthrax threat) were more likely to experience a violent or seriously violent incident than those that did not have any disruptions.
- Controlling for other factors, characteristics related to the prevalence of violent incidents included urbanicity, academic importance, number of classroom changes, number of serious discipline problems, and number of schoolwide disruptions.
- School characteristics related to the likelihood that a school would experience at least one *serious* violent incident included enrollment size, urbanicity, percentage of males, number of serious discipline problems, and number of schoolwide disruptions.
- Only 7 percent of public schools accounted for over 50 percent of the total violent incidents that were reported. Comparing the characteristics of those schools with the highest number of incidents to those with the lowest, school level, enrollment size, urbanicity, crime where students

live, number of serious discipline problems, and number of schoolwide disruptions were strongly correlated.

While I'm not offering a scholarly analysis here, and feel no need to footnote or cite, all of this comes from the U.S. Department of Education, office of research, and can be looked up.

Of course, school is only part of the story, although a heatedly over-documented part, but it's true that violence touches the lives of children today in and out of school. If you look, for example, at all youth homicide in the United States, young people committed 2,053 homicides in 2000–2002, but only 17 occurred on school grounds. In that same year, there were 1,777 youth suicides, only 5 at school. And while 18 percent of high school age students reported carrying a weapon at least 1 day during the previous 30 days in 2003, only 7 percent reported carrying a weapon to school.

And it's a fact that 1,400 youth are incarcerated in Illinois, for example, most of them for committing nonviolent crimes, and it's also a fact that just less than half will return to the system within five years.

On and on and on, statistic after dreary statistic—the numbers tell a story, but what story do they tell? If I were drawing this as a graphic report I'd insert here a wise-ass nerd holding a drawing of Edvard Munch's "The Scream" with a voice bubble saying "DUH!" After all, what do we know after studying the mind-numbing facts that we didn't know before? OK, violence is more prevalent in situations where "urbanicity" is a factor, and where violence is part of the neighborhood scene. Hmmm? Without rudely mentioning race and class, we get the idea—"poor Black folks are like that." There's a pervasive sense of wanting to nod dully, and then go to sleep, or at least to move on.

Indeed the facts mean nothing by themselves—they require a narrative to organize them and make them sensible, to circulate them and give them power. The popular narrative of youth violence—from "insane outbursts of rage" to "the revenge of bullied, alienated, and isolated nerds"—is inadequate. What are other possible narratives? And what's missing from the dominant narrative?

The missing can be found in two distinct directions: the first is context; the second is the meaning-perspectives of insiders. Becoming serious about context, foregrounding it as itself a social construction subject to intervention and change, and at the same time pursuing the insights of young people themselves, are essential if getting a truer picture of the phenomenon—and perhaps finding a relevant strategy of repair—is a reasonable goal.

Let's begin with the meaning-making of young people themselves.

I spent two years in the Cook County Juvenile Temporary Detention Center, the oldest and largest juvenile jail in the world, teaching and writing about the experiences and perspectives of those youngsters based on daily interactions and interviews. I called my report *A Kind and Just Parent*, the title taken from Jane Addams who, when she founded the first juvenile court in the world in 1898, said that it ought to act as "a kind and just parent would act for children in crisis." I liked the lofty and romantic sound of it, and I meant the title to be ironic, to show the ideal laid low by a system that was dysfunctional in a thousand ways, but, irony upon irony, I discovered in the juvenile detention center a host of people who were indeed acting out Jane Addams's dream—decent people, hard-working people, trying to lift these children up, while the entire world seemed to be pressing them down.

I remember attending a sentencing hearing for a kid named Jeff, someone I'd tutored in the detention center school. Jeff had killed a rival gang member two weeks past his fourteenth birthday, and there was a certain unsparing logic to the adult judgment that would fall upon his head that morning. Neither the chaos of his life nor the circumstances of his one murderous moment counted for much once he was caught and in the dock.

I had known Jeff for most of a year at the Audy Home school—formally the Nancy B. Jefferson School at the Cook County Juvenile Temporary Detention Center. He'd been called a "superpredator" again and again during his trial, creating a powerful image of an armed and amoral monster in sneakers, but the kid I knew was small and scared and mostly way too eager to please. He could, in turn, be charming or obsequious, agreeable or subservient. That he slavishly followed the orders of a gang boss is no surprise in retrospect; that he'd acted autonomously and willfully is unthinkable.

Still, another child was dead, and whatever else might be said, the victim, too, had claims that day. The dead child's mother took the stand, loss and pain upon her face, and no doubt a heavy price would have to be paid.

The scale of the thing was awesome: there were close to two thousand cases scheduled on that specific day in that particular courthouse in this one American city. The huge spectacle of crime and punishment moved dramatically across the stage, and this kid was, by any measure, a bit player.

"I'm in for murder . . . ," Jeff had told me easily, conversationally, one day, but his words were hard to comprehend. Murder. Of the armies of kids I'd known in detention Jeff seemed perhaps the least capable. I'd learned by now to take the kids as they were, to work with them exactly as they presented themselves to me, to suppress the obvious but unfair and inappropriate question: What are you in for? The question was automatic, instinctive at first because of the distinctive circumstances of the place: everyone here is charged with something.... What? But it was unfair because each kid was especially vulnerable here, and I had the inherent power of the adult, the privilege of freedom. And it was inappropriate because it was an aspect of their lives that I could play no productive role in whatever. I could eavesdrop, but I would be at best a voyeur. I tried to remind myself of the presumption of innocence—they are charged not convicted—and of the tradition of confidentiality in Juvenile Court. Better to meet each kid as a student, to resist the urge to know him through his criminal charge, to push all that to the background. Now, with Jeff at least, it was moving forward. I'd promised Jeff I would come to his sentencing hearing.

At 11:30 Jeff's case was called and he was brought out with another kid from lockup. I hadn't known there was a codefendant, and they were a contrast: Jeff, wearing his oversized white shirt and tie, a little boy in a man's world; the other guy, muscular, powerful, dressed in the Cook County coveralls. The white shirt covered most of the jailhouse tattoos Jeff had carved into himself the last couple of days, but not the raw, red letters on the knuckles of his left hand: H-A-T-E. It's a cliché, of course, but Jeff thought it was original to him.

I'd exchanged a few words with Jeff's parents earlier: his father, over seventy years old and blind, eager to find my hand and shake it when I told them I tutored Jeff in school and that he was always a good boy with me; his mother tense and incommunicative, her face revealing nothing. Jeff's lawyer—a private attorney whose fee consumed all of the family's savings along with everything they could borrow from more distant relatives—had seen us talking and joined in. When he discovered how I knew Jeff, he asked if I would testify at the hearing. We both knew it was just a gesture, possibly a ploy to prove to Jeff's parents that he'd tried everything and had earned his fee, but what the hell. Can it hurt?

Jeff is well liked in the school, I told the Court, a favorite of teachers and staff. He doesn't start fights and he gets along with the other kids. He's agreeable, nervous, a little shy. He is eager to please. He is making progress.

When I finished, the state's attorney started in with a vengeance: "Would you call shooting someone eight times at close range 'eager to please'?"

"Do you consider murder 'agreeable'?"

"Have you ever seen a body with eight bullets in it?"

I told him I knew Jeff only in the context of a classroom, and that we'd never spoken about the charges or the situation leading to today. I hadn't even known he was charged with murder until last week, and I knew nothing of the circumstances surrounding that charge. I'm thanked by the judge and told to step down.

A picture then emerged in the courtroom: Jeff had been a low-level street dealer for a large organization for about a year. He had stopped attending school and was easy pickings for the neighborhood branch of a big Chicago street gang. One day a boss and his lieutenant came around and invited Jeff into the car, and as they drove around, the boss told Jeff that there was a guy encroaching on their territory, a guy who had been warned but thought he was tough. "It's time to waste that motherfucker before everyone comes pouring into our territory."

The lieutenant put a heavy pistol into Jeff's hand. The boss stopped the car, pointed at a young man sitting on a low concrete wall near an alley, and said, "Now fuck him up."

Jeff got out, walked hurriedly toward the guy, and started shooting. Bam! Bam! Bam! Eight times. And then he ran. Two days later, he was arrested, picked out of a lineup by a witness, and charged with the first-degree murder of Joseph Woodford. The gang lieutenant was also picked up; he was the codefendant.

Joseph Woodford's mother was called by the prosecutor to read her victim impact statement. She looked remarkably like Jeff's mother—same age, same build. The strangest thing was that when she was seated next to the judge, the reflecting Plexiglass placed her next to Jeff's mom. And in that distorted image they were twins, both in their forties, both crushed with anger and sadness, sitting there side by side. And, it seemed, they told the same story, one back to front, the other front to back.

Joseph was Mrs. Woodford's oldest child, her favorite. She remembers how he helped with the other children in the family, in the building, and eventually in the neighborhood. He organized games for the kids, and everyone liked him. She cannot express the deprivation and bereavement she feels today, nor measure the loss to her family and community for all time. Such a waste. She shows the judge a picture of Joseph. Justice, in her view, demands balance, an eye for an eye. She wishes, she says, that the judge would execute Jeff.

Mrs. Woodford was entirely compelling. Her pain was trembling and alive. Mrs. Baron was equally inescapable. And there was Jeff: smaller, more frightened, more servile than I'd ever seen him—an unlucky speck of humanity writhing on the vast, pallid canvas of life. The spark was gone.

Jeff's attorney appealed to the judge for leniency: consider his youth— "He is just at the beginning of his life, and he *can* make a contribution if we help him"; and his lack of a criminal record—"This is his first arrest." Furthermore, look at his elderly, blind father and his sickly mother. He has no role models, he said, and no proper parenting. Jeff's first trip to Juvenile

Court had been seven years ago, he pointed out, but in that case he was accompanying his mother, who was cited in a neglect petition. Jeff is slow, perhaps retarded, his lawyer argued, and he began to paint a pathetic portrait of deprivation piled upon deficit. Of course, his purpose was to help, but I watched Jeff's father wince with every lurid word.

Several months ago I had heard Jeff say, in standard Audy Home parlance, "I caught this case . . . ," in the same style and cadence as "I caught the flu," but now he stood awkwardly in the court, head down, hands fidgeting, and tried to take some responsibility as he mumbled a barely audible apology to Joseph Woodford's family: "I'm sorry for what I did." His voice cracked. "It was wrong. I apologize."

"I wish I could believe you are sorry," the judge began, and it was clear that this would go badly for Jeff. "But you are a gun waiting to go off." The judge's voice was tired as he spoke of law and order and the destruction wrought by drugs. "Everyone in this scenario is a victim of the drug trade," he said sadly. "Both Mr. Woodford and Mr. Baron were involved in a deadly business, and both have reaped the results of that business. There are no heroes here, only victims." Mrs. Woodford, seemed stung by these words as she looked daggers at the judge.

"Some day you may be able to rejoin society and make a contribution as your lawyer has said you would," the judge continued. "But that day is not now." With that the judge sentenced Jeff, not yet seventeen years old, convicted killer of a rival drug dealer, to forty-seven years in prison.

Perpetrator victim, victim perpetrator. And where are the grown-ups? One kid in the jail school pointed out to me: kids don't make guns; kids get guns from adults. I then began asking kids in the detention center a hypothetical question: If I gave you $200, how long would it take you to get me a gun. The answer surprised me at first with its extravagance: $200? How many you want? I could get you two .38s this afternoon.

Let's turn to the second missing element in the litany on violence and youth, the many concentric circles of context: family, neighborhood, community, city, state, nation, and the world. As a teacher these contexts frame and shape my life with students.

Even as we reassure ourselves that as a nation and a culture we are a peaceful people, a child-loving people, and even as we insist that each of us personally abhors violence, the world (and many of us) watches with horror and anger as the country marches step by step toward a certain and definitive violent authoritarianism. It's not the whole story to be sure—but it is without a doubt a bright thread that is both recognizable and knowable:

- Violent empire resurrected in the name of a renewed and powerful patriotic and jingoistic nationalism.
- War without end.
- Identification of opaque enemies as a unifying cause requiring higher walls and more armaments.
- Unprecedented and unapologetic military expansion and militarism. "No Child Left Behind" legislation requires schools to grant access to recruiters and provide student names, phone numbers, and addresses to the military. Chicago leads the nation in militarizing its schools and creating the most massive junior military reserve program in the country with five military high schools, three dozen Junior ROTC programs and twenty middle school cadet corps programs.
- White supremacy intact and unyielding.
- Rampant sexism and organized campaigns to violate the rights of women and girls, and violence against women as a steady drum-beat in the B-section of every daily.
- Mass incarceration and disenfranchisement—over two million of our fellow citizens in prison, most for nonviolent crimes and disproportionately people of color, and over one hundred thousand youth in prison, just under half of whom will return to the system within five years of release.
- Intertwining of religious orthodoxy and government.
- Unprecedented concentrations of wealth.
- Overwhelming greed putting planetary survival in question, and abdication of responsibility for environmental catastrophe.
- The shredding of constitutional and human rights, and the hollowing out of democracy. Torture defended in the highest offices in government.
- Corporate power unchecked.
- The scapegoating of certain vulnerable groups, and the creation of popular movements based on bigotry, intolerance, and the threat of violence.
- Fraudulent elections.
- Disdain for the arts and for intellectual life.
- And on and on.

Our children are watching, so what is our response? What should it be? As Nina Simone might lament: "Why can't you see it?/Why can't you feel it?/I don't know,/I don't know."

A young African American soldier is taken to Walter Reed Army Hospital missing her legs and her face—shall I make a reservation for dinner and a show? A young Black man is shot in the back by the Chicago police—shall I take that vacation in Jamaica? Two more prisoners commit suicide at Guantanamo—shall I get that new car I'd been wanting? Four million Iraquis are refugees or internally displaced because of the U.S. invasion—shall I send a contribution to one of the rascals revving up his or her political ambitions?

And in this morning's paper:

- Northern Illinois University was closed because of a racial slur and a Virginia Tech reference scrawled on a residence hall bathroom wall. "Tell those [slur] to go home," it read. Virginia Tech was a problem, it went on, "having only one shooter...."
- Parents in a poor Chicago high school protested the heavy presence of military recruiters on campus. "They're here every day," said one mother. "Promoting violence as a solution. They build relationships with the kids they consider vulnerable, so it's like being recruited by a friend."
- A Chicago police sergeant was convicted of raping a neighborhood woman while on duty.
- An $11 million civil settlement with victims of police torture was approved by the Finance Committee of the City Council of Chicago.
- The CIA admitted destroying tape recordings of "enhanced interrogation techniques," torture according to the Geneva Accords.
- The Supreme Court agreed to hear another in the long line of cases arising from the extraordinary detentions without habeus corpus of foreign nationals at Guantanamo.
- Riot squad police were "savagely beaten" by twenty to thirty youth in a housing project on the outskirts of Paris, and no one knew if it was related to police beating youth in the same area a little more than a year ago.

We're reminded that privilege is always anesthetizing, and that the privileged are necessarily blind to their own blind spots. It's of course an effort for white people to see the obstacles placed in the paths of African Americans, for men to see the injuries visited upon women, for the able-bodied to feel the dislocation and banal discrimination experienced by the disabled, or for straight people to experience the pain of children routinely beaten and taunted and marginalized in our schools, of teachers asked to deny their identities, of parents pushed around in unfriendly settings, of human beings asked to hide their closest loved ones. And the privilege of exporting massive amounts of violence barricades us from the truth, and from our own responsibility.

The Bush administration announced on October 4, 2006, that it would host a conference in the following week to discuss the recent rash of school violence across the country. The idea was to bring together education and law-enforcement officials to talk about the nature of the problem and federal action that might help communities prevent violence. "The president is deeply saddened and troubled by the recent school violence and the shootings that have taken place in different communities across America," a spokesperson said. "It breaks America's collective heart when innocent children who were at school to learn are violently taken hostage and cut down in their own schools." That could have been written by the *Onion*.

The environment must become our focus. The culture of violence is the centerpiece: poverty, which includes unemployment and limited opportunities, the media, which includes prolonged exposure and sensationalism and Grand Theft Baghdad, disenfranchisement, millions with nothing to do, mistrust of youth, alienation, consumerism. Much of this is what the Catholic bishops called "slow-motion violence" in a 1994 pastoral letter—poverty, hunger, hopelessness. The Catholic bishops also pointed out that the U.S. is the world's greatest consumer of weapons and the world's largest arms exporter, and that the United States has a special obligation, then, to seek peace and promote justice.

Jose Saramago sketches a harrowing moral landscape in *Blindness*, his creepy allegory of a modern epidemic and the inevitable atrocities it unleashes. A man stopped at a red light in rush hour suddenly goes blind—a milky whiteness descends, and his sight is inexplicably gone. Around him horns honk, commuters become impatient and then enraged, a little chaos takes hold as people try to sort out what has happened. Someone helps the man home, and then steals his car.

By the next day it has become clear that an epidemic of "white blindness" is spreading, afflicting people at an accelerating pace. One after another, people open their eyes and feel as if they've plunged into a thick milky sea.

The authorities at first quarantine the ailing, locking them away in an empty mental hospital. When the guards go blind, their eyesight vanishing into the vast whiteness, the prisoners are abandoned, but not before a group of blind men organize themselves into a predatory gang, steal the food rations of the others, and humiliate and rape all the women, young and old.

When it seems the worst is upon them, when the brutality becomes overwhelming, one and then another and then all the people, just as suddenly, regain their eyesight. In jubilation, laughing and awkwardly hugging one another, they ask, Why? Whatever happened? Why did we go blind?

Where did the milky whiteness come from, and where has it gone? Why do we now see?

The woman narrator responds: "I don't think we did go blind, I think we are blind, Blind but seeing, Blind people who can see, but do not see." She is reminding them—and all of us—that the opposite of moral isn't always immoral—it's more often indifference. Ethical action on one hand, and on the other cool detachment, negligence, apathy, cynicism, inattentiveness, incuriousness, aloofness. Blindness. Were they really blind? And now, sighted once more, can they really see? Can we?

The beginning of moral thinking and ethical action is opening our eyes. Martin Luther King Jr. said: "I am convinced that if we are to get to the right side of the world revolution, we as a nation must undergo a radical revolution of values. We must rapidly shift from a thing oriented society to a person oriented society. When machines and computers, profit motives and property rights are considered more important than human rights, the giant triplets of racism, materialism and militarism are incapable of being conquered. A nation that continues year after year to spend more money on military defense than on programs as social uplift is approaching spiritual death. For years, I labored with the idea of reforming the existing institutions, now I feel quite differently. I think you've got to have a reconstruction of the entire society, a revolution of values."

It's important here to make a distinction between personal virtue—be honest, do your work, show up on time, be kind—and social or community ethics. Personal virtue is an undisputed good in almost every society, but we would be hard-pressed to say a slave owner—a participant in a vast and violent system of exploitation—who paid his bills and was kind to his wife, for example, was an ethical person. We need to think about how we behave collectively, how our society behaves, how the contexts of politics and economics, for example interact with what we hold to be good. Most of us, after all, most of the time follow the conventions of our cultures—most Spartans act like Spartans, most Athenians like Athenians, and most Americans like Americans. To be a person of moral character in an unjust social order, or to be a peaceful person living in a sewer of invisible or normalized or exported violence, requires us to work to change society. The only place for a just person in a slave state, Henry David Thoreau argued when it mattered, is in prison.

Bertolt Brecht, who knew something about the dark times, asked this question in his poem "Motto": "In dark times, will there also be singing?" And his answer: "Yes, there will be singing./About the dark times." Our work here and now is in part to sing the dark times. It is essential for us to begin with a particularly precious ideal—the belief that every human being is of incalculable value, each the one and only who will ever trod the earth, and that our work as teachers and citizens and artists and activists living in a democracy must be geared to helping every human being reach a fuller measure of his or her humanity. This ideal invites people on a journey to become more thoughtful and more capable, more powerful and courageous, more exquisitely alive in their projects and their pursuits. An unyielding belief in the unity of humanity—always revolutionary, and never more so than today—is never quite finished, never easily or finally summed up, and yet it is central to achieving a just society. Neither a commodity with readily recognized features nor a product for consumption, the democratic ideal is an aspiration to be continually nourished, engaged and exercised, a dynamic, expansive experiment that must be achieved over and over again by every individual and each successive generation if it is to live at all.

Those of us who are teachers engage in a front-line fight for a more human world—a world of mutual recognition, a world based on the principle that every human life is of incalculable value and that each is the one and only who will ever trod the earth—and we resist, then, all the hierarchies of human worth as base and ugly and in the end wrong in the sense of inaccurate and in the sense of immoral. Our stance must be identification *with* our students and community, not identification *of*—the latter moves dangerously toward surveillance. And we struggle as Jane Addams, another Chicago visionary, argued, to hold to the humanist idea, to the ideal of the unity of humanity, even—or perhaps especially—when humanity is represented by a delinquent boy, an alcoholic woman, a drug addicted teenager, or a gang banger. And so a commitment to education as the practice of enlightenment and illumination, education as the practice of freedom. Education as humanization.

Because every human being, no matter who, is a gooey biological wonder, pissing and shitting, pulsing with the breath and beat of life itself, evolved and evolving, prodded by sexual urges, shaped by genetics, twisted and gnarled and hammered by the unique experiences of living, and because every human being has a unique and complex set of circumstances that makes his or her life understandable and sensible, bearable or unbearable, we reject any action that treats anyone else as an object, any gesture that objectifies or *thingifies* human beings. This demands the recognition of the humanity of everyone. "The starting point of critical elaboration is the consciousness of what one really is," Antonio Gramsci wrote in his *Prison Notebooks*, "and is 'knowing oneself' as a product of the historic process to date, which has deposited in you an infinity of traces, without leaving an inventory." Gramsci articulates a sense of this critical dialectic: the infinite and the ineffable tied up inexorably with the concrete and the real.

We note here the casual disregard of the humanity of thousands and thousands—millions really—of young people, including the students most of us work with and worry about every day, who made the mistake of being born poor—or born the descendents of slaves or of Native peoples in a colonial nation founded on white supremacy—who hold no currency, have limited access and little recognition. We see dehumanization everywhere as both policy and practice, and we enter, then, the contested space of classroom and school. We want for our young people the miracles and the transformations, the hard efforts, the enduring hope, the generous investment that is the common place of the privileged. We work in ways that might allow them to become seekers after their own questions, authors of their own scripts rather than bit players in stories already written for them by others, actors in their own dramas rather than merely walk-ons in an oft-performed B-movie, artists and composers of their own lives.

We crawl toward love. And as we do, we engage a fundamental question, sometimes explicitly, often not: Who in the world am I? Who am I in the world? And from this: What are my choices? What are my chances? What will I do to make my way through? The thoughtful teacher, the ethical teacher, takes the questions as challenge and mandate.

We are mindful of the cry in Gwendolyn Brooks's masterful poem "Boy Breaking Glass": "I shall create!/If not a note/a hole. If not an overture/a desecration." But I shall create. This is the cry of every soul.

Our task in part is to provide opportunities to open creative possibilities so that the toxic options do not assert themselves and become the default position. Our task is to be the grown-ups: get the damned guns out of the environment; show how one uses words and not arms; represent dialogue, humility, and generosity in our practice. Our task is to hold the ground while youth make their grand mistakes.

CHAPTER
Six

"WE ARE ALL SEUNG-HUI CHO!":
American Social Psychosis and the Virginia Tech Killings

Stephen Pfohl

"We are all Hokies!" read the freshly painted sign on the outfield wall of the Boston College baseball stadium. These words echoed a declaration of mourning made at Virginia Polytechnic Institute and State University following the terrible murders that took place there on April 16, 2007. I teach at Boston College. Like Virginia Tech, Boston College is a member of the Atlantic Coast Conference. And shortly after the Hokies' campus was drenched in blood, its baseball team journeyed north to play our school in a game charged with goodwill and far less tragedy than the violent game of life and death enacted in Blacksburg a few weeks previously. During the baseball game, in a prayerful memorial service, and on the pages of our university's newspaper, the phrase "We are all Hokies!" rippled across our campus for a time this spring.

A similar embrace of Hokie identity took place at other colleges and universities across the United States. And, like them, Boston College (BC) not only allied itself symbolically with the thirty-two students and faculty members gunned down in Blacksburg, it also took practical measures to guard against the possibility of a violent massacre taking place on its own campus in the future. Within weeks, the BC administration announced that it had invested in new technology, enabling campus police to instant message students within seconds, should it be learned that a killer is on the loose at our own school. Aside from this fearful contingency plan, what other lessons are to be learned from the terrible events that took place at Virginia Tech?

There is, of course, something moving about public identification with the victims of the Virginia Tech massacre and by widespread expressions of compassion for the families and loved ones, classmates, and fellow faculty members, of those slain or wounded. In addition, in the weeks following the shootings both mainstream and new media outlets have taught their respective publics a great deal about the mixture of psychological, neurological, and environmental factors that leading experts view as contributing to the deadly actions of mass killers such as Seung-Hui Cho, the troubled Virginia Tech student and shooter. *Time*, for instance, quotes forensic psychologist Stanton Samenow, who notes, "They seem to have an unfathomable ability to shut off knowledge of the consequences, of the difference between right and wrong. It's critical for us to try to understand that worldview and its mental makeup."[1]

After concluding that mass violence typically combines "the dark hand of biology, life experiences, and the surrounding culture—plus the will to take lives in cold blood," *Newsweek* observes, "mass killers tend to be aggrieved, hurt, clinically depressed, socially isolated and, above all, paranoid. It is a specific kind of paranoia: a tendency to blame everyone but themselves for their troubles, to believe the world is against them and unfair."[2] This, of course, fits the profile constructed by the media of Seung-Hui Cho, the isolated, angry, and depressed killer. In the digital video manifesto sent to NBC News, Cho declared, "You forced me into a corner and gave me only one option. The decision was yours. Now you have blood on your hands that will never wash off."[3]

The Mind of a Killer

Many media stories about the Virginia Tech massacre have provided information about the so-called mind of a killer. Other than teaching educational institutions about how better to look for warning signs, while bolstering technological defenses against sudden outbursts of psychotic violence—what societal lessons might we take from the killings in Blacksburg? Of immediate importance is increased public awareness of the need for tighter interstate regulation of firearms and the banishment for private purchase of such weapons as the Glock 19 semiautomatic handgun and the hollow point bullets Cho easily obtained from local gun stores and on the web. These are weapons of violence, not instruments of sport.

Unfortunately, public awareness of the need for more effective gun control rises periodically, and then dissipates, following violent episodes such as that which took place at Virginia Tech. A spike in awareness and public outcry also occurred after the massacre at Columbine, but effective gun control remains legislatively derailed by powerful market forces and the corporately backed gun lobby. In addition, serious efforts to limit the availability of rapid-fire killing machines are hindered by populist social phantasms about the protection that deadly handguns and assault weapons can bring to law-abiding citizens. In the days following the shootings, conservative radio talk shows across America were replete with laments that more Virginia Tech students weren't carrying weapons. If they were, suggested fiery gun advocates, the killer would never have taken as many lives. Some other student would surely have taken Cho out before the killer completed his nightmarish rampage.

The Killings in the Context of U.S. History and Culture

More complex questions about the wider social context of the killings arose in two lengthy discussions of the Virginia Tech murders in my undergraduate class on Deviance and Social Control. Prompted, in part, by a compelling mixed-media presentation by Mike Cermak, one of my graduate teaching assistants, on the effects of consumer electronics in everyday life, some students wondered whether the same technologies that so quickly place us in communication with others might also estrange or alienate us from each other. Does the quick communicative fix provided by contemporary consumer electronics serve only to deepen our connections to one another? Or do these new technologies also carry the danger of an increased instrumental objectification of others? Is it possible that the same high-speed electronic devices that put in us touch, also shorten our attention spans and make us less able to connect with people in face-to-face relations? Was the evermore-intense technological mediation of daily life a factor in the distance that Seung-Hui Cho felt from others? Were the cruel effects of the bullying that Cho had experienced in school and in church groups amplified during his college years by his relative exclusion from the omnipresent technological "friendship" networks of MySpace and Facebook?

What about the disconcerting phone calls Cho made to a frightened woman student two years before his deadly rampage, or the annoying instant messages he sent to another? What about the troubling cell phone calls he made to his roommate Andy Koch? Cho once called Andy to say that he was not himself but "Cho's brother, Question Mark." Later, over Thanksgiving break in 2005, Cho phoned to say he was vacationing with Vladmir Putin in North Carolina. "I am pretty sure that's not possible Seung," replied Andy.[4] What, moreover, are we to make of the fact that Cho had photographed the legs of female students from underneath their desks? Was this further evidence of his objectified distance from others, distance fostered by the increasingly technological orchestration of everyday life and death? Dense streams of technological connections and disconnections were in evidence everywhere in the media-relayed story of the Virginia Tech murders. From the cell phone camera that captured chaotic images and the sound of gunfire from nearby Norris Hall to the incessant repetition of these same frightening images and sound on television, to the multiple video blogs recounting students' terror, and, of course, the digital media show produced for our consumption by the killer himself, technology and the trail of violence went hand in hand at Virginia Tech.

Sparked by a provocative lecture given by Jared Del Rosso, another of my teaching assistants, students in my class also pursued questions about whether societal reactions to some of Cho's previous behaviors may have prompted him to identify with, or even respond in a perversely affirmative manner to, the fear expressed by others that he fit the stereotype of someone likely to be a school shooter. Did Cho feel hemmed in or, perhaps, even brazenly emboldened by the reactions of others to his often strange demeanor, menacing silence, and violent classroom writings? Were the worrisome labels applied to Cho by teachers, school administrators, mental health officials, and his fellow students "contributing factors" that hastened his precipitous slide into unimaginable violence? Was Cho acting out a terrible—but socially ordained—drama, scripted ahead of time by the way that others had pigeonholed him in the past?

Sociologists and anthropologists have long observed that dramatic acts of deviance can be occasioned—even called into being—by the collective anxieties of the society in which they occur. Such anxieties may be so vexing and unspeakable that they bear no proper name; at least not until a label connoting deviance is burnt into the identity of a condemned wrongdoer. In intensely unequal societies, such as our own—hierarchically organized societies founded on deep-seated material and psychic injustices and the structured exploitation of some classes, or classifications, of people by others—the deviant who is called upon to functionally embody what that society most abhors is also often a perverse, or monstrously mirrored, figuration of shameful aspects of what that society itself—or, more accurately, those most blessed by power in the society—would deny or disavow. Socially figured as evil—a cold-blooded, emotionless, methodic, and empty-eyed killer—Seung-Hui Cho held up a psychotic mirror of mythic judgment to the society upon which he took aim. In the video message sent to us through NBC News, Cho declares, "You had everything you wanted. Your Mercedes wasn't enough, you brats. Your golden necklaces weren't enough, you snobs. Your trust fund wasn't enough. Your vodka and cognac weren't enough. All your debaucheries weren't enough. Those weren't enough to fulfill your hedonistic needs. You had everything."

Cho's video manifesto was followed up by the crack of a 9 mm, "the weapon of choice for cops and criminals, civilians and soldiers—and a sick young man in Virginia."[5] At first, most everyone thought it was the sound of construction, the erection of another university building, an architectural homage to global power and knowledge. Soon it was evident that this was the sound of something far worse—the sound of both a determined executioner and a symbolic message aimed at you and me. To treat Seung-Hui Cho's actions as bearing symbolic importance is not to romanticize or dignify Cho's violence. Cho was, after all, crazy. To explore the social symbolism of Cho's deadly rampage is, instead, to ask that we delve beneath the conscious surface of his psychotic actions and words, seeking in them symptomatic lessons about the way American society sets its social boundaries and how our society values some lives, while discounting others.

Several students in my class raised concerns about the possible effects of Cho's ethnic identity. As a native of South Korea, might Seung-Hui Cho's terrible deeds spur violence against Korean Americans and other Asians residing in the United States? This concern is of particular importance when set within the landscape of contemporary racialized privilege and a continuing global "coloniality of power."[6] Commenting on the relative ignorance of many Americans about our nation's decidedly contradictory history of involvement with Korea, one student even wondered whether the Virginia Tech murders might exacerbate existing tensions between the United States and North Korea. Despite the significance of such concerns, it is important to remember that, while born in South Korea, Cho spent his later childhood and young adult life in the United States, surrounded by the rituals of American culture and economic life.

Cho was, in a sense, "trapped in a generational warp, neither quite Korean like his parents nor American like his peers. His parents turned to the church for help within his emotional problems, but he was bullied in his Christian youth group, especially by rich kids."[7] Other students commented on the role that gender socialization might have played in Cho's horrific violence. Some pointed to Cho's troubled relations with women, while others pointed to how sadistic aggression is often "naturalized" in men in our culture as a learned response to situations of emotional turmoil, vulnerability, and relative powerlessness.

At this point in our discussion, another student in the Deviance and Social Control class made a connection between Cho's violence and recent U.S. history, speculating about mass public denial of responsibility for the horrors of the Iraq War as a haunting social context for the Virginia Tech killings. Without minimizing the tragic deaths in Blacksburg, the student reminded our class that on the same day in which NBC News reported on Seung-Hui Cho's media manifesto, "bombs ravaged Baghdad in five horrific explosions . . . killing at least 171 people in the deadliest day in the capital since the American-led security plan for the city took effect two months" earlier.[8] Nearly 230 people were killed or found dead in Iraq on that single day. Attention to the horror of these mass killings was, however, displaced by headline coverage of the Virginia Tech massacre. But more disturbing than this simple displacement may be the fact that virtually nowhere in the United States on that day, nor on any of the days following the 2003 American-led invasion and occupation of Iraq, have there been mass public expressions of grief and mourning even mildly approaching those produced by the terrible events at Virginia Tech. Why?

Social Psychosis from Baghdad to Blacksburg

I suppose it can be argued that it is only natural for us to mourn the deaths of those whose lives we identify most with. But why, as a nation, are we so manifestly unable to publicly identify with the lives, and mourn the deaths, of the hundreds of thousands of Iraqis killed as a result of the preemptive warfare unleashed by our country against Iraq? As mentioned previously, when attempting to account for the psychotic violence of mass killers, *Time* magazine quotes a leading forensic expert who states, "They seem to have an unfathomable ability to shut off knowledge of the consequences, of the difference between right and wrong. It's critical for us to try to understand that worldview and its mental makeup." This quote strikes me as being as applicable to the collective worldview and mental makeup of the United States, as it may be to the individual mental makeup of a psychotic mass killer. Both the individual killer and the killer nation display an uncanny ability to "shut off knowledge of the consequences" of one's violence.

The continuing Iraq War must be understood as a primary historical context by which to make mythic symbolic sense of Seung-Hui Cho's horrific actions—the social psychosis of a nation engaged in an enormously violent, thoroughly illegal, and strategically unprovoked campaign of preemptive warfare, the formal justification of which is nothing short of paranoiac. This is a war brought about—much like Cho's preemptive attack on his teachers and classmates—not to defend against actual acts of aggression, but by the manufacture of psychotic fear of a very specific kind—a tendency to blame everyone but ourselves!

In attempting to make sense of the paranoiac violence of mass killers, *Newsweek* quotes James Alan Fox, professor of criminal justice at Northeastern University. According to Fox, "They see others as being responsible for their problems; it's never their fault."[9] In attempting to justify the Iraq War, officials in the Bush administration repeatedly display a related form of psychotic reasoning, blaming imagined demons for unleashing the terror of mass killings—nonexistent weapons of mass destruction, nonexistent connections between the 9/11 terrorist attacks and Saddam Hussein, nonexistent connections between al Qaeda and the government of Iraq, and nonexistent attempts by Iraq to secure materials for nuclear weapons to carry out a supposed imminent attack on the United States. Today the problem is said to be Iran. Tomorrow, perhaps, Syria, Pakistan, or Sudan will be blamed.

Evoked as a moral guide to U.S. foreign policy and the "war against terror," the paranoiac "axis of evil" pictured by President George W. Bush is as flexible and subject to psychotic mutation as the viral vectors of fast capitalism upon which it parasites. Each exhibits ritual denial of the historical actualities of an ascendant global order of things set into motion by institutions of power and profit such as the International Monetary Fund, World Bank, and U.S. military. It's never our fault! It's never our responsibility! It's never the result of fast corporate capitalist interests! It's never the outcome of Northwestern geopolitical designs on the oil-rich territories of the Persian Gulf! To paraphrase Seng-Hui Cho's own paranoiac self-justification for righteous violence—it was their threats, not our historical actions that forced us into a corner and gave us but only one option. The decision was theirs. As such, it is them, and not us, that have blood on their hands that will never wash off.

The analogy I am making here between pathological individuals and social expressions of psychosis is rooted in Teresa Brennan's discerning theoretical analysis of the confounding of imaginary psychic projections and the violent social history of modern capitalist/colonialist expressions of power (1993:1, 9–10). Brennan traces social psychosis in the West from its psychic origins in a "foundational fantasy" that makes the ego of modern "Man" appear as if "self-contained" and destined to exert control over the fields of living energetic matter upon which it depends economically for sustenance and survival. This sense of fundamental separateness of the self from the world of living energetic matter is a core feature of what Brennan refers to as the modern "era of the ego" (1993:3) This signifies the historical emergence of an intensely masculine form of collective social psychosis, a "warped psychology" that accompanies the rise of modern science and the increasing dominance of a capitalist "coloniality of power" in the seventeenth century (Brennan 1993; Quijano 1998).

Making use of critical psychoanalytic theory, Marxist-feminist thought, and a wide range of historical data, Brennan identifies social forces enabling the realization of a long-standing "foundational fantasy" about matter (and mothers) as destined to be exploited as "natural resources" by men, "denying any notion of indebtedness or connection to origin" (1993:167). Forces facilitating the realization of this aggressive fantasy include both the ascendance of profit-driven capitalist logic and new technologies of measurement, manufacture, and transportation permitting an increased objectification and appropriation of earth's energies. In this, "fantasy is made into reality, as commodities are constructed to serve their human masters, to wait upon them, at the expense of the natural world. These commodities are objects to be controlled: they are nature transformed into a form in which it cannot reproduce itself, nature directed toward human ends" (Brennan 2000:9).

Psychotic because it is literally out of touch with material actuality, the technological enactment of the foundational fantasy also begets a haunting collective feeling of paranoia—a repressed awareness of the sacrificial violence enacted by modern men of power in the name of economic and scientific progress. This paranoia leads to further cycles of aggressive cultural projections and action aimed at domination, locking the global Northwest into a self-enclosed death culture of masculine and imperial violence. Brennan describes the dynamic behind this perpetual cycle of technologically fueled aggression in the following way.

> The aggressive imperative involved in making the other into a slave, or object, will lead to territorial expansion (territorial imperialism). This is because the objectification of the other depends on establishing a spatial boundary by which the other and self are fixed. But this fixing of the other leads to the fear that the other will retaliate, which in turn leads to a feeling of spatial constriction. Moreover, the feeling of spatial constriction is related to the physical environment. These changes have physical effects on the psyche, which in turn alter the psychical perception of the environment, and of one's boundaries. With spatial constrictions, one's boundaries are threatened, and the resultant fear increases the need to control the object. (1993:8)

The popular U.S. capitalist cultural archetype of "the self-made man" is a good historical example of the foundational fantasy at work. This man shows little gratitude to anyone but himself. He falsely imagines that he has pulled himself up (above others) by his own bootstraps, even when this is manifestly not the case. In truth, this mythic man's real history is of far less self-congratulatory sort. This man forgets who actually made his bootstraps and where in the world his boots were produced, at what price, for whose profit, and at whose expense. It is not that the man forgets entirely. The harsh and exploitative realities buried beneath the man's foundational fantasy return to haunt his psychic well-being, his dreams, desires, and half-thoughts. This makes the supposedly self-made man of American mythology paranoid. Afraid of his own historical shadow, he is always watching his back, looking over his shoulder, fearful that what he has taken energetically from others will, in turn, be taken away from him. This puts him on guard, makes him defensive, and fuels his movement toward violence and war.

A projective distortion of material actuality, the foundational fantasy that drives this archetypal leading man of American historical drama gains steam and spreads across the globe by the twin forces of modern technological domination and the speedy advance of fast capitalist/colonialist practices of commodification (Pfohl 2006). The result is a perilously aggressive fixing and depletion of natural energetic connections to others and the world. Bolstered by denial and laced with false memories, the collective historical enactment of this fantasy represents a psychotic disconnection and divorce from reality, a malaise that Patricia Williams (1991:15) associates with a singularly American form of "social amnesia."

For Canadian social theorist Arthur Kroker, the social psychosis theorized by Brennan also assumes a distinctive American cultural form, one steeped in anxiety and resentment and justified in religious terms by a long-standing Puritan ideology. Kroker portrays leading vectors of American society as plagued by a kind of bipolar cultural personality disorder—a repetitive and compulsive oscillation "between two extremes—between the 'war spirit' and spirit of 'acedia'" (Kroker 2007:23). This oscillation is symptomatic of a disturbing cultural bifurcation that has haunted America from the time that Puritan invaders first claimed this land their own. With the Puritans came an aggressive theology that wed the sacrificial violence of conquest to a religious vision of a people chosen by God to redeem the very world they laid waste to. This suggests a "classically split consciousness veering between a raging 'war spirit' (which, as de Tocqueville noted, set out to conquer the continental wilderness with a bible in one hand and an axe in the other);

and panic fear (tempered by melancholy self doubt) concerning the imminent dissolution of the boundaries of the self" (Kroker 2007:23).

This split American consciousness is cloaked beneath the veneer of the country's dominant "political theology"—a vision of the United States as a nation blessed by God. But, for Kroker, this is only one side of the bifurcated American mind. While providing a religious justification for several centuries of U.S. contributions to world cultural, economic, techno-scientific, and military history, this vision of an America as a nation blessed by God has also helped keep from common sight and collective memory legacies of a far grimmer sort. Baptized out of a popular U.S. cultural imagination of itself are the more troubling historical realities of genocide against indigenous peoples, the violence of slavery without reparations and the continuing market-based disenfranchisement of the vast majority of people of African descent, the theft of Mexican lands and territories once controlled by Spain in the Pacific and Caribbean, and the virulent suppression of women in many realms, as well as the repression of erotic expressions, bonds, relations, and identities that challenge the putative "naturalness" of hierarchical kinship patterns headed by white heterosexist men of power.

Also blocked from mainstream religious discourse and cultural symbolism is the recurrent alignment of the U.S. state—domestically and in foreign policy—with the interests of mostly wealthy white men and the corporations they command; not to mention a demonstrated American willingness to use weapons of mass destruction, including nuclear weapons, to incinerate civilian populations and send messages of terror to its enemies the globe over. When telling a story of America's "born again" political theology and the split consciousness it engenders, Kroker places particular emphasis on the bivalent character of dominant American religious sensibilities. These sensibilities oscillate between boundless optimism about God's plan for America and panic; between optimism about America's role in the world and recurrent tremors of panicky fear, rooted in a denial of historical actuality and a collective failure to own up to and mourn the suffering to others caused by a legacy of unexamined greed and lust for imperial power.

A Hokies' Lament

Social psychosis, social amnesia, and split consciousness—these are ways of describing the paranoiac culture of historical denial and preemptive warfare that enveloped the psyche of Seung-Hui Cho from the outside in. This is not to claim that Cho's violence was simply caused by American culture. It is, however, to suggest that the nihilism of each represents a complex and disturbed mythic mirroring of the other. In his media manifesto Seung-Hui

Cho both lashed out at and identified with the sacrificial religious spirit of American culture, condemning what he perceived as the hypocrisy of U.S. Christianity, while likening himself to the suffering Christ. In refusing to recognize and make reparations for the violence we have collectively unleashed in Iraq and elsewhere across the globe, and in refusing to reckon with the guilt-ridden realities of socially structured inequalities here at home, U.S. society similarly lashes out with resentment at those it views as enemies. At the same time, America dresses itself up in the imaginary garb of a god-like suffering servant. This is evidence of a profound social psychosis. But while leading experts on the psychology of aggression remain plagued by an inability to predict individual psychotic outbursts of violence, the same need not be true at a societal level.

The terrifying social forces that make all Americans complicit with mass killings abroad and aggressive inequality within the boundaries of our own country will not be curtailed by new technologies of control aimed at instant messaging us when killers are on the loose. We may all be Hokies. But, perhaps, we are also all Seung-Hui Cho. To shed this terrible killer side of our split collective consciousness, it is necessary to begin to disassemble the warring social order to which we contribute daily. This order is rooted in a relentless search for speedy profit and a paranoiac denial of responsibility for the violence engendered by our collective actions in history. Ending the unlawful occupation of Iraq will not instantly rid our country of the nihilistic social impulses that fuel psychotic outbursts of violence. But it may help, particularly if stopping the war is but a first step toward waging a renewed campaign of global justice and peace. But paranoid about secret killers among us, and afraid of our own historical shadows, it seems more likely that America will continue to deny the violent social psychosis that holds our entire country hostage to a culture of war. This is a tragedy that far exceeds that of the terrible Virginia Tech killings. This is a Hokies' lament.

Notes

1. Jeffrey Kluger, "Why They Kill," *Time*, Vol. 169, no. 18 (April 30, 2007): 54.

2. Sharon Begley, with Anne Underwood and Mary Carmichael, "The Anatomy of Violence," *Newsweek*, Vol. CXLIX, no. 18 (April 30, 2007): 43.

3. Excerpt from video message sent by Seung-Hui Cho's to NBC News. (www.cnn.com/2007/US/04/18/vtech.shooting/index.html). Retrieved May 29, 2007.

4. These and other details pertaining to the Virginia Tech murders are available in the *Wikipedia* entry for Seung-Hui Cho (en.wikpedia.org/wiki/Seung-Hui_Cho). Retrieved May 29, 2007.

5. Jerry Adler, "Story of a Gun," *Newsweek*, Vol. CXLIX, no. 18 (April 30, 2007): 37.

6. The term "coloniality of power" is used by Peruvian sociologist Aníbal Quijano to suggest that no aspects of contemporary culture or economy are entirely free of the haunting shadows of colonialism and the complex ways that colonial formations of power impact upon virtually all social processes, from the social constitution of what counts as valid forms of knowledge to the meaning of such diverse matters as pleasure, pain, and subjective experience. See, for instance, Quijano (2000).

7. Evan Thomas, "Making of a Massacre," *Newsweek*, Vol. CXLIX, no. 18 (April 30, 2007): 24.

8. Kirk Semple, "Bombs Rip through Baghdad in Wave of Attacks, Killing 171," *New York Times*, Vol. CLVI, no. 53, 919 (Thursday, April 19, 2007): 1.

9. James Alan Fox, quoted in Sharon Begley, with Anne Underwood and Mary Carmichael, "The Anatomy of Violence," *Newsweek*, Vol. CXLIX, no. 18 (April 30, 2007): 43.

References

Brennan, Teresa. 1993. *History after Lacan*. New York: Routledge.
———. 2000. *Exhausting Modernity*. New York: Routledge.
Kroker, Arthur. 2007. *Born Again Ideology: Religion, Technology and Terrorism*. Victoria, Canada: CTheory Books/ NWP.
Pfohl, Stephen. 2006. "New Global Technologies of Power: Cybernetic Capitalism and Social Inequality." In Mary Romero and Eric Margolis, eds., *The Blackwell Companion to Social Inequalities*. Cambridge, MA: Blackwell Publishing, 456–592.
Quijano, Aníbal. 2000. "Coloniality of Power, Ethnocentrism, and Latin America." *NEPANTLA*, Vol. 1, no. 3: 533–80.
Williams, Patricia. 1991. *The Alchemy of Race and Rights: Diary of a Law Professor*. Cambridge, MA: Harvard University Press.

CHAPTER Seven

SATIRE, GUNS, AND HUMANS:
Lessons from the Nacirema

Steve Kroll-Smith and Gwen Hunnicutt

> The real trouble with this world of ours is not that it is an unreasonable world, nor that it is a reasonable one. The commonest kind of thought is that it is nearly reasonable, but not quite. Life ... looks a little more mathematical and regular than it is; its exactitude is obvious, but its inexactitude is hidden; its wildness lies in wait.
>
> —Chesteron 1909:81

In early spring 2007, a student at Virginia Tech University shot and killed thirty-two students and faculty. He wounded an, as yet, untold number. He finished his massacre by shooting himself dead. Dead students, dead faculty, and guns, it is not a new story. It is how the story is told that gives us cause for concern.

Expressed in the official White House response to this particular slaughter is the paralyzing language of the absurd, speech so incongruous, so ridiculous it must be a cruel joke: White House Conference Center Briefing Room, 12:58 PM, EDT:

MS. PERINO: Good afternoon. I have several announcements and then we'll go to questions. The President was made aware of the Virginia Tech shootings. He was horrified.... As far as policy, the president believes that there is a right for people to bear arms, but that all laws must be followed. And certainly bringing a gun into a school dormitory and shooting

... obviously that would be against the law and something that someone should be held accountable for."[1]

"And certainly bringing a gun into a school dormitory and shooting... obviously that would be against the law...." Indeed. Press Secretary Perino appears unaware of her banal statement. She does not seem to grasp how unaffected and ham-fisted she sounds. When faced with tragedy we might expect more from language: more nuance, more empathy, more reason.

Amidst a pandemic of gun violence, however, we listen numbly to a progressively superficial chain of clichés and vacant phrases, emptied of any meaningful substance. There is a kind of dance, a gavotte, between stale and clichéd language and the spectacle of gun violence; as if weary language "drained of significance" becomes an accomplice to mayhem.[2] Facile language become part of the public drama of expiation that inevitably follows a massacre, like the denouement that serves to bring the story's climax to conclusion, re-creating a sense of normal. Here is how it works: First the shooting, then the catharsis expressed as:

- *a story of a troubled soul*, "The shooter was deranged"
- *solutions*, "Close the gun shop loopholes," or "If we were all armed..."
- *good, positivist, social science*, "Rarely in social science do you ever get two variables that explain so much. Young men commit most of the violent crime in the world today" (Kimmel 2005, United Nations)
- *political mantras*, "the president believes that there is a right for people to bear arms."

A public language expressed in ritual cadence brings an act of aberrant carnage to a normal conclusion, resetting the stage for another shooting. Perhaps it is only when language forfeits its primeval power to bring us to the table of common sense that the mayhem of gun violence begins to appear routine.

This essay borrows the lingual coin of the jaded, to wit, *satire*, to create, as Nietzsche might say, a folly in service to the truth (1960). We adopt Marcuse's counsel to "revive the desperate laughter and the cynical defiance of the fool as a means of demasking the serious ones who govern the whole" (1969:63–64). To follow is a story of humans and violence, told as if we were strangers in a strange place. It is written to be at once irreverent and provocative, a calculated disordering, recalling Rimbaud, of our readerly senses. Placed side by side is the contradiction of human character and the metal tubes from which projectiles are fired at unimaginable velocities.

A Swift Prelude

Born November 1667, in Dublin, Jonathan Swift would spend his life ministering to believers as a clergyman of the Church of England while writing barbed, satiric essays—the best of their kind—about the hapless human quest to be reasonable, sane, and wise. In 1704 he published "A Tale of a Tub." In telling the tale, Swift introduces a figural representation of the folly of human reason:

> There is in Mankind a certain**********************
> Hic multa****************desiderantur. ***********
> ******And this I take to be a clear Solution of the Matter.
> (Roscoe 1850:32)

If satire lashes at vanity, Swift carried a good size whip. But it was in the better known *Gulliver's Travels* (1726/1999) that he mortally wounds the human pretension that "Mankind," above all others, is capable of behaving reasonably (rationis capax). Many of us read Gulliver as children, though it was not Swift's intention to write a story for kids.

In his fourth voyage to discover the nature of humans our gullible Lemuel Gulliver comes ashore on a distant island. He is immediately set upon by several vulgar and violent creatures that both beat and shit on him. Rescued by two Houyhnhnms, Gulliver finds himself in a society of gentle creatures who appear to be living dignified, peaceable, and, above all, reasonable lives. He was troubled, however, by the nature of these creatures. The Houyhnhnms, you may recall, were not human but equine. As horses, they could not read, but they were capable of speech. As Swift listened to these beasts he heard a sensibility that he had not encountered in any of his previous journeys. A horse becomes the embodiment of reason.

As our human converses with horses he tells them of England's last war with France and the legions of men who die in battle. The horses are appalled. Unaffected, Gulliver continues, recounting the reasons humans kill one another, among them, ambitions, jealousies, vain quarrels. Without reflecting on the peaceable nature of his audience, he boasts of clever humans who invent "Cannons, Culverins, Muskets, Carbines, Pistols, Bullets (and) Powder" to make killing on so grand a scale possible. The horses don't understand Gulliver, but they forgive him. He was, after all, human.

Living alongside and serving the Houyhnhnms were the loathsome and fearful Yahoos. It was a gang of Yahoos who attacked Gulliver when he came ashore. Obsessed with pretty stones, the Yahoos were ever ready to kill one another to possess them. Most troubling to Gulliver, the Yahoos looked a lot like him. If reason took the shape of a horse, senseless violence appeared in the form of a human. Gulliver quickly realized that Yahoos were in essence humans bereft of a capacity to behave in a civil, peaceable manner. As Gulliver sails from the island he concludes that the Houyhnhnm, the illiterate horses, embody the spirit of reason while the Yahoos, the humanoids, rage, fume, and storm through life.

With time, the Houyhnhnm, the wise horse, is forgotten. The Yahoo, however, appears in such diverse places as the letters of Daniel Boone, scrawls sent from David Berkowitz, the "Son of Sam," to the New York Police Department, as a contemporary caricature of a less than sensible person given to raucous, disorderly acts, and, of course, as a popular Internet search engine. Ignoring this latter use, the Merriam-Webster dictionary currently defines a yahoo as "a boorish, crass, or stupid person."[3]

Swift, of course, thought there was a little Houyhnhnm and a lot of Yahoo in each of us. Indeed, he found humans capable of reason, but not likely to exercise it. At our best, we pretend to reason while the alchemy of our passions works its magic without our awareness or consent. At our worst, we are Yahoos. Freud must have read Swift.

If we are both Houyhnhnm and Yahoo, we are also at times like Gulliver himself who felt compelled to think about the nature that makes us peculiarly human. On April 16, 2007, in a spectacular display of violence, a young man at Virginia Tech University killed thirty-two students and faculty before shooting himself dead. His instruments: two pistols, a semiautomatic Glock 19 and a Walther .22 caliber. As we write this essay, the number of wounded is not being released to the public.

The magnitude of this carnage and its location at an institution of "higher learning" shatters complacency and sends many of us on a journey to make some reasonable sense of the human well-springs of violence in a society awash in guns. Like Gulliver, we are invited to ponder the nature that is inside of us. Recall his quest. To seek the nature of human nature Gulliver did not go to the library or meditate in his favorite chair; he set upon a hazardous journey. Like him we will travel—though without the guiding genius of Swift—to a queer and perplexing place. It is here, in the land of the Nacirema, that we will make some sense of the acute senselessness of guns and humans.

Gulliver among the Nacirema: A Report from the Field

You may recall Professor Linton's discovery of the Nacirema more than fifty years ago. Horace Miner popularized her discovery in his now famous essay,

"Body Ritual among the Nacirema" (1956). Though obsessed with health, the Nacirema, like the Houyhnhnm, appear to value reason and sense-making. Indeed, they have created thousands of places where natives can go and learn the art of sound, sensible thinking. We located 4,140 such places. Consider how one such place advertises itself:

> Penn takes pride in being a place where students and faculty can pursue knowledge without boundaries, a place where theory and practice combine to produce a better understanding of our world and ourselves.[4]

In addition to their collective commitment to reason, the Nacirema are an information or "fun fact" rich society. Close to 90 percent of their households subscribe to cable television; a "watcher" has more than five hundred channels from which to choose; and there are millions of "watchers" among the Nacirema. More than fourteen thousand radio stations beam sound waves to the nooks and crannies of their day-to-day lives. Satellite radio boasts fourteen million subscribers. For the "readers" among them there are more than nineteen thousand magazines and, as of 2003, slightly less than one thousand five hundred newspapers (Thierer 2007; Newspaper Association of America 2004).

Together, a commitment to reason and an abundance of easily available information might be expected to work in tandem to foster a deep and abiding mindfulness toward the pressing issues that beset the Nacirema. But if sense and reason abound in this curious place, it is difficult to find. Consider these troubling patterns:

Sixty million Nacirema live on less than 7 "srallod" (pronounced *srallod*) a day. A srallod is a unit of Nacirema "yenom." (Like the Yahoo's obsession with pretty stones, the Nacirema are fixated on their yenom.) In our currency a srallod has the purchasing power of $.80. Together, 7 srallod are worth $5.60 in our spending money. To assist with this comparison, the cost of living in the United States is proportionate to the cost of living among the Nacirema.[5]

Poverty has become so desperate the Nacirema now make a distinction between the "extreme poor" and the merely "poor." One in five Nacirema live in, what they call, "extreme poverty." The extreme poor live, if one can call it that, below what the Nacirema call the "absolute poverty line." Absolute poverty is defined, rather confusingly, as living without the necessities of life. How one does that is not at all clear.[6]

In 2005, 38 million Nacirema were "food insecure," that is they could not count on having enough yenom to purchase food.[7]

Curiously, the Nacirema are less focused on making sure that everyone has enough to eat than they are in making sure that most everyone can acquire something they call a "nug." (More than one is referred to as "snug.") A nug is an instrument with a long tube capable of projecting metal objects at extraordinary speeds. Some Nacirema enjoy pointing these tubes and shooting the metal objects at animals, others shoot them at other Nacirema, and still others shoot themselves. Odd, by any standard, there are almost as many guns as there are Nacirema (approximately 220 million). Nacirema can boast of owning one-third of all nonmilitary snug in the world (Cukier and Sidel 2006:8). Perhaps this explains our final observation. Both the rate and the real number of nug deaths among the Nacirema are far higher than in any other postindustrial society.[8]

So, how do we make sense of this conundrum: a society with a seeming commitment to sensible, reasonable behavior, and an apparent readiness to create and sustain a perverse amount of misery and carnage? An approximate answer to this question requires more inquiry into the nature of the Nacirema and their social arrangements.

Demons, Ghosts, and Spectacles

To make reasonable sense of the paradoxical temperament of these people we must, at the very least, inquire into one of their most implausible habits of mind, to wit, a lively belief in the supernatural. Accompanying that belief and intertwined with it is the Nacirema's passion for the spectacle. We begin with their ready embrace of phenomena that fall well outside nature's laws.

A Pervasive Belief in the Supernatural

With regularity, the "learneds" among the Nacirema will opine on how individuals acquire a readiness to work from a certain ethic embedded in the religious beliefs of their ancestors. Perhaps this is so. But along with acquiring a taste for work, the Nacirema also adopted their predecessors' beliefs in powers that exist outside the fixed boundaries of the physical world. The mystical and numinous vies with yenom for the attention of the Nacirema.[9]

A striking 68 percent of them believe in what they call "the lived," a vile-spirit that takes the shape of a cloven hoofed humanoid with a taste for fire and eternal damnation. Forty percent of Nacirema between the ages of twenty-five and twenty-nine believe they are reincarnated, that they were once someone else. A whopping 84 percent believe in "selcarim" (pronounced as it sounds), events that are inexplicable by both the laws of nature and common sense. Over 50 percent of all Nacirema believe in the existence of human like creatures with no physical bodies that glide about as if blown by the breeze. Typically invisible, these shades now and again reveal themselves, at times announcing their presence with a "Boo" like sound.[10]

Caught between reason and a pervasive belief in the supernatural, it is perhaps not surprising that many Nacirema attribute magical qualities to their snug. Recently, for example, a young Nacirema told a reporter

> He feels pretty safe when he goes to ... University ... but he takes no chances. He brings a loaded 9 mm semiautomatic every day. (See "handnug" above.) "It's not that I run around scared all day long, but if something happens to me, I do want to be prepared," said the twenty-four-year-old business major, who has a concealed-weapons permit and takes the (handnug) everywhere but church.[11]

Other than his holy place, this young Nacirema, who, we can assume, believes in "the lived," selcarim, shades, and perhaps reincarnation, reckons he can be only truly safe in school, with his friends, indeed, perhaps on a date if he is packing a semiautomatic weapon. Magic of some kind would be required to conflate safe with snug. After all, more than thirty thousand Nacirema shoot one another or themselves to death annually. (Only in Brazil, another country with a strong belief in the mystical—particularly spirit possession—are more people killed annually by guns.)[12]

Miracles and Spectacles

An omnipresent belief in the supernatural coupled with an unusually high number of nug deaths works in tandem with another curious feature of Nacirema culture: its passion for the spectacle. A conscious space for the mystical and magical would seem to allow for the grandiose and exaggerated. Spectacles, it is reasonable to assume, are likely to thrive in any society where more than eight out of ten people believe in the magic of selcarim. To borrow from Debord (1995), for the Narcirema, society is spectacle.

One might say that the Nacirema live from spectacle to spectacle, from one combustible moment to another. Think of a spectacle as an isolated event, incident, or occasion bounded on either side by a beginning and an end. It is the separateness of the spectacle that gives it a kind of totality, one that demands all attention and all consciousness (Debord 1995:12).

Some spectacles are purposely created by the Nacirema, like their annual garish and extravagant Lowb Repus (pronounced as it sounds). A queer ceremony, the Lowb Repus takes place on a long narrow field cross-marked with white lines. On this field, twenty-two Nacirema dressed in an odd assortment of armor line up, eleven on one side, eleven on the other. Following an unintelligible incantation, twenty-two Nacirema smash headlong into one another. Most everyone falls down; everyone down gets up. The two groups of eleven re-form, often patting each other's bottoms in a playful display of what, exactly? We have yet to inquire.

Aside from these planned and commodified bursts of "collective effervescence" (Durkheim 1912/1995) that occur at predictable times in the Nacirema calendar, there are unplanned and unforeseen spectacles. Often violent in nature, these unscheduled spectacles solidify public attention, directing consciousness to the seeming totality of the moment. As we write, a tornado wiped a small town from the face of the earth, leaving only a vague footprint to represent what was once a Nacirema community. If violent nature is the source of an increasing number of spectacles, so are the violent outbursts of the Nacirema themselves.

Even though school shootings make up only 1 percent of the total number of youth murdered in their society, the school "rampage" holds a particularly strong valence for the Nacirema (Center for Disease Control 2007). "Rampage" shootings are a subset of all school shootings that include the essential elements of dramatic spectacle. The "rampage" is a targeted attack against an educational institution perpetrated by a former or current member of the school. The incursion is played out on a public stage in front of an audience. The rampage turns out multiple victims, some of whom are selected for their symbolic representations (Newman 2004).[4]

The media reconstruction of these spectacles evokes archetypes of the loner, the alienated youth, the rejected, and the mentally ill (Herda-Rapp 2003). The vilification of the shooters and the romanticization of the victims accentuates the allure of the spectacle. Further, the shooter is almost always portrayed as seeking revenge. These rampage reconstructions borrow from the familiar cultural script where ultimate vengeance is carried out by showy, public violence, with school shootings becoming a distinct "signature of terror" (Mehta 2006). For the Nacirema, the Rampage is now "normal," assuming a life and inevitability of its own. Sixty percent of them believe that school shootings will continue regardless of preventative measures (Mason 2005).

The allure of the spectacle, linked to a robust belief in the uncanny and implausible, shapes the unusual quantity and quality of nug violence among the Nacirema. The irony of the spectacle is its capacity to direct all attention and concern to a single, horrific event; as if this occasion is the site upon which all collective concern and meaningful discussion about shooting both themselves and one another *must* occur. The spectacle of mayhem and bloodletting is at once brutally real and an illusion. As deception, it is a sleight of hand trick that substitutes this one-off event for the relentless, far more mundane, regularity with which the Nacirema shoot themselves and others. The spectacle paralyzes the power of ordinary perception. Expecting spectacle, knowing little else, the typical Nacirema simply does not perceive what to us, as observers, appears so brutally stark.

If we bracket the irregular spectacle of nug slaughter among the Nacirema, a sensible observer would conclude that everyday, each day, is a dramatic episode of nug carnage. Consider, for example, a normal day among the Nacirema: in one twenty-four hour period, an average of eighty-one people die and one hundred and seventy-six are wounded by nug fire. Together that is two-hundred and fifty-seven Nacirema killed or wounded by nug fire daily. That amounts to ninety-two Nacirema killed or wounded every hour of every day. In 2004, 29,569 Nacirema died by nug fire, another 64,389 were wounded.[13]

Why? A Hypothesis

Blessed with the faculty of reason, you must wonder aloud, dear reader, how a society can solidify its collective attention and anguish on a single, spectacular killing scene, but cannot or will not "see" the daily accumulation of carnage that occurs with brutal regularity. In mistaking the one-off part for the brutal whole, the Nacirema appear able to live surprisingly easy with the specter of nug death. There are likely many explanations for this conundrum. Perhaps the Nacerima are a species more constitutionally organized around Thanatos than Eros.

A more pedestrian explanation would point out that snug are "big yenom" for the Nacirema. Last year alone, nug sales were worth 2.1 billion srallod.[14] Knowing, as we do now, the visceral attachment of the Nacirema to their srallod, perhaps they prefer their yenom to life; it is possible. (Theorizing in this manner would give us a neo-Marxist insight into Freud, if that matters at this moment.)

But there is another reason, not incompatible with the admittedly absurd "give us yenom, we'll live with death" argument. It is rooted in the steady attrition of anything we might call a civil society among the Nacirema coupled with their fierce defense of the self-interested individual. For decades now the Nacirema—or the more powerful among them—have been busy dismantling civil society, gutting both the programs and ideas that fostered (if never achieved) a reasonable and humane public life. A good friend of the rich and powerful among them recently summarized their success. For the Nacirema she declared:

there is no such thing as society. "There are individual men and women, and there are families.... (The Nacirema) must look to themselves first." (Thatcher 1987)

Concluding that society does not exist has at least one obvious result: Citizenship among the Nacirema takes the peculiar form of a radical individualism. A famous early observer of this society, Sixela Elliveuqcot (pronounced elli-veu-q-cot), was compelled to invent the word "individualism" to hammer home his point that if the Nacirema are anything they are self-centered (de Tocqueville 1835/2001). Simply put, with little or no expectation that something greater, more powerful, and humane than the person exists, it is left to the individual to secure his or her survival.

Returning from the Field: A Note on Species-Lag

"What a long strange trip it's been," to quote the late Jerry Garcia (who was quoting poet Robert Hunter). Back among our own we are struck by the similarities between ourselves and the exotic practices and beliefs of the Nacirema. We suspect that you too, dear reader, saw some similarities between the two cultures. One question strikes us as unavoidable, like the Nacirema are we too unpredictable a species to own guns? If our "wildness lies in wait" how can we be sure it won't appear when we have a gun in our hands?

A rhetorical question, to be sure. But it does suggestion an idea. The gun, perhaps, is an example of what we might call species-lag. Recall Ogburn's prescient idea that values typically change far slower than our capacity to make things (1964). Coining the phrase "cultural lag" he taught us that inventing stuff is often far easier than revising our heartfelt standards and ideals. Stem-cell research, for example, promises a new world of medical miracles, but faces a massive rearguard assault by groups whose beliefs oppose any medicine that puts a microscopic spherical bag of proteins—a fertilized egg—at risk.

Species-lag takes Ogburn's notion of pause to a more primordial level by pointing to a disjuncture between the makeup of an organism and the ways it fashions or makes the world. It is an idea that asks us to consider the possibility that a life form might create an environment, or part of one, that puts its own existence at risk. Importantly, it assumes that no matter how much a life form tries to accommodate to the altered environment it cannot overcome its own creaturely limitations and achieve a healthy adaptation. In other words, species-lag is more stridently determinant than its cognate, cultural lag. Inherent in the idea of cultural lag is the possibility that values will catch up to technology. We purposely connect species and lag with a hyphen to make the point that there is no catching up. From the vantage point of species-lag, a gun is a cultural artifact that humans cannot use without deadly consequences.

Swift used Gulliver, Houyhnhnms, and Yahoos to help us see the antinomian character of human beings. Freud used the image of the Id to convey the uncontrollable in each of us. Nietzsche scolded Socrates for assuming that the imposition of reason would save Athenian society; it didn't. Thoreau disconnected reason from our incorrigible search for happiness: "We are made happy," he concluded, "when reason can discover no occasion for it" (1960:41). Einstein reflecting in his later years concluded: "We all are ruled in what we do by impulses" (1950:15).

Lest you think that only ministers, philosophers, writers, and physicists reason in this fashion, consider a well-known sociologist who argued convincingly that sociology does not have the answer to the Hobbesian question of how human beings become tractable and well-mannered. For Dennis Wrong, there is a significant part of each of us that will always fall outside the watchful eye of the Panopticon (1961). And for Harold Garfinkel, reason is always little more than a trope used to explain the emotion-laden, situation-determining nature of human conduct—deployed after the fact but "conspicuous by its absence" in "everyday affairs" (Garfinkel 1967:114).

Inventing a gun was easy. And following Darwin, we may well ask "Might we evolve into a species mature enough to use it?" Or is that the wrong question? Perhaps we should ask: "If we evolve into a species mature enough to shoot guns, would we care to?" In the meantime, in a culture bereft of a meaningful civic life but awash in miracles and spectacles, too many of us live and die by the gun.

Postscript

On a Sunday, as we finished this paper, a story of another rampage style spectacle splashed across cyberspace: "Three Dead in Idaho Church Shooting." A local police officer observed: "He was just shooting at anybody he could...."[15] To paraphrase Press Secretary Perino: "And certainly, bringing a gun into a church and shooting ... obviously that would be against the law and something that someone should be held accountable for."

Notes

1. See www.whitehouse.gov/news/releases/2007/04/20070416-1.html.
2. The phrase "drained of significance" is borrowed from Richard Harvey Brown, 1987, p. 173.

3. See www.m-w.com/dictionary/yahoo.
4. See www.upenn.edu.
5. See www.povertyinamerica.psu.edu.
6. See www.povertyinamerica.psu.edu.
7. See www.povertyinamerica.psu.edu.
8. See www.gun-control-network.org/GF01.htm.

9. Religious devotion sets the United States apart from some of its closest allies. Americans profess unquestioning belief in God and are far more willing to mix faith and politics than people in other countries, AP-Ipsos polling found.... Only Mexicans come close to Americans in embracing faith, the poll found. But unlike Americans, Mexicans strongly object to clergy lobbying lawmakers, in line with the nation's historical opposition to church influence (*USA Today*, June 6, 2005. "Poll: Religious devotion high in U.S.," p. 1).

10. Data cited on religious beliefs can be found at *The Harris Poll*® #11, "The Religious and Other Beliefs of Americans 2003," February 26, 2003. www.harrisinteractive.com/harris_poll/index.asp?PID=359.

11. *Deseret News*, April 28, 2007: 1–2.

12. See www.nytimes.com/imagepages/2007/04/21/weekinreview/20070422_MARSH_GRAPHIC.html.

13. See www.nytimes.com/imagepages/2007/04/21/weekinreview/20070422_MARSH_GRAPHIC.html.

14. See www.nssf.org/news/.

15. See Time/http://www.time.com.

References

Brown, Richard H. 1983. "Dialectical Irony: Literary Form and Sociological Theory." *Poetics Today* 4, 543–64.

Center for Disease Control. *School Associated Violent Deaths*. Retrieved May 20, 2007 from www.cdc.gov/ncipc/sch-shooting.htm.

Cukier, Wendy, and Victor W. Sidel. 2006. *The Global Gun Epidemic*. Westport, CT: Greenwood Press.

Chesterton, Gilbert K. 1909. *George Bernard Shaw*. Rockville, MD: Wildside Press.

Debord, Guy. 1995. *The Society of the Spectacle*. D. Nicholson-Smith, trans. New York: Zone Books. (Original work published 1967.)

de Tocqueville, Alexis. 2001. *Democracy in America*. New York: Signet Classics. (Original work published in 1835.)

Durkheim. Emile. 1995. *The Elementary Forms of Religious Life*. K. Fields, trans. New York: The Free Press. (Original work published 1912.)

Einstein, Albert. 1950. "On the Generalized Theory of Gravitation." *Scientific American* 182, 13–17.

Freud, Sigmund. 1900. *Interpretation of Dreams*. London: Hogarth Press.

Garfinkel, Harold. 1967. *Studies in Ethnomethodology*. New Jersey: Prentice Hall.

Harris, Louis. 2007. *The Harris Poll®* #11, "The Religious and Other Beliefs of Americans 2003." Retrieved April 17 from www.harrisinteractive.com.
Herda-Rapp, Ann. 2003. "The Social Construction of Local School Violence Threats by the News Media and Professional Organizations." *Sociological Inquiry* 73 (4): 545–75.
Kimmel, Michael. 2005. *Masculinity and Gun Violence: The Personal Meets the Political*. United Nations. Retrieved April 1, 2007 from www.womenwarpeace.org/issues/smallarms/docs/kimmelspeech.
Marcuse, Herbert. 1969. *An Essay on Liberation*. Boston, MA: Beacon Press.
Mason-Keiffer, Heather. 2005. *Public: Society Powerless to Stop School Shootings*. The Gallup Poll Tuesday Briefing, 57–59.
Mehta, Deepak. 2006. "Collective Violence, Public Spaces, and the Unmaking of Men." *Men and Masculinities* 9 (2): 204–25.
Merriam-Webster Dictionary: www.m-w.com/dictionary/yahoo.
Miner, Horace. 1956. "Body Ritual among the Nacirema." *American Anthropologist* 58, 503–7.
National Shooting Sports Foundation. Retrieved April 25 from www.nssf.org/news/PR_idx.cfm?PRloc=common/PR/&PR=060506.cfm.
New York Times. Retrieved May 11 from www.nytimes.com/imagepages/2007/04/21/weekinreview/20070422_MARSH_GRAPHIC.html#.
Newman, Katherine S. 2004. *Rampage: The Social Roots of School Shootings*. New York: Basic Books.
Newspaper Association of America. 2004. Retrieved April 16 from www.naa.org/info/facts04/interactive.html.
Nietzsche, Friedrich. 1960. *Joyful Wisdom*. New York: Frederick Ungar.
Nugent, Ted. 2007. *Gun-free Zones are Recipe for Disaster*. Retrieved April 20, 2007 from www.cnn.com.
Ogburn, William F. 1964. *On Culture and Social Shange*. O. D. Duncan, ed. Chicago and London: University of Chicago Press.
President of University of Pennsylvania: Retrieved April 18 from www.upenn.edu.
Swift, Jonathan. 1704. *A Tale of a Tub*. New York: Signet.
———. 1999. *Gulliver's Travels*. New York: Signet. (Original work published in 1726.)
Thierer, Adam. 2007. "The Media Cornucopia." *City Journal* (Spring), www.city-journal.org/html/17_2_media.html.
Thoreau, Henry David. 1906. *Journal of Henry David Thoreau*. Cambridge, MA: Riverside Press.
Thatcher, Margaret. 1987. "Interview," in *Women's Own*, October 31, 1987: 4.
"Three Dead in Idaho Church Shooting." Retrieved April 16 from www.time.com.
USA Today. June 6, 2005. "Poll: Religious devotion high in U.S.," 1.
White House Conference Center Briefing. 2007. Retrieved April 30, 2007 from www.whitehouse.gov/news/releases/2007/04/20070416-1.html.
Wrong, Dennis. 1961. "The Oversocialized Concept of Man in Modern Sociology." *American Sociological Review* 26, 183–93.

CHAPTER Eight

S/HE'S LOST CONTROL?:
Damaging a Body of Knowledge

Tara Brabazon

I am being sucked back into that moment. It was marinated in a saturating sweat of fear, empathy, confusion, and anger. It did not start this way. It did not finish this way. But the metaphoric box cutter slicing through my teacher's body has stayed with me.

The week before semester ended, my first year students were in the crazed and gasping day-before-the-assignment-is-due-and-I-don't-know-what-I'm-doing-please-help-me-or-I-will-fail panic. They were queuing outside my office when I arrived at 7:20 AM. But this hyperventilating stream stopped by 5:15 PM. I quietly started to pack my briefcase to drag my exhausted body home, my bones so tired they could hardly support the flesh.

At 5:28 PM, a drunk, crazily crying, agitated, angry, and aggressive student stumbled her way around my door frame. She said she'd been cutting herself (forearm held up as evidence), and was going home to kill herself. This young woman had been a troubled soul throughout the semester. She had been institutionalized. Her (former) boyfriend was in jail. There was a history of child abuse. These spicks and specks of her life had been revealed in the middle of a crammed auditorium of fellow students, in tutorials where scholars were trying to understand semiotics not social dysfunction, and in endless personal meetings with me. It got to the point where I was seeing her on a daily basis. When hearing her voice, my skin crawled. I wanted to help. But the line between helping and complaining, support and stalking, was being transgressed.

Now, I was alone in the building with this young woman. She was not there to talk about the assignment or the course. She was there to talk about herself to me. She was seeing a counselor as well, and children's services had removed her daughter from the home. Clearly, she was after something I could not give. However—by 7 PM—when I finally calmed her and stopped the ragged tears and began to call her father, she produced a box cutter. It was pointing at me.

Certainly—like most academics—I have handled students with "issues." Most of us have taught students managing schizophrenia, depression, manic depression, anorexia, bulimia or suicidal thoughts. Students have followed me home, followed me to the shops, followed me to the gym, followed my car, and interrupted my family having time together. But for an excruciating second, I thought that this student was going to slice me open. However—somehow—I twisted the knife from her. Only then did I drag my body home, more than tired, wondering what had just happened. Was she handing me the knife? Was she aiming it at me?

I will never know the answer to these questions. She dropped out from the university at the end of that year and was taken into care. The last time I saw her, I was walking around my local park. She ran over to me with her little daughter in tow, wanting to talk and spend time with me. To my shame, I greeted her, said I was busy, and ran back to my house and locked the door. I lacked courage to be better. I lacked consciousness to do better.

University academics teach scholars who are moving through transitions in their lives.[1] We either instruct mature-aged students trying to forge a different path for themselves, or we work with the best and brightest of a younger generation as they try to change the world, while not becoming too burnt and bitter in the process. The volatility of passionate, dynamic, charismatic education is—and must be—immersive. The tether between emotion and intellect cannot be quashed by curricula on empiricism, methods, rationality, or ethics. There is a heat to the best debates between self and society, identity and history. We need this energy to prepare and propel the next generation of scholars to challenge and change the acceptance of war, terrorism, and xenophobia, which will be our bequest to their future.

Managing the line between excitement and scholarship—respect and transgression—is becoming increasingly difficult. Obviously the relationship between teachers and their students is always a site of controversy. One of the charges against Socrates was that his influence on the young damaged the social fabric of Athens (Plato 2003). Even in the popular cultural configurations of teaching, the teacher who becomes too close to students is punished: *Dead Poet's Society*, *Mona Lisa's Smile*, *Good Will Hunting*, and *Wonder Boys*.

This chapter enters the wreckage of Virginia Tech's shootings with an agenda. I probe the death of educators via the hands of students. The costs and consequences of Virginia Tech resonate long after blood has been cleaned from carpet, psychologists have been appointed and released, and public relations consultants have "managed" the crisis and moved to their next assignment. Whenever we "manage" or "handle" a troubled student after April 16, we carry the legacy of the colleagues we have lost. The "massacre" remains a crisis point, a moment of change, where the lectern and library were no longer pedagogic prophylactics or edifices of respect and disaffection. But the point of my chapter amidst the immediate and volatile scholarship in this collection is to confirm—with tentative disquiet—that the violence of Virginia Tech was not an isolated incident from a disaffected young man with a mental illness. It is not an act isolated to the geographical territory of the United States. As Timothy Luke confirms in this collection, the mass shootings in schools, universities, and workplaces feed into the continual loops of news. There is a morphology to this bloody folktale (Propp 1968). Whatever the setting of these violent acts, there is a narrative arc enfolding a troubled redundant worker, war veteran, or student who shoots his (too often it is a he) way through a narrative of hatred, revenge, or rage (DiPiero 2002). Cho's movements were given choreography by news broadcasters who arched back to Charles Whitman's shootings at the University of Texas in 1966. Universities still seem a place apart, disconnected from life. When everyday life arrives on campus, the tabloid media follow.[2]

Instead of being pulled into this macabre modern folktale, I pull the curtain back on the daily struggles confronted by faculty that have little to do with curriculum, andragogy, or assessment and everything to do with how we as scholars—quietly—manage the personal struggles of our students. One young man with guns destroyed lives. Many young women and men—each day—destroy themselves and others, but because they lack a gun are invisible to journalism. Yet if we can use the April 16 events at Virginia Tech as a window, then we see the role of an academic's body in the development of a body of knowledge, and the complex student struggles that we mediate on a daily basis.

Love Will Tear Us Apart

It is a tough to be a teacher with a body. The corporeal form of educators has been stripped of the cane, de-gowned and threatened with sexual impropriety. These necessary legislative and social interventions in teaching behavior and practice have transformed the teacher's body into a dangerous, scrutinized cultural formation. We all have stories—gossiped whispers in the corridor—detailing sexual impropriety between students and staff. As we titter into our long black coffee, teachers become increasingly conscious of limiting their bodily gestures, repressing enthusiasm for ideas, people and places, and always leaving their office door open for all to see the banal routines of education. Many of the goals of contemporary higher education either implicitly or overtly separate staff from students. Quality assurance strategies, the administrative "revolution" of universities and online education all increase the mediations between faculty and students. Through such monitoring, we are hiding—denying—what makes education important and memorable.

One of the reasons it has been so easy to celebrate online education is because there have been so few theorizations or even personal admissions of how flesh, blood, and bone function in our classrooms. In the startling white glow of the PowerPoint projector, we dart around the glare and surveillance of our students. Virginia Tech captured the violence and complexity of this surveillance and layered intimacy between staff and students. It is significant to note that Seung-Hui Cho was enrolled in a sociology class, "Deviant Behavior," during the spring term in which the shooting took place. Yet with the managerial and administrative attention placed on research, the daily struggles and complexities of teaching difficult students challenging material are often displaced and demeaned. Cho had caused problems for both teachers and students in a writing course in 2005 and was under care by mental health experts, after a court order ("Trying to make sense of the massacre," 2007:40–42). Handguns were only obtained in the months before his shootings in 2007. Prior to the atrocity, he was one student of the 35,000 people who traveled onto a campus of a rural college town. But his video "justification" generalized blame:

> You forced me into a corner and gave me only one option. The decision was yours. Now you have blood on your hands that will never wash off.... You had everything you wanted. Your Mercedes wasn't enough, you brats. Your golden necklaces weren't enough, you snobs. Your trust fund wasn't enough. Your vodka and cognac weren't enough. All your debaucheries weren't enough. Those weren't enough to fulfill your hedonistic needs. You had everything. (Cho 2007)

Could teachers have prevented the violence that framed and followed these statements? The mental health issues were recognized by teachers, students, and deans. Their consequences could not have been predicted. But this lack of connectivity between words and actions is explained—not justified—

through the ambiguity and impulsiveness of teaching encounters. Strange events, actions, and statements emerge in classrooms. How they are handled varies by the staff member, university, and time. Politicians and educational administrators talk a great deal about teaching, without detailed knowledge of the volatility of educational contexts. The shootings at Virginia Tech were a bloody reminder that academics have bodies (of knowledge), but that our universities are filled with caring teachers who will literally put their body in the line of gunfire. The vulnerability of the teacher's body needs to be discussed and often. A "massacre" suggests a singular destructive act.[3] This chapter tries to bring education, scholarship, teaching, and learning back to this tragedy to show that disturbing and dark events are part of higher education, not an occasional aberrance.

Those of us who teach are locked in isolated classrooms, lecture theaters and tutorial spaces. We rarely share our concerns, fears, or experience. The experiences of joy, sadness, and frustration we confront each day never make it into government reports or press releases. With the intense demands on academic life, collegial and group discussions about the tremulous moments of teaching are rare. All teaching is part of a system, and has a context and a history. My words offer a taste of the vulnerabilities of corporeality in education. It is also a continuance of bell hooks' project of rerembering teaching bodies.

> Individuals enter the classroom to teach as though only the mind is present and not the body. To call attention to the body is to betray the legacy of repression and denial that has been handed down to us by our professorial elders, who have usually been white and male.... No one talked about the body in relation to teaching. What did one do with the body in the classroom? Trying to remember the bodies of my professors, I find myself unable to recall them. I hear voices, remember fragmented details but very few whole bodies (1994:113).

Hooks has always been forthright—indeed passionate—in her love for students. There is little space in administrative structures for her ardor and commitment. Feminist pedagogy is a significant corrective in debates about education (Probyn 2004:21–43). The corrosion of mind and body transforms academics into textured selves, rather than disembodied texts. The teacher's body is—to offer a suicidal metaphor—where the rubber meets the road. We feel the pain, disappointment, sweat, anger, and passion. It is our corporeality that creates an affective, transformational space.

Education is a struggle with powerful ideas and a fight over meaning. I remain deeply moved by hooks' realization that, "even when students are desperately yearning to be touched by knowledge, professors . . . allow their worries about losing control to override their desires to teach" (118). It is the desperate yearning to feel more, live differently, and activate an alternative way of being that is the point of education. The invidious, seething anger of the current political environment—which our students bark back at us when they complain about fees, teaching quality, or feedback—is based on the cool, clear realization that the market is not going to save us, and a shareholding citizenry offers few entries into justice. As Cho seethed in his statement, "you had everything" (Cho 2007). Through this despair, our responsibility as educators is to connect the individuality of our students to a community conscious of inequality and social dysfunction. Students do spend time thinking through their lives and the barriers and borders between themselves and their teachers.

> From: CA
> Sent: Mon 15/10/2007 11:56 am
> To: Brabazon Tara
> Subject: Tick Tock
>
> Hello Tara,
> Regardless whether you have the time to read this or not I'm going to write this anyway as i have a lot to say and you're very much this person that i have feeling about, in the sense that you're vital to me—its a very strange feeling/thing to say but if you can see through my eyes—i don't think I've met anyone more important to me in the sense of development and creativity, then you. and please don't get freaked out, i hope you see that as a massive compliment.
>
> I write songs and i write blogs but since i've been here man i've got some harsh block on my mind . . . and when i cant express myself be it singing or writing i get quite restless and generally cloudy and downbeat—expression is both the love yet the bane of my existence.
>
> University ay, what a strange place there's so much to interpret and analyse—people all as alien as the other. I've had quite the naff time at school in growing up so this whole "new place new people same boat thing to me is as old news as it is new news". . . it is strange, would you believe me if i were to tell you that i almost didn't even come to university as i couldn't overcome old insecurities and

fears . . .? But i did and im so happy, to think what i'd be missing out on if i went with my feelings.

Im this fellow, whos proper friendly, love having a laugh, loves all friends and family—gets on with virtually everyone. . . . Underneath Tara, there's this machine that doesn't stop working—always analysing, always reading, always thinking—long live deep thinkers but its the depth of thoughts that are killing us softly, ha ha sweet irony (btw at this juncture i thought i'd just tell you, that this isn't like a sad gloomy email, i just want you to know more about me).

I'm awfully tired, perhaps this is where this email has come from—but there has been intent on emailing you for a few weeks now. I could write all day about myself but i'll leave this here cos im scared that you're scared, and that you'll call the fuzz as im being an utter nutter as im sure you think..
A few questions for you. . .
What is the Popular Culture Collective?
What are your views on the club culture?
And do you love Green Day?
Sorry if you find this extremely weird but i feel if anyone has a depth understanding or recognisation its you.
:-) CA x

CA was not weird. He was reaching out—stretching—working out his limits in a new environment. The future—an imagining of what could be—is written in our students' bodies with shoulders back, eyes forward, and head up. There is knowledge of and in the skin that is not placated or bent by conservative politics or imperializing nations. Sherry Shapiro's realization is a significant one: "what is rarely found in such work is a pedagogy where the body/subject as a lived medium becomes part of the curriculum" (1999:143). The taste, touch, and smell of life are part of our teaching. Living truths can emerge, provoking questioning, activism, and writing. It is the disconnection that creates fear and hatred.

Education is a passionate formation, triggering deep, lasting change. Classrooms are sites of challenge, confusion, and passionate dialogues about ideas. Considering the feminine domination of the profession, it is surprising that much of the fear and concern about sex in education is aimed at the men who hold power in schools and universities: the headmasters and professors. This fear does have some basis. William Kerrigan, Professor of

English at the University of Massachusetts, acknowledged his sexual conquests with pride:

> I have been the subject of advances from male and female students for twenty-five years. I've had them come at me right and left. I've had people take their clothes off in my office. And there is a particular kind of student I have responded to. . . . I'm talking about a female student who, for one reason or another, has unnaturally prolonged her virginity. . . . There have been times when this virginity has been presented to me as something that I, not quite like another man, half an authority figure, can handle . . . these relationships between adults can be quite beautiful and genuinely transforming. It's very powerful sexually and psychologically, and because of that power, one can touch a student in a positive way. (Kerrigan in Botstein, Boswell, Blythe, and Kerrigan 1993:35–36)

This statement captures actions that are repulsive. I am not sure which "half" is an authority figure and which half is "not quite like another man," but such behavior breaches the trust that our students require from us. Teachers are not the equal of students, and friendships can only be formed much later, not in the educational oven of tutorials and lectures. The reason for this distance is that teachers are required—often repeatedly—to demonstrate credibility in their field. If students trust us as teachers, then they will follow us anywhere. But the excesses of Kerrigan's fantasy life raise troubling questions. Is the only solution for such unforgivable actions to withdraw the body completely and retract to the corseted self of the keyboard, bulletin board, and chat room? It is a safe mode of teaching and keeps troubled students away from us, but is education—in the best sense—ever safe? The line between modeling intellectual leadership and mentoring student change is never as cleanly drawn as we may hope. A teacher's interest in ideas can be read as an invitation for a different type of intimacy. While I have never had students remove clothing in my office—perhaps because I leave my door open and they may become either cold and/or embarrassed—they become agitated, emotional, and obsessive on a daily basis. It would be easy—very easy—to take advantage of the power that we as teachers hold. To do so would not only be unprofessional, but destructive of the potential we have to channel that passion and commitment for educational imperatives. Through our bodies and voices, students construct knowledge in an educationally relevant way. By granting attention to teachers' bodies, a critical rupture cuts through the teacher-knowledge-student relationship.

Digital

Teaching operates across the boundaries of nation, class, justice, and desire. It is not surprising that interdisciplinary approaches from cultural studies and critical pedagogy challenge the language of insiders and outsiders, citizens and foreigners. Seung-Hui Cho has been treated as an individual pathology and paranoia (Chew 2007). Cultural studies' history of research into deviance and violence demands alternative analyses and hypotheses (Hall, Critcher, Jefferson, Clarke, and Roberts 1978). There is a strong argument that cultural studies was built through teaching. While the canonical texts rarely cite the politics of pedagogy, the references and beliefs are revealed when scratching below the theoretically chiseled prose and the references to Althusser, Gramsci, Deleuze, and Foucault. Lawrence Grossberg remembered that:

> All of the founding figures of cultural studies (including Richard Hoggart, Raymond Williams, E. P. Thompson, and Stuart Hall) started their careers, and their intellectual projects, in the field of education, outside the university, in extramural departments and adult working-class courses (1994:3).

The role of web-based education in such a history remains ambivalent (Brabazon 2002, 2007). Education initiatives have been increasing in their frequency, but significant follow-up questions need to be asked. Is change motivated by cost savings, a commitment to alternative modes of teaching and learning, a fear of teaching bodies, or disquiet at student behavior? The mobilization of online educational resources privileges some learning styles (and some learners) over others, and prioritizes hardware over peopleware, and software over cultware (Kent 2005, 2008). But is it safer?

To celebrate the freedom and flexibility of technology is to block the systematic recognition of the intangibilities of learning that are of the body: the nod, the smile, the praise, and the wink. To assess educational technology requires a language of resources, efficiency, cost, and interactive delivery. Human resources are often absent from this model. As Daniel Chandler laughingly reminded us, "the world is divided into those who divide people into two types, and those who don't" (2000). The intellectual desire to codify, classify, and order means that the messiness of (other) bodies of scholarship—or scholarly bodies of the other—rarely receives attention. Funding online education displaces discussions of power and societal transformations by stressing a new array of "basic skills." Not all disciplines and paradigms are based on easily assessable content. Many require multiple mediations of content with form. Students want to feel moved, they want to change and grow, and they want approval.

From: Mike
Sent: Sun 18/03/2007 10:01 pm
To: Brabazon Tara
Subject: HAPPY MOTHERS DAY TARA

A big shout to Tara,
I don't mean to trouble you too much on this late Sunday evening but I'm worrying about a future career—specifically mine. The trouble is—I have aspiration! But the small city I'm from just outside Wales has no room for this "ungrateful attitude"—people like me (of which there are few) get spat at in the streets for ever daring to deviate from the celebrated farming heritage ageing Herefordians so proudly thrust upon any stranger curious enough to venture into this peculiar and forgotten city.

Two possible options exist for me there, either work in Bulmer's brewing close to 80 percent of England's cider—an attractive possibility for most I assume, I have no doubts that there are rooms in this factory where the fumes are enough to put the less experienced in a coma for months! Or alternatively we have Sun Valley, which prides itself on slaughtering chickens to provide McDonalds with over 50 percent of the chicken used in its chicken nuggets throughout ALL of Europe! (The moral implications of the latter worry me—The Sun Valley Company is scrutinized by Greenpeace, reports show it actually cleared 10,000 sq miles of Amazon forest just for Soya crop farming—which is then in turn used for chicken feed, it's called "the 7,000 km journey that links Amazon destruction to Hereford.")

In all fairness Tara to be honest with you that pretty much SUCKS big-time and I don't want to spend the rest of my life a hardened alcoholic or aspiring to be "Head Chicken Slaughterer"—even though the lure of knowing how to instantaneously kill a poor critter with ninja like stealth just with my eyes is attractive it's something I'm not too enthusiastic about.

So my dilemma is what am I going to be, I know where I'd like to be and I'm pretty sure I have the means and dedication to get me there—but how?—I don't even know where to start. I'd love to present on Blue Peter!—But I guess the chances are pretty slim. Alternatively I find writing and ramblings such as this therapeutic, which is more than encouraging. So if you feel like helping out a lost sheep (of which I see a lot of living on the outskirts of Wales!) then anything you have to say will be much appreciated.

Many thanks

A slightly daunted and drifting Mike.

x x x

P.s. Am I good writer?

A truth of my teaching life is to talk to students where they are rather than where I want them to be. Mike needed to be heard and validated. I needed to understand his life and environment. Such a process is reinforced by the word and work of Henry Giroux and Roger Simon.

> By ignoring the cultural and social forms that are authorized by youth and simultaneously empower or disempower them, educators risk complicity silencing and negating their students. . . . Educators who refuse to acknowledge popular culture as a significant basis of knowledge often devalue students by refusing to work with the knowledge that students actually have to eliminate the possibility of developing a pedagogy that links school knowledge to the differing subject relations that help to constitute their everyday lives (1989:236).

The delights and passions of life are not convenient. Why should the passions of education be any different? The enthusiasm and excitement of the classroom disrupt lives, promoting ruthless debates between partners, friends, and parents. It should be exciting, distracting, and highly inopportune. Education should be politically worrying and personally shattering. It is an affective, agitated environment. It is the confusions, difficulties, and frustrations that allow students to learn and make significant connections. The point of a great teacher is to grant meaning and context to the hard work, drudgery, disappointment, and repetition that is required of scholarship. Body knowledges are messy: they leak, are squashed into (metaphorically) too-tight trousers, fashion disasters, and bad hair days. This type of consciousness is outside university strategic plans and educational goals of consumerism, productivity, and marking criteria. As universities increase the size of their marketing departments and develop corporate plans, they are much more vulnerable to the promises of public relations consultants and online profiles. Through user-generated content and social networking sites such as Facebook, there are (too) many student voices to control, shape, and interpret to create a clean marketing image. Jamal Albarghouti's mobile phone footage that provided a slice of the Virginia Tech horror for the world through the CNN portal allowed "us" to hear gunshots and see the panic from the police ("Virginia Tech School Shooting Phone Vid"). CNN called him an "I-reporter." This phrase captured his amateurism, his modernity, his luck, and his e-literacy. It also showed the terror and the violence through the shaking of his hands gripping the camera phone.

Technology is not the salve of risk in teaching. It will not prevent the difficult students lashing outwards to create injury. I do understand the attraction of disconnecting teaching and learning from bodies, emotion, and danger. But throughout my professional career, I have not worked in an environment where guns circulate through the population. It is startling—as someone who has taught in three countries with strict gun control—that the behavior of students is disconnected from the behavior of the rest of the population. There are 270 million guns held by the 300 million people of the United States ("Morning of Terror" 2007:44–45). Virginia Tech has a Corps of Cadets and is a senior military academy. It is one of the few public universities in the United States maintaining these "training" functions. Militarism is an ideology that damages the social fabric of civility, debate, and discussion, validating rage, revenge, and violence. Meanwhile, a war in Iraq releases a death count each day. I am not the first here to note that on the day that Cho discharged his pistols, 171 people died in Iraq (Semple 2007:10). There is no causality between cadets, Iraq, and Cho. A climate where violence "fixes" complex problems does not salve or solve the disquiet and anger of young people.

Cho's actions are reified by focusing on his race. Very early in the media coverage, he was labeled an "Asian male" or "Korean." Such descriptors were racist and—as with all racisms—convenient. The Columbine shootings demonized young white men. Most of the difficult students facing challenges that I have taught have been white and female. There certainly are young men who are angry at "the system."

> From: Phil
> Sent: Mon 15/10/2007 2:56 pm
> To: Brabazon Tara
> Subject: [SPAM?] bored inbetween lectures
>
> Had a crazy weekend mixed with some deep thought so i thought i'd share with you lol. As human's we are each only given one chance to live our life and enjoy it. So what gives politician's the right to act in the controlling manner they do, implementing laws that take

away rights and possessions that might actually make life enjoyable and interesting, often because they are to scared of how it might affect their power in government. To me, they are the weak one's, they seem too power hungry and blinded to genuinely care about the country and the public, more putting into place restrictions than offering opportunity. Admittedly, that's a pretty naive view on politics as it's based on my opinion and i probably only know very little of what actually goes on in the government, not actually knowing how much they hide from the public. It's something that i've thought about before but pushed to the back of my mind, probably because i realised it's almost impossible to change anything and maybe because i didn't want to think about it. And it does seem to be an impossible situation, to live in a fair society there obviously needs to be some sort of government and in an ideal world there would be a viable political structure that is an alternative to anything out there today, Communism is obviously a great concept but filled with so many flaws, there's always going to be a hierarchy of power. Unfortunately the majority of the public are too ignorant to think about the way the live, maybe people are ignorant, maybe people are happy with their lives as they are and that's fine. I'm not overly sure what i have a problem with, i don't think it's the money side of things, that's always going to happen and can't be helped, but i think it's the fact that an individual or group of people you've never met can have such control over your life when at birth everyone is equal, nothing in this world makes someone better than someone else. Politician's have no right to restrict the way we live our lives as they are no different to us, apart from some words that might be next to their name which ultimately, to me personally, shouldn't given them anymore power in this world. I suppose in some sense you could relate bits of what i've said to today's lecture/seminar if you look at the way we personally choose to live our lives, myself, i'd be content with a job or lifestyle that allows me to be lead a life where i'm happy but possibly one which allows me a form of expression.

Admittedly not much thought actually went into any of this, just sort of poured out and the majority is much a highly idealistic view of way we live, but it's a view that can offer no answers. Maybe if people listened to more Radiohead (just an example, obviously many socially and politically active "artists," but you can see by their lyrics and website how they try and push people into thinking about the world) and took more drugs, the public would be more active and the world would be a better place, bit of a shit way to phrase it but rushing as got seminar in 5 minutes lol. Just look at the 1960's. I could probably talk much more bullshit than that but must be off.

How was I to handle this e-mail? The attacks on the government and politicians did worry me. But the e-mail emerged from nowhere. The young man had never contacted me before, so it seemed important to involve him in a dialogue.

From: Brabazon Tara
Sent: Tue 16/10/2007 5:50 am
To: Phil
Subject: RE: [SPAM?] bored inbetween lectures

Hey Phil—great to hear from you!!!

You've always had some pretty amazing thoughts on these issues. I hope you're going to write this down in detail a bit more!!!

But—I'm interested—I'm generally in favor of a legal system. I see it as part of the building blocks of civilization. I do think—and you are making me think—that there should be circumscriptions on behaviour—rules and guidelines that are in place through historical precedence. And the government is part of making these rules.

You probably disagree with that :) It's the issue about if and then how humanity patrols its limits. You can tell me about this!

T XXX

I was obviously worried how this young man was handling these issues. Therefore, how he would reply to my correctives was interesting. He simply dismissed his earlier e-mail, like it was never sent.

From: Phil
Sent: Tue 16/10/2007 10:04 am
To: Brabazon Tara
Subject: RE: [SPAM?] bored inbetween lectures

i dunno man, i obviously agree that there needs to be a legal system otherwise society would collapse, i think i was just generally pissed

This was a strange e-mail dialogue. A young man thinking about society and social change blaming politics and politicians for social problems. When asked about his ideas, he shut down the discussion. It was right to probe and test his views, to learn about him. Kristin Goss recognized the value of such knowledge in the context of Virginia Tech: "Who was the shooter?" (2007). The question I raise in this chapter is why there are not more shooters in our schools and universities. Cho produced disturbing plays that alerted faculty to problems ("In morbid plays," 2007). While these documents are brutal and disturbing, those of us who mark, assess, and judge have seen suicidal and homicidal poetry and prose with great frequency. Rarely have I notified university authorities. I have tried to help, but often been silent. Virginia Tech's shootings mean that we all must take these random e-mails, jottings, and musings more seriously than we have in the past.

Don't Walk Away in Silence

This chapter has punctuated a discussion of Virginia Tech and the damaged teaching body with Joy Division, or more precisely Ian Curtis's lyrics for the long-defunct band. Joy Division, as a band, was dissolved without the whimper of lawyers and accountants or a Yoko-Ono scapegoat. Instead, Curtis committed suicide on the eve of their American tour. In the subsequent decades, death has not destroyed them or their music, but fed the myth of a misunderstood young man whose music screams of loss, confusion, and danger. Violent death creates a moment of pause and reflection, even in the midst of accelerated modernity. For one of my former students—who was also a self-harmer—Curtis provided a way forward in her own life.

> From:
> Sent: Thursday, 19 May 2005 12:30 pm
> To: Tara Brabazon
> Subject: A "New Order" in my life
>
> Dear Tara,
>
> Well, it sure has been awhile! I have been wanting to write to you for awhile, but i have so much to tell you that i didn't know where to start! What made me get off my arse and finally write to you was something that happened last night . . . but i will start at the beginning. Over the past couple of months i feel like i have had a huge awakening, or an epiphany or something. it sounds so cliched but it is seriously like i have been born again! As you know, i have had a

few issues over the past couple of years, and these all came to a head 2 months ago, when i attempted suicide. A couple of weeks after that i went to Melbourne to stay with my step brother for a couple of weeks, and it was there that my whole outlook on life changed. i had many conversations with my bro and his housemate, and through these i came to finally accept myself as a person and the world as imperfect but full of amazing experiences. i have spent too long fighting life—complaining about things, being depressed about things and basically not taking responsibility for my own happiness. i used to have such a bleak and cynical outlook on life—i have never been religious so have never had that as a comfort blanket to give me meaning, so i basically just believed that its all pretty meaningless. But now, through reading and talking (and maybe experimenting with various substances!) i have discovered spirituality; not in religious terms really, just a peace within myself, and a peace with the universe. To put it simply, i guess i have am growing up. I am no longer self destructive—i eat healthily and exercise regularly, and i have stopped cutting myself for MYSELF, not for anyone else, because i finally see that more than anything i was hurting myself (and certainly not just physically).

So anyway, back to why i finally wrote to you... last night i was at my brother's house (who i couldn't be closer to) and we were listening to music, as we do. i have to admit, i used to be a bit of a music snob—i had my (narrow) likes and wouldn't really step outside the square. But, with the help of my brother, my new attitude and a few herbs, i am appreciating so much more music now. so last night, we were listening to New Order, which i have never liked until last night. i loved what i heard, but knew nothing about them, and when my brother educated me on ian curtis's suicide i finally realised the significance and the powerfulness of the music. it made me think of cultural studies and what you taught us about pop culture and i feel like i understand so much better now. i wanted to tell you all of this, as it feels as though the things you said to me back in first year, and the things we talked about both in class and out of class mean so much more to me now.

i always wanted someone to "fix" me, to give me the answer, i didn't think i had the strength to do it myself, but here i am! This is all my own doing . . . the psych didn't do it for me—you were right—it was something i had to do when i was ready, and i did it.

Virginia Tech was and is an opportunity for educators to think again about our responsibilities and how our actions impact on the lives we teach. We have a choice. We can isolate and demonize students like Eric Harris, Dylan Klebold, and Seung-Hui Cho, or we can ponder how our teaching and learning promises respect, care, and consideration, but sometimes does not deliver these aspirations. We can validate the market economy and vocational education or we can log the disappointments confronted by generations of scholars who were promised the world but left with a McJob. We can repeat the categories of educational psychology—codifying normality and deviance—or we can place mental health issues in historical and social context.

From: Tina
Sent: Fri 13/04/2007 02:21
To: Brabazon Tara
Subject: RE:

Hey Tara,
I'm sorry for this email. To be honest I am a little drunk right now. You said in you email earlier that you can answer any question to do with the course or life. Mine is relative to life. Right now I feel like I could end it all. Theres no reasons for it which is why its so annoying, but Im constantly depressed . . . my brain cant fathom it and I dont want to have to deal with it anymore. I hate feeling distanced from my brains and actions.

I cant see a point in anthing anymore and I feel worthless. I dont think I have any controle and Im at a lost at what to do. I dont know who to talk to about this and I am fuckijng scared :[

Tina X

From: T.M.Brabazon@brighton.ac.uk
To: Tina
Subject: RE: Date: Fri, 13 Apr 2007 10:35:52 +0100

You got me, my darling girl. Now remember—the world out there deserves your talent, your ability—and you.

All I ask is that you follow the old blonde's advice. HANG IN THERE.

However crappy a night is—the sun does come up the next day. I promise you.

And remember I NEED YOU to work with me for the next decade at least. AT LEAST. You can do anything—and always know that I believe in you completely . . .

So always email me. Always talk to me. I'm not going anywhere—O.K.???

T XXX

From: Tina
Sent: Fri 13/04/2007 12:47 pm
To: Brabazon Tara
Subject: RE:

Thanks for your support Tara but it's so hard. The pain in my head is constant, even when I seem happy I'm just continueing to rot inside and I just feel stuck.

I have no drive for anything. I cant see a point in anything. Despite what you say, I dont feel I have talent or ability in any areas and I dont see where I fit in.

I hate myself. I hate the people around me. I've felt this way for a long time but now I can feel myself cracking.

Tina XX

It is easy to demonize the rage of young men at university as crazed, aberrant, or abnormal. It is harder to acknowledge that academics "manage" student traumas most days. Many are serious. Some are suicidal. Schools and universities are troubling environments. Part of my task in this chapter reviewing the myriad sites/sights of pain and anguish of which Virginia Tech is a metonymy and as someone old enough to remember analogue education is to ask once more if the risk of corporeal teaching is worth its benefits. In 1969, an education textbook reported that "for all our general or professional involvement as teachers, we still have difficulty in describing and analyzing what it is we are doing and what influences we are having" (Morrison and

McIntyre 1969:45) Remembering the deaths and difficulties of contemporary education, can the online environment provide the salve for scholarship in difficult times? In offering allegiance and compassion to our faculty colleagues who have lost their lives protecting students, it seems important to recognize that Cho was not an aberrance. He was a challenged young man who could not manage the disturbances in his life. On an almost daily basis, we try to assist students who cannot align life and study, emotion and scholarship. While asking why Cho started shooting, perhaps a more poignant realization is why more students have not started shooting. As Ben Agger argues in this collection, "Cho wasn't evil; he was damaged." Most of us have taught plenty of damaged students through the years, men and women, of various ages and races. What is significant is that Cho blocked those who followed him from providing simplistic answers to the complex questions of his life. His cell phone and computer hard drive were never recovered after the shootings ("Investigators leave Tech duck pond empty-handed"). He prevented easy "answers" or justifications for violent behavior, like gaming, pornography, or childhood abuse. The digital collaboration/cop-out was destroyed.

While the other remarkable chapters in this book explore the spectacle, language, and mediations of Virginia Tech, it is important to recognize the bodies of knowledge that link teachers and students. Liviu Librescu was killed while trying to wedge the door shut on Cho, providing crucial seconds for his students to escape. Jocelyne Couture-Nowak tried to protect the students in her French classroom, sending her students to the back while she attempted to barricade the door. Kevin Granata moved his twenty students from a classroom and locked them in an office. He then returned to investigate the disturbance and was killed. All his students survived.

While these academics died protecting students and gain status as scholarly heroes, it raises the everyday risk of scholarly life that most of us do not consider. We encourage dialogue and dissent, yet five academics died alongside the twenty-seven students. For the death of our colleagues to mean more than the dreadful by-product of a mental health patient, we must use Virginia Tech's shooting to talk more honestly and passionately about education, teaching, and learning. This event of homicide and suicide is also a scholarly space for change, growth, and renewal. In losing control, we must gain insight.

Notes

1. Tom Bentley stated that, "young people in many Western societies are having more trouble perhaps than ever before in making the transition to adulthood.

Persistent and unpredictable change in economy, demographics, technology, culture, values, and relationships throw doubt upon the institutions we have created to deliver education," from "Learning beyond the classroom," from Hargreaves and Christie (1998: 80)

2. A remarkable "guide" to preventing violence on campus—that predates the Virginia Tech shootings by six years—was Nicoletti, Spencer-Thomas, and Bollinger (2001), *Violence Goes to College: The Authoritative Guide to Prevention and Intervention*. This book presents a way to "manage" violence in a university.

3. Significantly, Wikipedia does not have an entry for "Virginia Tech shootings." Instead, it has an entry for the "Virginia Tech massacre" and redirects searchers to this entry.

References

Bentley, Tom. 1998. "Learning Beyond the Classroom." In Ian Hargreaves and Ian Christie, eds. *Tomorrow's Politics*. London: Demos, 80–85.
Brabazon, Tara. 2002. *Digital Hemlock*. Sydney: UNSW Press.
———. 2007. *The University of Google*. Aldershot: Ashgate.
Chandler, Daniel. 2000. "Biases of the Ear and Eye: 'Great Divide' Theories, Honocentrism, Graphocentrism and Logocentrism." www.aber.ac.uk/~dgc/litoral.html.
Chew, Kristina. 2007. "Seung-Hui Cho's Diagnosis." *AutismVox*. August 30. www.autismvox.com/seung-hui-chos-diagnosis-selective-mutism.
Cho, Seung-Hui. 2007. "Virginia Tech Shooting." *YouTube*. www.youtube.com/watch?v=0rT8G8QvB2U
DiPiero, Thomas. 2002. *White Men Aren't*. Durham, North Carolina. Duke University Press.
Giroux, Henry, and Roger Simon. 1989. "Popular Culture as a Pedagogy of Pleasure and Meaning." In Henry Giroux and Roger Simon, eds. *Popular Culture, Schooling and Everyday Life*. Granby, MA: Bergin and Garvey, 236–52.
Goss, Kristin. 2007. "Aftermath of a Tragedy." *The Chronicle Review* (May 4): 53.35. chronicle.com/weekly/v53/i35/35601001/html.
Grossberg, Lawrence. 1994. "Bringing It All Back Home—Pedagogy and Cultural Studies." In Henry Giroux and Peter McLaren. *Between Borders: Pedagogy and the Politics of Cultural Studies*. New York: Routledge, 1–28.
Hall, Stuart, Chas Critcher, Tony Jefferson, John Clarke, and Brian Roberts. 1978. *Policing the Crisis*. London: Macmillan.
hooks, bell. 1994. "Eros, Eroticism and the Pedagogical Process." In Henry Giroux and Peter McLaren, eds. *Between Borders: Pedagogy and the Politics of Cultural Studies*. New York: Routledge, 113–18.
"In Morbid Plays, Cho's Characters Dreamed of Killing." April 18, 2007. *CNN.com*. www.cnn.com/2007/US/04/17/vatech.writings/index.html.
Joy Division. 1999. *Heart and Soul*. London: London Records.

Kent, Mike. 2005. *The Invisible Empire*. Doctor of Philosophy Thesis. Murdoch, Western Australia: Murdoch University. www.lib.murdoch.edu.au/adt/browse/view/adt-MU20051222.112058.

———. 2008. "Cultware." In Tara Brabazon, ed. *The Revolution Will Not Be Downloaded: Dissent in the Digital Age*. Oxford: Chandos, 103–10.

Mallory, Anna. June 30, 2007. "Investigators Leave Tech Duck Pond Empty-handed." www.roanoke.com/news/nrv/wb/122648.

"Morning of terror." 2007. *Newsweek* (April 30): 44–45.

Morrison, Arnold, and Donald McIntyre. 1969. *Teachers and Teaching*. Harmondsworth, England: Penguin.

Nicoletti, John, Sally Spencer-Thomas, and Christopher Bollinger. 2001. *Violence Goes to College: The Authoritative Guide to Prevention and Intervention*. New York: C. C. Thomas.

Plato. 2003. *The Last Days of Socrates*. Harmondsworth, England: Penguin.

Probyn, Elspeth. 2004. "Teaching Bodies: Affects in the Classroom." *Body and Society* 10 (4), 21–43.

Propp, Vladimir. 1968. *The Morphology of the Folktale*. Austin: University of Texas Press.

Semple, Kirk. 2007. "Bombs Rip through Baghdad in Waves of Attacks, Killing 171." *New York Times* (April 19): 10.

Shapiro, Sherry. 1999. *Pedagogy and the Politics of the Body: A Critical Praxis*. New York: Garland Publishing.

"Trying to Make Sense of a Massacre." 2007. *Time* (April 30): 40–42.

"Virginia Tech School Shooting Phone Vid." 2007. *YouTube*.

CHAPTER
Nine

WHEN RHETORIC FAILS:
The Heroic Teacher and the Basic Communications Course

Matthew Levy

A burglar who holds a gun to my head and calmly expresses an intention to rob me may induce my cooperation, but not by means of rhetoric.

—Erika Lindemann, *A Rhetoric for Writing Teachers* (2001:41)

College as America once knew it—as an incubator of radical social change—is coming to an end. To our generation the word "radicalism" evokes images of al Qaeda, not the Weathermen. "Campus takeover" sounds more like Virginia Tech in 2007 than Columbia University in 1968.

—Nicholas Handler, (2007), Class of 2009

April 16 was Holocaust Remembrance Day. In 2007 on this day (according to CNN) Virginia Tech Professor Liviu Librescu was showing a slide show to his engineering students, when the shootings began. Librescu's students say he acted quickly, blocking the door with his body in order to give them time to escape out the window. It is assumed that Seung-Hui Cho shot and killed Librescu through the door. Two students in this class were wounded, but all survived.

Like others, I am awed by the courage of Librescu and the students and other professors who mustered the clear-mindedness and courage to save others. Sitting around the lunch table, I have listened to coworkers talk about the Virginia Tech massacre, largely in conjunction with anecdotes from the "lock down" training they have been given at other universities, training that they said advises fleeing but not resistance. One professor said, "I like to think I would try to protect my students anyway." This care for students seems basic to the *ethos* of a good teacher, even if the care is wrapped in toughness, as students said of Librescu. Another professor said, in a statement I think basic to the *wisdom* of an experienced teacher, "I don't think any of us know how we will behave in that kind of situation."

I am struck by the poignancy given to Librescu's story by the fact that he was a survivor before he was a teacher-hero. Without diminishing the deserved honor of those that sacrifice themselves for others, I believe that this poignancy (which is real) underscores the fact that heroism is the stuff of narrative. How could we escape assigning meaning to the heroic death of a survivor on Holocaust Remembrance Day, and why would we want to? Without evidence, I find myself assuming that his earlier experiences somehow contributed to his decisive action. Then, I remind myself that others without his experience blocked doors and saved lives.

I watched Seung-Hui Cho read his statements on YouTube and considered how powerfully the habit of narrative seemed to contribute to his malevolent actions. Feeling wronged or excluded is not uncommon; however, Seung-Hui Cho, for whatever reason, wrote such feelings into a narrative of martyrdom and revenge. I think it is plausible that Seung-Hui Cho called on the meaning-making power of narrative in order to convince himself that his suffering was as significant to the world as it felt to him. When we read Cho's horrific acts as an expression of narrativized narcissism or megalomania, there is the temptation to blame them on a steady diet of ultraviolent video games and melodramas, especially those that involve saving the world. One could imagine that they instill a kind of thinking in which, "My story only matters at all if it matters to everyone." And this thinking can be dangerous, since it seems to be much easier to impact people in a negative way than in a positive one. Yet, the power of narrative also fuels positive contributions through its ability to expand and condense the scope of our influence. It creates order and meaning and allows us to feel agency, which is necessary if we are to believe those who tell us "one person can make a difference." (For instance, narrative allows us to link mundane household habits to ecology.) Likewise, narratives about the meaning-making power of language attracted me to my profession of writing teacher and explain why I believe the way we teach writing has serious consequences beyond just raising our students' income potential: political, social, and psychological consequences.

The Figure of the Teacher-Hero

My Advanced Composition for Teachers course watched *Freedom Writers* together as we began reading Berlin's *Rhetoric and Reality: Writing Instruction in American Colleges, 1900–1985*. I chose to show the film because Berlin was concerned about the historical narratives we tell about writing and instruction. Popular culture is another powerful force in shaping our narratives about writing and teaching. In the film, Erin Gruwell (played by Hillary Swank) uses journaling to overcome the fractious and divided nature of her English classroom. The name *Freedom Writers* puns on the rides taken by civil rights activists across state lines to test the 1960 Supreme Court decision *Boynton v. Virginia* (which deemed laws segregating interstate travel unconstitutional). As Gruwell's classroom becomes a safe place for the students, they make friendships that cross a different set of borders: borders enforced not by Jim Crow laws but by neighborhood gangs. Building upon the students' journaling experience, Gruwell uses *Diary of Anne Frank* and a study of the Holocaust to expand on these lessons about discrimination, violence, and shared human dignity. After watching, we brainstormed together a list of bromides about teaching expressed in the film:

- Remember that students are people
- Never stop learning
- Recognize that everyone's experience contains wisdom
- Be independent in your approach to teaching
- Go against the status quo (carefully!)
- Be passionate
- Give models and texts students can relate to
- Help students to support one another
- Don't give busy work
- Use writing to engage interests
- Treat each class as new
- Use unconventional means if conventional means fail
- Don't give up if students don't understand
- Don't use students' bad attitudes as an excuse to quit trying
- Create a safe learning environment

- Know students can teach you too
- Maintain high standards: low expectations yield low outcomes

I noticed with approval that my students were able to identify ideas about teaching inculcated by this and all the teacher-hero films, at least those in which the students are not privileged and the teachers succeed at some risk to themselves: *Lean on Me, The Ron Clarke Story, Stand and Deliver, Dangerous Minds, Teachers,* to name a few.

One student summed up our list by repeating a maxim, "Teaching is a passion not a profession." The rest of the class applauded his statement. I had to agree that it takes a great deal of energy to maintain a commitment to the needs of every student through a lifetime of teaching. This must be all the more true when teaching under terrible conditions. And I like seeing teachers honored in major films and attention given to the personal sacrifices made by teachers for students.

Nevertheless, even as I said this, I was troubled by the way the film's narrative makes the public disaster of our education system into a private matter, something best addressed by one teacher-hero rather than through collective action. It is already easier, I think, for new teachers to imagine themselves finding creative, individual means to beat the system and teach well than to imagine a movement that would allow them to participate in a wholesale transformation of public schooling. In *Freedom Writers,* the extremely unsympathetic senior teacher who tries to thwart Gruwell at every turn uses her own experience and tenure as a justification for her antistudent attitude. Given the public discourse about public schools and the way popular culture narrates the victory of teacher-heroes, I must admit that I was also uncertain about what kind of values new teachers might seek to express in any new arrangement they helped to create. They say, "Teaching is a passion not a profession." Does this mean they would help conservatives undermine the meager professional benefits teachers currently enjoy? This is similar to "every man for himself," modified to "every teacher for *the self,*" in keeping with the American ideology of the individual, in which people act against their own interests in the name of individual freedom.

Luckily, class time ran out before I climbed up on this soapbox. Saved by the bell, I had time to develop what I hoped would be a less accusatory and more useful response.

The report of the panel appointed by Virginia governor Tim Kaine suggested that the Virginia Tech Massacre was not only significant as an individual act of violence, that it also represented a political and institutional failure. Without somehow suggesting that writing instruction also contributed to that horror, I believe rhetorical instruction can play a role in environments that do or do not give rise to violence. In the days after the Virginia Tech shooting, when the media was whirling with discussions of the writing of Seung-Hui Cho, more than one person asked me if I believed that writing teachers could somehow help with this problem, perhaps by flagging students who showed the capacity for violence. I didn't see how. After all, as I understand it, a number of Cho's teachers had recognized that he was troubled, but no effective action was taken, due in part to a perceived need to protect his privacy. The people who asked me whether I thought writing teachers could somehow play the role of the canary in the coalmine of the university were not themselves writing teachers. If they had been, I'm not sure they would have ventured this idea. After all, writing teachers sometimes invite students to investigate troubling areas. To then rush to diagnosis would seem like a trap. Only once when I received discomfiting writing did I feel the need to ask my student if she was OK and tell her about available counseling services. When she said she had the help she needed, I felt I had to take her word for it.

This "flagging" function, however, is not the only possible institutional role writing teachers could help play connected to these questions. The idea that rhetorical instruction is relevant to the Virginia Tech Massacre is predicated on the idea that violence results from failures of rhetoric. While it would be hyperbole to say that *all* violence comes from an inability to communicate and express oneself in a healthy way—or, of course, that writing programs could put an end to violence—the idea that good communication can reduce violence and perhaps ameliorate other social problems was a basic presupposition of the 1940s University of Denver program that I want to discuss here, which I will call the Basic Communications Course (even though there were other versions of this course at other schools). Many of its features have become commonplace in current writing programs; however, the course was also criticized and even ridiculed for the grandness of its motivations, the way it tied mental health concerns to communication problems, and the holistic attitude it brought in its attempt to replace Freshman English. I believe there is more to be learned from this effort, especially during this period when many schools are investigating possibilities for creating better-integrated first-year experiences for students by drawing upon the talents of more members of the academic community. I have observed such efforts at the University of Texas at Arlington and at Pacific Lutheran University. Making such changes is difficult. It involves convincing people outside of English to devote their energy and giving them say in what is often considered the domain of the English department. It involves reassessing the university's structure of disciplinary specialization and addressing concerns about privacy. Devoting the necessary resources means giving writing (and communication, generally) a different, perhaps more central, role in the narratives we tell about private and public life.

History: An Angel Blown Backwards into the Future

So, I let the student's statement, "Teaching is a passion not a profession," stand until a few meetings later. This intervening time was spent trying to help students understand the importance of Berlin's contribution in *Rhetoric and Reality*, which most of them found to be less than delightful. When I called the book *R&R*, one student said, "Not hardly," which it took me a few beats to understand: For her, this was no page turner, no rest, and no relaxation.

Nevertheless, *Rhetoric and Reality* is a comeback narrative, every bit as much as teacher-hero tales like *Freedom Writers*. It is a history of the revival of rhetorically sophisticated writing instruction in the twentieth century after its decline in the nineteenth (detailed in Berlin's previous book). It tells of the groundwork laid through brilliant failures, innovative programs like the Basic Communications Course that came and went before wide-scale change was finally accomplished through a national investment in education (made, according to Berlin, in some part due to the Russian's launch of Sputnik) and through a rediscovery of the value of rhetorical research and practice. This renaissance brought back to writing instruction a sense of the value of writing not just to individuals but also to society. For teachers who embraced these "new rhetorics," writing instruction was no longer a purely aesthetic endeavor reserved for the elite or a remedial grammar fix from which the elite could be exempted. Many colleges and universities seemed to own up to the fact that none of the incoming students were prepared to do the kind of writing expected in college and that even the writers who had no grammar problems still had much to learn about the relationships between rhetoric and reality that could be taught beneficially in writing courses. Soon, enough had been changed for the better—such as a new emphasis on teaching writing as a process rather than just emphasizing the form of the product, the de-emphasis of teacher authority in favor of collaborative peer groups, the reintroduction of invention (getting and developing ideas), and a consideration of social contexts—that it was possible to write articles about the inevitability of progress with optimistic titles like "The Winds of Change." This was a communal narrative of redemption, a society-wide version of the teacher-hero story.

Though, as Richard Young had already pointed out in 1980, some "disharmonies" remained in the new rhetorics. Berlin identifies three major camps according to their epistemologies: subjective rhetorics find truth within the individual, a private perception that can only be imperfectly conveyed; objective rhetorics find truth out in the material world, reproducible phenomena observed through correct scientific method; transactional rhetorics find truth emerging in the interaction between self, other, language, and world. Berlin sees these epistemologies as yielding political outcomes. While many subjective rhetorics are self-consciously progressive, their stress on the individual makes collective political action more difficult. Objective rhetorics, with their uncritically positivist attitudes, tend to think "what is" is "true," reinforcing the status quo as "natural." Berlin finds transactional rhetorics the most politically promising, because they show that we and our world are in development and can be changed. So, in addition to telling a comeback story in which the political and institutional bodies of the United States rediscover the value of writing instruction, Berlin also suggests that important choices remain about how we will teach it.

One of the high points for me in Berlin's story is his discussion of the Basic Communications Course. When we were going over this passage, I remembered the questions I had been asked about the Virginia Tech Massacre. Here was a program where writing teachers actually were put in the position of thinking about the mental health of students and not merely in terms of flagging "problem cases." Based on the assumptions of General Semantics, this writing program attempted to treat many communication problems as mental health issues. Here also, the institutional response to student writing and mental health revealed a concern for privacy. In a way fascinating to me, this issue of privacy contributed to a disciplinary argument about the nature of writing: writing as social adjustment, writing as creativity, writing as political engagement.

The Basic Communications Course

Levette J. Davidson and Frederick Sorenson published an essay in *College English* in November 1946 about "The Basic Communications Course" after it had been "developed over a period of six or seven years" (83). As you will hear, it did not last much longer; however, their article bursts with optimism about the accomplishments of the program. Even then, some commentators found naïve the goal of the course, which sought to bring together the best methods of "modern science" from psychoanalysis to propaganda analysis in order to bring about a less violent world. Forty years later, Berlin found the need to give an ambivalent assessment of the course for very different reasons: "It shows the remarkable range of innovation that the communications course could engender as well as the unfortunate excesses that it could occasionally encourage" (100). In particular, Berlin found in the goal of "integrating" students better evidence of a conservative desire to create conformism (100). Now, with sixty intervening years, the program may seem quaint and bizarre rather than progressive or conformist. Yet, I find its strangeness to be part of its appeal, since I believe what seems normal to us also seems broken.

Supporting the Basic Communications Course in the 1946–1947 school year, a staff of fifty teachers and fifty clinicians worked at the University of Denver with over 2,500 students. Representatives from English, speech, philosophy, and library science developed the course collaboratively, which was concerned with "the integration of reading, writing, speaking, and listening." Special emphasis was placed on listening, because, with the exception of the "ororverbalized," "that is what people do most frequently" (83). One can only assume that Davidson and Sorenson had orators like Hitler and Mussolini in mind when they write, "Students in these perilous times must be taught how to avoid being duped by persuasive speakers" (83).

The goals of the course were broader, however, than just teaching students to develop what Neil Postman and Charles Weingartner—echoing Hemingway—would later call good crap detectors (Postman and Weingartner 1969:3). Davidson and Sorenson explain:

> The most distinctive feature of the University of Denver basic communications course is the breadth of its objective. Necessary as the four skills just mentioned are, they are only a means to an end. They are the tools. The major objective of this course is to secure the best possible adjustment of the individual in the complex field of human relations, and the principal method used to help the student attain such adjustment is general semantics. Clarity in writing, for example, depends on clarity in thought. Hence we train students to live and think by means of the best modern methods. (83–84)

If the phrase "best modern methods" seems humorously dated, some of the clichés from the article do not: "At the University of Denver we teach individuals to help themselves. We do not teach texts" (86). I have often repeated this idea myself: "Don't teach the paper, teach the student." In keeping with this value, the Denver program pretested each student in order to understand individual needs and kept the results in files in clinics staffed by graduate students. These were not CLEP exams. High scoring students were not exempted based on the interesting assumption that the high grades of "oververbalized, intensionally oriented students" does not indicate adequate "adjustment into the field of human relations" (84). They may be "egocentric extroverts" who received As in competitive speech or "egocentric introverts" who received As in English. These students may have "bad habits" and need more help. Thus, the program aimed to teach all of their students, from the weakest to the strongest.

Many colleges now have writing centers that can trace their lineage back to this program; however, the Denver program had three other clinics as well for reading, speaking, and psychiatry. The clinics used Rogerian methods:

> It is felt that the student who considers himself a non-writer is blocked by fears similar to stage fright in the speaking situation. It is the task of the various clinics to find (if possible) the causes of the student's particular blockages and to help him to overcome them. (84)

Not only the idea of writer's block, but other ideas that retain currency are shared, such as the idea that students suffer under self-imposed standards that can impede progress and that the student clinicians have success with fellow students because they are closer to peers than teachers and don't assign grades. It would take many schools thirty more years to follow Denver in eschewing standard grammar drills and "themes" in favor of papers and speeches "of a particular length for a given purpose and audience" (85). These innovations and their influence are remarkable; however, the scope of the goals of the program is even more remarkable, ranging from individual mental health to world peace:

> At the University of Denver we teach cooperative thinking rather than competitive thinking. We are attempting to help build such habits of mind as will make a world state possible. That is the only way that we can see to avert the onset of another war and the consequent destruction of modern civilization as we know it. (85)

This program of instruction started with a first quarter "observing and reporting" about the self in a long "almost psychoanalytical" autobiography; the second quarter focused on national and international issues in a research paper; and the third quarter focused on "methods of securing 'interest and emphasis'" through a study of literature, which Davidson and Sorenson describe as "that inquiry into the person-as-a-whole in his environment-as-a-whole" (85). Like other innovations of the course, this movement from a focus on the self to broader and broader concerns is a staple of contemporary writing courses.

Also very contemporary, it seems to me, is the idea of language being central to "private" personal wellness and "public" political wellness. Less taboo surrounds the subject of mental health than in the 1940s. Large numbers of U.S. citizens take medication for one mental, emotional, or cognitive reason or another. The language of psychology also plays a big role in mainstream public discourse. You can watch accessible discussions of the "fascist personality" on the History Channel. Familiarity with mental health issues allow for more nuanced discussions in which people are not merely sane or insane. All people engage in various communicative behaviors that seem more or less healthy given the context. Perhaps the intervening time in which psychological language has permeated our culture has prepared the ground for a return of some of the ideas of General Semantics and some of the programmatic strategies of the General Communications Course.

While I am impressed by Davidson and Sorenson's program, the weirdness of its description in their article is not altogether lost on me. The discussion of General Semantics must have seemed rather alien to many readers of *College English* at the time. You could say that their essay was ripe for parody. In December 1947, it became the target of a vicious piece of satire by Samuel Middlebrook. Speaking of English I (as it was still taught in most of the United States) as if it were something from a gone era, Middlebrook begins by providing "a bit of background," a tongue-in-cheek description of how "rusty ancients with faded diplomas" remember writing being taught to them (140):

> It was a college sweatshop where harried young men, vaguely patterned on Robert Louis Stevenson, writhed in agony over stacks and stacks of "themes." A "theme" was a disguised exercise in punctuation or in whatever the sainted E. C. Woolley thought was good grammar. Or sometimes it was an exercise patterned on the dubious insights of the soul of the disappointed young author who handled the particular "section" one happened to be in.
>
> Composing "themes" taught confused college students to write with clarity, force, and elegance. The catalogue said so; and in those days we believed what we saw in print. Later we had doubts that we can summarize briefly: themes did no such thing. Themes stank. What we thought incessant reading of themes did to the instructors we forbear to mention. (140)

The tone of this passage continues throughout the essay, and like a lot of reactionary cynicism, is quite charming and humorous until one realizes its elitist (or otherwise regressive) viewpoint and its unfortunate effects. Like an aging member of the most prestigious fraternity, Middlebrook looks back on writing "themes" like many do on hazing. Yes, he admits, themes do not teach what they are supposed to. Yes, writing them stinks. Yes, reading them is worse. That does not necessarily mean, though, that he would excuse newcomers from the exercise.

Especially not if this would mean replacing themes about literature with assignments with a rhetorical focus on real-world contexts. Middlebrook continues with irony:

> So we are glad that they have banished themes from the University of Denver. Instead, the students "write papers of a particular length for a given purpose and audience." Even more challenging, the whole of English I has been changed: it has become "The Basic Communications Course" of the university.
>
> As we get it, this new course seems to be fruit of a marriage of the English and speech departments, plus some sound advice on when to shut up. (140)

This reference to shutting up is meant to lampoon Davidson and Sorenson's discussion of "ororverbalized" students. Middlebrook continues, making fun of both the idea of "adjustment" and the scientism of the University of Denver course, again by comparing "old" to new:

> It was regrettable that a few of the graduate students [who "once" taught English I]—to say nothing of their charges—could never seem "to secure the best possible adjustment of the individual in the complex field of human relations." These misfits did deplorable things: some got drunk, some wrote poems, some made passes—all disappeared. Now and again one of them would turn up in an editorial office, or as a public relations counsel, or as a living, honest-to-God novelist like Thomas Wolfe.
>
> It sounds as if the Denver doctors have changed all that. . . . The Augean stables of English I have become the spotless dairy barns where the milk of human contentment is produced under the care of watchful men in white—a product that should be sterile, non-curdling, and wholesome. (141)

In this passage, Middlebrook manages to create an opposition between the all-in-good-fun misbehavior of his literature fraternity, on the one hand, and the scientific factory farm of the democratically motivated Communications Course, on the other. Oh the good old days (before the marriage between Speech and English departments ended romance)! Middlebrook goes on to suggest that being well-adjusted would have been the ruin of the romantic poets: "When they got the kinks out, they might have got the writer out of the boy too" (143). While I appreciate the point that we often see great writers as great because of their unique visions, the more important point here is the assumption Middlebrook makes about college writing. Even where concerning first-year writing, only the aesthetically brilliant counts. Only *literary* writing counts.

Now Middlebrook's contempt for both new and old approaches to writing instruction becomes more understandable. Middlebrook fits squarely into the group Berlin called "the proponents of liberal culture," literary scholars who felt that either writing should not be taught at all or it ideally would be reserved for a few students with special promise. As Berlin explains, "The proponents of liberal culture . . . looked upon the university as the preparatory school for an elite, aristocratic group of individualists. Rather than being trained in the ways of a profession, students were to be immersed in the traditional learning of literature, language, and art. . . . [T]he purpose of the English teacher was to cultivate the exceptional students, the geniuses, and, at the most, to tolerate all others" (71–72). It is no wonder that, coming from this perspective, Middlebrook would heap scorn on a program designed to prepare all students. Literature, for Middlebrook, testifies to the sanctity of the individual and the private creative act; the Basic Communications course saw writing, like language itself, as something inherently shared, something social and public, something political.

Sadly, in "The Basic Communications Course Reconsidered," wherein Sorenson responds to Middlebrook's essay, Sorenson distances himself from even the best innovations of the program (calling the Writing Clinic a "tragic semantic blunder"), declares himself to have been unsatisfied in both Communications programs he collaborated in, vaguely blames the downfall of the program on "reasons which Mr. Middlebrook wisely surmised" (325), and asserts that he has discovered a new focus on "Reading" to be the answer. Sorenson criticizes Middlebrook for mocking without offering real solutions and defends the experimental spirit of the program; however, the implicit charge of being a philistine who does not recognize the value of literature was too much for Sorenson. It is creepy how effective Middlebrook's literary peer pressure was. Licking his wounds, Sorenson writes, "I should like Mr. Middlebrook to know that I have taken special pains to study what real writers do and how they work, having been married to one for a long time and having the advantage of a good many literary friends along with the profound love and respect for literature which caused me to choose my particular field for a life's work" (327). Sorenson does not even count himself among real writers because he does not write in a literary mode.

To bump up his upper crust English credentials, Sorenson attacks the "Speech men," ostensibly including those from the Communications department with whom he ran communications skills programs. He refers to training in persuasive speaking, a staple of Speech and Communications as the

"I-tell-'em attitude." "Reading," of course, signals a return to appreciating literature as the central purpose of English departments, or, at the very least, a signal that other communication skills should be taught by first seeing the examples of the great masters.

> Perhaps the "I-tell-'em" program is all right for Michigan, or even for the West. But here in the South [Sorenson has moved to Alabama] one gets a new point of view. I understand now why the University of Florida program is based upon Reading. We know down here that we don't yet know it all and that we seriously need this basic tool of communication. (327)

Sorenson writes in 1949. How interesting that Sorenson makes this argument about the purposes of writing instruction—persuasion in Michigan and Denver, reading in Florida and Alabama—into a new War Between the States. I have lived most of my life in North Carolina and Texas, but, nevertheless, for me, this bizarre turn in Sorenson's essay only underlines the reactionary nature of this movement to tear apart the collaboration between English and Communications.[1]

The dominance of literary aesthetics, the same "profound love and respect for literature" that sent Sorenson into retreat, helped to destroy the emphasis on general communication skills that marked the Basic Communications Course. Sharon Crowley writes, "Despite the intellectual excitement they briefly generated . . . communication skills courses were moribund in English departments by 1960. They were killed by literary scholars, who succeeded in returning instruction in the first-year composition course to the Arnoldian humanist foundation that had been its stock-in-trade since the late nineteenth-century" (2004:6).

While I obviously find this to be a wrong turn in the history of writing instruction, I do not mean to suggest that the General Communications course as deployed at University of Denver is the course we need today. It had its problems. For instance, Berlin says that "Denver fell victim to the 'life adjustment' emphasis that appeared after World War II" (100). "Life adjustment" refers to a movement that replaced some traditionally academic subjects with studies like home economics, leisure, physical education, and psychological health in the interest of creating good citizens, good spouses, good workers, and so on (Kleibard 1982:57). He cites Arthur N. Applebee, who called the "life adjustment" emphasis a departure from the "traditional concern of progressive education with the continuing improvement of both the individual and society" (Applebee 144). In other words, given the notions of what it meant to be a good citizen, spouse, and worker at the time, better integration might have meant, effectively, not mental health but conformity to a repressive culture. Also, the life adjustment movement gained an anti-intellectual reputation by questioning the value of traditional academic subjects. There is no reason, however, that a current notion of cross-disciplinary and even psychological integration needs to support "life adjustment" in the mode of the 1940s. The idea of writing as a public, social act once again has purchase in English departments due to the growth of the Rhetoric and Composition specialization. Unfortunately, the division between so-called rhetorical and so-called literary writing still characterizes much of the thought about first-year writing. For instance, in the Dallas-Fort Worth area, where I taught until recently, the universities discourage the assigning of literature in composition courses while the community colleges commonly use literature as part of a traditional modes-of-discourse approach to writing instruction. Perhaps the word "integration" could today serve as a slogan for overcoming the false oppositions and disciplinary boundaries that stand in the way of the ability of first-year programs to teach the whole person: composition/literature, private/public, English/Communications, and so on.

"The Posteverything Generation"

I hope you have found this little excursus into the history of writing instruction in the United States more interesting than did my students in Advanced Composition for Teachers. I still cannot say conclusively why they put up resistance throughout our reading of Berlin. Was it only because of his dry writing style—burdened as it is with long lists of necessary-but-not-necessarily-relatable supporting examples? Or was it also because the happy ending of the story rings false twenty years later? Even if Berlin tried to make the narrative more cinematic, even if he made it overly flashy like the Broadway production of *Les Miserables*, we would still know what comes next: in *Les Miserables*, the guillotine; in writing instruction, the ramping up of counterproductive forms of assessment. Writing instruction at the college level is still far from what it should be, and I have yet to meet a writing instructor who believes increasing the pressure for assessment will make things better.

Of course, the students of my course will be teaching in public elementary, middle, and high schools, schools with curricula sanctioned by No Child Left Behind that still insist upon a detestably limited vision of writing and communication, typified and enforced by the five paragraph essay.

I think we all sighed in relief when we had finished reading Berlin together, but even after I knew *Rhetoric and Reality* had fallen flat, I continued trying to get them to see why I find its narrative so important now. One strategy was returning to my misgivings about the movie *Freedom Writers* and their summation of its values, "Teaching is a passion not a profession." I gave a little speech along these lines: "Are these movies an alibi for not doing anything as a nation to fix our schools? Along with all of those good morals about teaching, are we also being told that only a heroic teacher can make education work? This teacher-hero arrives at a site of failure with little or no training and makes a difference in the lives of her students not by changing the system but by becoming an exception. For instance, Gruwell is allowed to teach upper-level courses, despite her inexperience and against the objections of our tenured villains, so that she can keep working with the same students. As audience members, we are happy for these students who won't lose hope in education as long as they have this teacher. Do we feel an equal regret for the incoming class that now will not encounter our hero? Not if the narrative has its way. Gruwell's new gang is formed *across* racial lines, but it still excludes. Only a small group can get into Gruwell's educational lifeboat, and it is too bad for the rest. And what of our educational Titanic? I think we should be concerned about the narrative device that pits the untrained new teacher-hero against the tenured cynics. Doesn't this prepare young movie goers to accept the political argument that the problem with our educational system is tenured teachers who don't care, that teacher's unions are the problem, that further professionalizing teachers with fair pay and adequate training would be throwing good money after bad? Sure, teachers should love their students, but is it bad of them to want to be able to support their families as well? Why can't teaching be a passion *and* a profession?"

Given the discomfort that had been in the room due to my excitement about Berlin and their lack of interest, I was nervous about how they would respond. Part of me, though, wanted a confrontation that would support my hypothesis that their dislike of Berlin was primarily a matter of politics. I perversely wanted them to take the side of *Freedom Writers* against me and my hostility to the ideology of the individual. Yet, my future teachers responded that they only meant teaching wasn't a profession in the sense that it didn't pay like other professions; if you go into teaching for the money, you must be a fool. Your commitment to your subject and your students has to carry you through rather than the financial rewards.

The earnestness of this group reflects a trend I have noticed in the last few years. In fact, I have to admit that the relative lack of cynical attitude in my recent students, especially here in the Pacific Northwest, has left me a little disoriented. As it turns out, I'm not sure whether the ideology of individualism or a pessimism about collective action are much of a stumbling block at all with these students. These students collaborate admirably in peer critique groups and on projects. Largely, they prefer to work together. Significantly, they do not have to be convinced that writing matters in the workplace and in other areas of life. While it comes from a different region, I recognized my students in this passage from Nicholas Handler (2007), the winner of the *New York Times* magazine's College Essay Contest:

> How do we rebel against parents that sometimes seem to want revolution more than we do? We don't. We rebel by not rebelling. We wear the defunct masks of protest and moral outrage, but the real energy in campus activism is on the Internet, with websites like moveon.org. It is in the rapidly developing ability to communicate ideas and frustration in chatrooms instead of on the streets, and channel them into nationwide projects striving earnestly for moderate and peaceful change: we are the generation of Students Taking Action Now Darfur; we are the Rock the Vote generation; the generation of letter-writing campaigns and public interest lobbies; the alternative energy generation.

Handler concludes by saying: "Perhaps when our parents finally stop pointing out the things that we are not, the stories that we do not write, they will see the threads of our narrative begin to come together; they will see that behind our pastiche, the post generation speaks in a language that does make sense. We are writing a revolution. We are just putting it in our own words." Maybe there is reason to accept what Handler says about his age group, that they are capable of making new narratives that can bring about much-needed change. They have always been on the Internet. They have always been hooked up. They are wired together, wired for collective action. It is easy to recognize the flip side of this generational togetherness; it must make feeling ostracized by your peers that much more painful, whether this exclusion is real or imagined. Of course, this does not begin to explain what happened at Virginia Tech.

Handler's essay gave me pause about the pessimism I often have about the future place and character of writing instruction. After all, the narrative of the teacher hero as told in *Freedom Writers* does not just demean experienced teachers. It also testifies to the power of the classroom to teach more than just skills and the power of writing, especially, to address social ills. The *New York Times* essay contest that Handler won asked writers to respond to Rick Perlstein's essay, "What's the Matter with College," which bemoans the fact that college campuses no longer have a central role in U.S. political culture due to a lack of student activism. Entitled "The Posteverything Generation," Handler's essay is, in part, a reflection on postmodernism. I don't know if my students feel a Lyotardian "incredulity to metanarratives" (xxiv–xxv), but I haven't failed to notice a new incredulity at my sometimes-negative humor. They don't seem to share the same brand of cynicism that characterizes my Generation X. Maybe that is because they are genuinely optimistic and believe that the global and local problems that seem so insurmountable to me can be managed. Few of them seem to recognize that my ironic jokes betray a real, if somewhat disappointed, sense of political hope. Or maybe they just recognize what I should have sooner: being earnest at heart does not justify being bitter out loud (like Perlstein's essay). If my students can find reasons to be encouraged, I pledge not to discourage them. Among other things, for me, this means trying to find other ways to be funny. (I'll keep you posted.)

In her song, "The Dream Before (for Walter Benjamin)," Laurie Anderson has something to tell us about the relationship between narrative and history:

> Hansel and Gretel are alive and well, and they're living in Berlin. She is a cocktail waitress. He had a part in a Fassbinder film. And they sit around at night now drinking schnapps and gin. And she says: "Hansel, you're really bringing me down." And he says: "Gretel, you can really be a bitch." He says: "I've wasted my life on our stupid legend. When my one and only love was the wicked witch. She said, "What is history?" And he said: "History is an angel being blown backwards into the future." He said, "History is a pile of debris. And the angel wants to go back and fix things, to repair the things that have been broken. But there is a storm blowing from Paradise. And the storm keeps blowing the angel backwards into the future. And this storm, this storm is called Progress."

Hansel and Gretel live in a narrative told by others. Wracked by regret and resentment, Hansel can't get out of his cups long enough to retell the story for himself. There are things to be done other than blaming Gretel. Even though the Basic Communications Course fell into debris, writing teachers managed to retrieve some of its valuable parts as they were blown backwards into the future by the "Winds of Change." More authentic assignments. Writing centers and peer tutoring. More focus on processes of writing. Less obsession with class-based norms of surface correctness. An awareness that, in addition to reporting, writing helps us to make meaning and negotiate our places in the world. It is too easy, though, to regard all of the changes that have occurred as "progress" in the sense of beneficial development. The winds have ripped rhetoric in two with a pointless division between Communications and English. "Progress" is giving us a distracting rather than clarifying focus on efficiency and assessment.

It is too much to blame the Virginia Tech Massacre on these events. Yet, these institutional dysfunctions distract us from what could be accomplished in integrated first-year programs. If these programs function well, they can help students transition into the university and form learning communities that are also effective support networks. My recent students have inspired me to do what I can to contribute in any small way to the continual reshaping of first-year programs and, with humility, to not think too small, either about writing or about how I might be able to contribute to its instruction. But I am not trying to write myself into this story as another teacher-hero. In the narrative I want to shape, some "we" enacts a social process. Maybe one of the best things we can do to encourage college students to engage in activism is to engage in a little bit ourselves, to seek out ways that can revitalize universities through collaborations that cut across disciplines and specialties. I think if we stretch, we may be able to reach back to discover more of value to such an enterprise among the discards of the Basic Communications Course, at the very least to be inspired by its attitude of innovation.

Note

1. See Crowley, "Communication Skills and a Brief Rapprochement of Rhetoricians" for more discussion of opportunities missed for collaboration between rhetoricians separated by university structure, especially English vs. Speech/Communications.

References

Berlin, James. 1987. *Rhetoric and Reality: Writing Instruction in American Colleges, 1900–1985*. Carbondale: Southern Illinois University Press.
Crowley, Sharon. 2004. "Communication Skills and a Brief Rapprochement of Rhetoricians." *Rhetoric Society Quarterly* 34 (1): 89–103.
Davidson, Levette J., and Frederick Sorensen. 1946. "The Basic Communications Course." *College English* 8 (2): 83–86.
Freedom Writers. Dir. Richard LaGravenese. Perf. Hillary Swank. 2007. DVD. Paramount.
Handler, Nicholas. 2007. "The Posteverything Generation." *New York Times* (November 2). essay.blogs.nytimes.com/2007/09/27/the-college-pastiche.
Kliebard, Herbert M. 1982. "Education at the Turn of the Century: A Crucible for Curriculum Change." *Educational Researcher* 11 (1): 16–24.
Lindemann, Erika. 2001. *A Rhetoric for Writing Teachers*. Oxford and New York: Oxford University Press.
Middlebrook, Samuel. 1947. "English I in Cellophane." *College English* 9 (3): 140–43.
Postman, N., and C. Weingartner. 1969. *Teaching as a Subversive Activity*. New York: Dell Publishing.
Sorenson, Frederick. 1949. "The Basic Communications Course Reconsidered." *College English* 10 (6): 324–28.

CHAPTER
Ten

THERE IS AN UNKNOWN ON CAMPUS:
From Normative to Performative Violence in Academia[1]

Patricia Mooney Nickel

> Was he free? Was he happy? The question is absurd:
> Had anything been wrong, we should certainly have heard.
>
> —W. H. Auden

For many, academic life is regarded as known and knowing in every last aspect except for that which would be the basis for transformation. Like W. H. Auden's (1940) anonymous subject in *The Unknown Citizen*, who is known administratively and thus according to predetermined categories of normality, the unknown on campus is treated by those who refuse to think otherwise either as an absurdity or as a basis for authoritative intervention. The inaudible knowledge inherent to everyday life on campus is rendered unknowable by an administrative ontology and methodological logic that cannot withstand its existence. Normative attempts to eliminate through the quest for a performative unknown what we know as our lived experience on campus are refusals to acknowledge those experiences which cannot be known without necessitating change.

This essay is constructed of my observations at Virginia Tech and elsewhere in academia, from which I draw the conclusion that the palpable administrative anxiety in the aftermath of the Virginia Tech Massacre was misdirected toward capture of the unknown, thereby further embedding a quiet culture of normative violence endemic to academia at the expense of a recognition of the transformative potential of vulnerability (Butler 2006). My first observation is that the strident chorus of "we are Hokies, we will prevail" was a pressurized ontological fiction that obfuscated the realization that something had changed. My second, and contradictory, observation is that a parallel public release of previously unknown emotions stemmed from the fact that there was already something wrong. My third observation is that from the intersection of these two confused releases, one of defiance of the unknown and one of confession of the unknown, emerged a performative violence which demonstrates how expressions of pain resulting *from* the ontology of academia are subjugated to expressions of pain resulting from damage done *to* the ontology of academia.

Observation One: We are Hokies, We Will Prevail

Stop all the clocks

—W. H. Auden

The days and weeks following the "Massacre at Virginia Tech" on April 16, 2007, seemed to me to be lived under the pressure of an ontological fiction imposed by the media, the Virginia Tech administration, and the "Hokie Nation." By ontological fiction I mean that, despite the complete violence done to "the normal" there was an immediate attempt to return to something that no longer existed, if it ever did exist. The imposition began when, at about 11 AM on April 16, 2007, the local media reported first "several" people shot dead, then as many as seventeen shot dead, then over twenty shot dead, all under the stylized graphic "The Tragedy at Virginia Tech." The national media quickly contributed the escalated title "The Massacre at Virginia Tech" which, we learned, was qualified by thirty-two confirmed deaths. Finally, less than a week later, we were given our story: this is not part of "our" reality of nationhood and family, but an isolated and exogenous accident over which "we will prevail." In the following days and weeks prevailing would become the administratively determined endpoint of all thinking, feeling, and action.

Prior to notifying faculty and students about how the academic semester would proceed, the Virginia Tech administration began the process of notifying "Multiple Recipients" of how "our" story would proceed. On Friday, April 20, 2007, President Charles Steger sent an e-mail that hurriedly began the process of "ontological stabilization" (Luke 1999). The e-mail, to

"Multiple Recipients" (an odd addressee given the intimate tone) was titled "We Will Prevail" and concluded: In closing, I can only echo a few of the stirring words of Nikki Giovanni: "Through all our sadness . . . we will prevail."

To criticize this quick capture and release of what would become "our" story is not to criticize Nikki Giovanni's Convocation Address, delivered on April 17, 2007. Indeed, the very fact that she wrote these words—her own words—at what could only have been a deeply sad moment (Seung-Hui Cho was a student in Giovanni's classroom and she had previously expressed concern about him) and, while the world watched, spoke them the day following The Massacre was not only an act of personal fortitude, but also of kindness. There can be no doubt that when she delivered her Address it was comforting to many people in ways that we may not understand. What I am concerned with is the very specific performative trajectory of her words afterwards. The phrase, now divorced from its context and therefore no longer an Address, quickly spread in various incarnations:

- On Saturday, April 21, President Steger closed an e-mail with: We will prevail . . . we are Hokies!
- On Sunday, April 22, Provost Mark McNamee repeated by e-mail: We are Virginia Tech. We will prevail.
- On April 22, an unsigned e-mail sent from Virginia.Tech.news@vt.edu, repeated: We are Virginia Tech. We will prevail.
- On April 22, The Student Leadership of Hokies United repeated: As a community, we have the strength to prevail.
- On April 23, Larry Hincker, Associate Vice President for University Relations, repeated by e-mail: We are Hokies. We will prevail.
- On Tuesday, April 24, Larry Hincker repeated by e-mail: Thank you for your continued strength and resolve. We are Hokies. We will prevail.
- On Thursday, April 26, President Steger repeated by e-mail: We are the Virginia Tech family, and we will prevail. But along the way, each of us will have good days and bad days. So, let's be sensitive to each other's needs and take care of one another. I'm proud of all of you. We will prevail.

The "Hokie Nation" is located in Blacksburg, Virginia. Blacksburg is a small town and even if one did not check their e-mail for the official Virginia Tech message of reality, eventually one had to eat. Within days one could observe joggers in their tragedy uniform, a maroon T-shirt[2] with "We Will Prevail" emblazoned on the back. Reminiscent of football Saturdays, "We Are Hokies/We Will Prevail" appeared in bright orange letters on the back windows of passing vehicles. The dry cleaners on Main Street changed their marquee to read, "We Will Prevail." The local Kroger supermarket parking lot was plastered with leftover bright orange, jagged-edged "Sale!" signs on which someone had used the clearance marker to declare "We Are Hokies! We Will Prevail!" One began to hope that one's mind would prevail over the now thoughtless message of 99-cent prevalence, reminiscent of the days following 9/11, sloganeered with "These colors don't run."

As more and more "Hokies" began to transmit this unified "message," interpretation and transformation seemed almost to be reserved for the grief elite, who were charged with official sense-making and impression management. Giovanni's Address became susceptible to fast capitalism's tendency to "degrade every concept quickly, celebrating its novelty and then dispensing it to name things that live as a parody of what concept was meant to criticize" (Agger 1989b:84). "The Hokie Nation" was "swallowed by its slogans" (Agger 1989b:83). As the phrase was increasingly divorced from its passionate Address on April 17 and increasingly conflated with administrative e-mails, it became more and more unthinkable to disagree with the prevalence of the We. Yet, in the impersonal chorus of strident determination, it was difficult to know what it was that we were meant to prevail over. In the days following Giovanni's Address it sometimes felt as though the phrase "We will prevail!!" was taking on a competitive tone as it took on more exclamation points. As a small town where Saturday mornings frequently involved getting hyped up on football and chugging beer at parking lot tailgate parties where grown *women* disempowered themselves in "Hokie Girl" T-shirts, Blacksburg could seem like an aggressive place before The Massacre; after The Massacre, there were times when the words "we will prevail" began to sound more like "we will conquer." I became unsure of what prevailing even meant or whom or what I was to prevail *over*. With no enemy other than the denial of the ontological certitude that was the Hokie Nation united without exception, suffering seemed to me to be a bit more realistic as a course of action following a massacre. I certainly did not want to rush out and buy myself a new "We Will Prevail" massacre T-shirt that would label my body as belonging to this "We," label the event as something immediately comprehensible, and also convey my thoughts on the event as being part of one singular and sovereign voice shared by me, the President of Virginia Tech, Hokie Girls, and the local Kroger store. Even if I wanted to be "normal," purchasing a T-shirt would have been difficult given that the stores were overcrowded with media personalities shopping for orange and maroon Hokie Massacre souvenirs, which quickly sold out.

I was not sure that those who had so quickly transformed Giovanni's Address into a slogan had thought things through. Not that they were given the opportunity to do so; no one was more pressured to *do some-*

thing than the Virginia Tech administration and it is not hard to imagine that they grasped at the poetic as some way to humanize their response to immediate demands for information and answers. My hesitance can only be considered a luxury to those who suffered the violence of the wholly unnecessary consumptive speed of the media. Note well that the Virginia Tech administration was sending these e-mails on Saturdays and Sundays, a time that we would have hoped that they could have been resting; instead, they clearly had not slept for days and seemed to be cracking under the pressure of the media's demand for something new to report; in a slower world, one press conference per day surely would have sufficed. Instead, as in our academic careers, producing *anything* that stabilized, was visible, and contributed to national rankings, was valued over that which was composed of thoughtful consideration, local circulation, and resulting in transformation brought forth by the destabilization of the fictitious image that everything is okay.

I want to make clear that I think that in their efforts to respond, the Virginia Tech administration did as well as any university administration could have been expected to and probably even better than most. This is not to say that they did everything right, I think that they did a lot of things wrong, but that in the current academic environment *no one possibly could have*. I remember quite clearly that I was sincerely afraid to speak to the media, even to send an e-mail to a friend, because every mistake made at Virginia Tech was at a global premium. It is nearly impossible to explain the pressure of the media presence in Blacksburg; their monstrous gaping cameras were everywhere and everywhere one went one had to sidestep them. One of my former students living in the Washington, D.C., area e-mailed me to tell me that he had seen me on the news and was glad to see that I was alright. I never consented to being on camera and, more importantly, I never walked in front of a *visible* camera. From my perspective, the media attention was not at all comforting and neither were the media personalities. I found the gaze oppressive and, as Foucault (1995) would argue, disciplinary. I can only guess that Virginia Tech's administration must have felt something of a similar resentment, though it would likely be taboo for them to say so. It was only a few hours after the shootings that they were forced in front of the camera; the world having come to a halt in Blacksburg and my classes cancelled, I had the momentary luxury of solitary space for processing what had happened before carefully constructing e-mails to my students; Virginia Tech President Charles Steger had no such luxury, forced into a room with journalists eager to make their big break by breaking him. A friend said to me on April 26 that he had just seen Steger and that he looked as though he had "aged ten years in ten days." It was callous and calculating for the media to treat this person as an administrative machine rather than as a suffering human being who was horrified by the murder of thirty-two of his students and the suicide of another. Perhaps it was his job to respond to overwhelming demands for information and perhaps this is precisely the problem. Fast capitalism is often cruel in its demands for instantaneous processing under pressure, leaving no time to find, let alone convey, the full humanity of a situation. I thus make the following observations not of a specific individual, but rather of the *environment* that has resulted in the demand that they comply with this unnecessary administrative glut, thereby producing an administration of sense-making.

Within the cacophony of media judgment, Operation Hokie Nation Stabilization seemed to be aimed at getting "our" story straight. On April 21, 2007, Hincker sent to "Multiple Recipients" the official bullets:

———Original Message———
From: Unirel@vt.edu [mailto:Unirel@vt.edu]
Sent: Saturday, April 21, 2007 8:27 pm
To: Multiple Recipients
Subject: Thoughts on responding to interview requests

April 21, 2007

Dear Colleagues,

When we reassemble on Monday, April 23, discussions pertaining to last week's tragic events are sure to take place between and among students and faculty. It is our hope that these conversations will facilitate the healing process when classes resume. At the same time, we also expect the media to again be on campus, and many of you have asked how to respond to them. So that everyone feels comfortable participating in the conversations they choose to have, here are some general guidelines about the media, and information on our own communications policies.

First, concerning the continuing media presence on our campus:

Media are never allowed in the classrooms without faculty permission. Academic buildings, normally open to the public, will be off-limits to the media. Notices have been posted on all academic buildings stating this rule. In addition, the big satellite trucks we saw last week will no longer be allowed.

However, ours is an open campus and the press will still be present. Reporters on campus may ask to interview you. If you are approached, it is entirely up to you if you want to speak them. Feel free to say, "Thanks, but no thanks." But, keep in mind that the majority of the media are genuinely concerned about the Virginia Tech community and want to let our many supporters know how we are coping with last week's events.

Next, I want to share with you the messages we think are important to convey. These messages are part of Virginia Tech's continuing efforts to support one another as our community regroups to grieve, heal and move forward:

1. We will not be defined by this event.

a. First, as an academic family we will endeavour to analyze, learn and, ultimately, come to some understanding of the event. Our Principles of Community remain our values.

b. Virginia Tech—our traditions, community, history, and promising future—will prevail. Our motto Ut Prosim (That I May Serve) underscores our spirit.

c. Finally, everything we do as we move forward will commemorate, honor, and respect the numerous individuals affected by this tragic event.

2. Invent the Future

"Invent the Future" captures our role and spirit as a world-renowned research institution. Nothing in the events of last week will alter who we are and what we represent. When classes resume, our academic excellence, the commitment and talent of our students, and our clear role in shaping a positive future for the world will again be apparent. Hokies are, and always will, embody learning, discovery and engagement.

3. Embrace the Virginia Tech Family

a. We are a unique, special family—more enduring and closer to one another than a typical university community.

b. Assisting the families and friends of those injured and bereaved is our focus. We are also committed to the assistance and support of one another.

c. We will nurture the legacy of the 32 Virginia Tech family members we lost. The Virginia Tech family will celebrate their lives and accomplishments. Our memorials to them, both public and private, will reflect those sentiments.

It is also our intention to do whatever we can to promote the healing process within our community. We consider our communications to be a critical element of that process. We are regaining control of the Virginia Tech reputation and legacy, and believe these messages are crucial to accomplishing that goal.

Please contact us with any questions or concerns you may have. We want you to have everything you need to promote constructive, healing conversations among all the constituencies of our community.

We are Virginia Tech. We will prevail.

Lawrence G. Hincker
Associate Vice President, University Relations

The message clearly states that I am not to be defined by this event, but apparently I *am* to be defined by Virginia Tech's AVP of University Relations. Hincker's directive on how we were to publicly make sense of The Massacre put pressure on "Multiple Readers" to declare his version of what exists in Blacksburg as true and unchangeable. The statement is a political declaration, "[O]ur analysis of what 'exists,' is also, immediately political" (Passavant 2004:17). Thus, Hincker's statement that "Nothing in the events of last week will alter who we are and what we represent" is not only obviously inaccurate, it is distinctly political (see Agger [2007] on the politics of the shootings). The murder of thirty-two students on our campus *should* have instigated a transformation of "who we are" and "what we represent." We could have done something as simple as declaring that we were now a university staunchly opposed to violence. As Butler (2006) conveyed in *Precarious Life*, violence and our reaction to it are not as simple as Hincker's message insists that they are:

> Perhaps, rather, one mourns when one accepts that by the loss one undergoes one will be changed, possibly for ever. Perhaps mourning has

to do with agreeing to undergo a transformation (perhaps one should say submitting to a transformation) the full result of which one cannot know in advance. There is losing, as we know, but there is also the transformative effect of loss, and this latter *cannot be charted or planned*. One can try to choose it, but it may be that this experience of transformation deconstitutes this choice at some level. (21, *my emphasis*)

In stark contrast to Butler's (2006) recognition of violent loss as a source of political transformation, Hincker's directive tells us that the stabilizing narrative (damage control) is how we ought to construct our mourning process: "These messages are part of Virginia Tech's continuing efforts to support one another as our community regroups to grieve, heal and move forward." Yet, the official message is clearly not one of grief, but of control: please remove yourself from your responses to the media and convey the official (authorless) response. This is distinctly antitransformational, as Agger (1989b) explains: "Domination not only resists its authorization but also defies other versions of it" (82). Hincker's version of what I experienced in Blacksburg is wrong, but it is the legitimated and official version, which discourages me from deeper reflection. While I do think that in countless ways Virginia Tech should be proud, there are other *unknown* versions of how life at Virginia Tech was experienced in the year leading up to The Massacre. April 16, 2007, was not the first, but the fourth Monday of the 2006–2007 academic year that classes had been cancelled due to the threat of violence on campus. By the time that Cho took his first victim I had already received nearly a dozen e-mails in fewer than a dozen months warning me variously of a gunman on campus, multiple bomb threats to the building in which I was teaching, and violent physical attacks on campus.

The myth of the "unique Virginia Tech Family," which presumably included me, the reader of the message, is itself a violent exclusion (see Butler 2004). Hincker asks us to communicate to the media that we will *unconditionally* "Embrace the Virginia Tech Family.... We are a unique, special family—more enduring and closer to one another than a typical university community." Such a message must be suffocating for anyone who feels exceptional in relationship to the Hokie Nation, as Cho likely did. The identification of Virginia Tech as unique among university communities, especially on the issue of familial relations, could not be further from the truth for those who were reading these messages as an insistence that *what they were experiencing* was wrong and thus they must not belong. The message is that one must accept the myth of the Hokie Nation or be excluded.

Not only was our sense of what existed and what would exist prescripted, but we were assured that "We are regaining control of the Virginia

Tech reputation and legacy, and believe these messages are crucial to accomplishing that goal." One might read this statement as "we are protecting your investment." The very idea of *regaining control of reputation and legacy* as a goal in April 2007 is outrageous and, despite the ubiquitous black and maroon ribbon in Blacksburg, which we were told symbolizes "remembrance," Hincker's message is one of *forgetting*, not the victims, but our actual transformative experience as a result of this loss. As Butler (2006) writes, "Perhaps we can say that grief contains the possibility of apprehending a mode of dispossession that is fundamental to who I am.... If I do not always know what it is in another person that I have lost, it may be that this sphere of dispossession is precisely the one that exposes my unknowingness, the unconscious imprint of my primary sociality. Can this insight lead to a normative reorientation for politics?" (28). If we had been willing to let go of who "We" supposedly were as "Hokies," perhaps we would have responded with insight rather than insistence.

Butler (2004) asks "what forms of community have been created, and through what violences and exclusions have they been created?" (225). Such a question can hardly be dismissed when one considers that the Hokie reaction to The Massacre was to clearly delineate the boundaries of the Hokie Nation, the Hokie Family, and the Hokie Reputation: "We will not be defined by this event.... Our Principles of Community remain our values.... Virginia Tech—our traditions, community, history, and promising future—will prevail.... Nothing in the events of last week will alter who we are and what we represent.... We are a unique, special family—more enduring and closer to one another than a typical university community." Such "logics of exclusion" are fictional, "an image reinforced by the negative image of the marginals who are excluded from it ... the marginals are in fact internal to the bourgeois system ... the purity of society is already contaminated by a blight it would prefer, for its own protection, to consider as external" (Ryan 1982:127). The continual reassertion of the image of the Hokie Nation, a family united and unique, seemed to be an attempt to consider not only Cho, but *all* violence and suffering as something external not only to Virginia Tech, but to the idyllic image of academia.

Observation Two: Virginia Tech's Other Tragedy: Everyday Life Shoots Through

> The consul banged the table and said,
> "If you've got no passport you're officially dead."
>
> —W. H. Auden

The pressure to prevail was intense, but so was the pressure to crack. As of April 16, 2007, it was acceptable to have an emotional breakdown on the Virginia Tech campus. Indeed, tears were not only acceptable, they were encouraged:

Thursday, April 26, 2007

Dear Colleagues,

Although classes are back in session and we are all trying very hard to move forward, we are also coming to realize that it will take a very long time for our university community to recover from the most traumatic event in our history. On the surface, things may seem normal, but they're not. Even those among us who seem to be coping well are often struggling internally.

So, I want to encourage everyone to please talk with one of the counselors who are available—if only for a few minutes. If you personally don't feel the need to speak with a counselor, you still may find it helpful to spend a few minutes talking about ways you can help co-workers, students, and even your family members, who may be having a difficult time. Information about the counseling services are available can be found at the bottom of this note. Most of all, be assured that the counseling sessions are completely confidential.

We are the Virginia Tech family, and we will prevail. But along the way, each of us will have good days and bad days. So, let's be sensitive to each other's needs and take care of one another. I'm proud of all of you. We will prevail.

Sincerely,
Charles W. Steger

Counseling Information

For confidential access to telephone counseling or referral to a local counselor for private visits, faculty and staff can contact ValueOptions at 1-866-725-0602 anytime, 24 hours a day.

Human Resources has compiled a number of informational and support resources which remain available to our entire community at www.hr.vt.edu/supportresources

> Human Resources will continue to coordinate counselor availability for department or workgroup meetings. Contact 231-7772 for more information.
>
> Counselors and Human Resources representatives will continue to be available for walk-in visits on the third floor of Squires Student Center—this Saturday (April 28) from 10 a.m. to 3 p.m., and Monday through Friday from 8 a.m. to 5 p.m.

The Virginia Tech administration seemed to be saying that no expression of pain was unacceptable (although, Hincker's April 21 e-mail, "Thoughts on responding to interview requests," seemed to contradict this). Suddenly I heard from varying Virginia Tech faculty members about heartbreak, stress, guilt, rage, difficulties sleeping, financial troubles, overmedication, alcoholism, extramarital affairs, fatigue, and career suicide; none of these expressions of pain were specifically related to the shootings, but were instead preexisting—only the permission to discuss them was new. I also heard from Hokies a concern not previously expressed; this is not to say that Hokies were not previously warm—many often were—but that in the days and weeks following The Massacre, feelings that previously went unexpressed suddenly were released. This was not the currency-concern of the national media personalities reporting on The Massacre, which quickly faded when the line for a cappuccino or t-shirts was long. It was not the marketing concern of the visiting volunteers who walked through coffee shops interrupting intimate conversations between friends with marketing offers for free T-shirts, CDs, and website addresses. The concern that I observed was a local and interpersonal, yet latent, warmness that previously had been suppressed by "professionalism" and "aspiration." Now, suddenly, professionalism and aspiration did not exclude genuine concern for one another.

There were moments of lucidity among those who had prior to the shootings suffered the everyday tragedy of Virginia Tech and countless other universities. It was not that the shootings had necessarily made anything clearer, but that it was now momentarily acceptable for the inaudible to become audible. There were audible signs of stress, audible signs of pain, audible signs of addiction: the unspeakable of academia was suddenly speakable. Many of the Virginia Tech faculty members who spoke with me in the days following the shootings shared with me deeply painful and moving stories, but very few of these stories were "about" the shootings. Instead, these stories, some of which were as many as ten years old, were about the pain that faculty had experienced in relationship to the everyday violence of campus life in the United States. The myth of the Hokie Nation, shared by a chorus of universities declaring "We are all Hokies today," seemed finally to have given way to the reality of everyday life in academia; with thirty-three dead bodies on campus people seemed no longer willing to tell the "right" story.

Academia normally suppresses these emotions and the academic career informally forbids them. In 2005, during my Ph.D. program in Texas, I heard a story about a junior professor who began crying during class. She was discussed as weak, unintelligent, unfit for the classroom, and was, according to the violent gossip that surrounded this event, brutally attacked in her evaluations. On April 23, 2007, as I went back into my classroom at Virginia Tech, I heard countless stories of faculty who began crying before, during, or after class. They were not discussed as weak and unfit for the classroom and their evaluation was now optional:

Wednesday, April 25, 2007

Dear Faculty Colleagues:

With the support of the colleges at every level, we are making good progress in resuming classes in a way that enables students to make good choices about how best to complete the semester. I appreciate the extra effort the faculty is making to adapt to this new set of policies. The response of the students in terms of both attendance and commitment is truly inspiring.

Not surprisingly, we are getting some questions. One set of questions revolves around student evaluations of teaching.

Normally, these are required. Under the circumstances, flexibility appears to be a reasonable approach. I think each faculty member should work with their department and decide if, when, and how to obtain student feedback. The students may want to let you know how much they appreciate your efforts and your dedication, so I encourage you to obtain feedback.

You may decide that a process other than the standard SPOT form is appropriate this semester, but the choice is yours. We will note officially that the Spring 2007 evaluation process is optional when considering all future actions associated with merit increases or the Promotion and Tenure process.

Best wishes for all you do.

Mark McNamee
University Provost

This message only highlights the way in which ranking and evaluation overtake everything in academia. In the midst of everything else, it was absolutely necessary to immediately determine how The Massacre would impact evaluation and promotion and tenure. Promotion and tenure and the associated numbers cannot be ignored no matter what the personal or public crisis. Promotion and tenure stay on everyone's mind all of the time. Not even the murder of thirty-two people on campus will put an end to the demand for absolutes in relation to promotion and tenure. Virginia Tech's administration of emotional turmoil in reaction to the shootings missed the point entirely, which is that administration was already in emotional turmoil. The preexisting anxiety surrounding evaluation was strong enough that a sudden unknown in relation to how we would be judged could not wait for a full two weeks after The Massacre before it had to be addressed. "We will note officially that the spring 2007 evaluation process is optional when considering all future actions associated with merit increases or the promotion and tenure process." Though, note well that "the choice is yours" is frequently academyspeak for "not doing so will count against you when someone else does" and "official" means that you will be judged, albeit informally.

I do not know why the junior professor in Texas began crying during class; she might have been tired, overwhelmed, or perhaps she knew someone who had been murdered. We are more likely as human beings to cry when we are stressed and sleep deprived and we are more likely to be stressed and sleep deprived when we work in an unforgiving academic system that attacks emotion, as it did the emotions of the junior professor in Texas who probably was a good instructor who just had a bad day. I also do not know why the professors at Virginia Tech began crying during class, but I do know that The Massacre brought a lot of emotions to the surface. Crying in the classroom may have been a reaction to The Massacre, but it also may have happened because in the days, weeks, or years *prior* to the shootings things, in Steger's words, "appeared normal on the surface, but they were not." All junior faculty members at Virginia Tech and every other research university in the United States are under pressure to "appear normal, even when they are not." A brief scan of the *Chronicle of Higher Education*'s "Careers" section will reveal countless articles and columns from Ms. Mentor (gag) about how to "appear normal" and anyone who wants tenure must act as though the system in which they find themselves is normal.

That the junior professor in Texas was so brutally attacked for having a bad day is reason for concern. Perhaps I also would have cried in my classroom at Virginia Tech if I did not have the knowledge gleaned in Texas that when a young female professor cries in the classroom her evaluations deem her unfit for academia and thus significantly and negatively impact her evaluation for promotion and tenure. I agree that an instructor regularly crying in the classroom probably is not a good thing; however, this misses the point, which is that academia makes a lot of junior faculty members want to cry—after years of investment in one goal academia seems incredibly high stakes; our time to either fail or succeed is short and competitive and there are no runners up; we are wholly and powerlessly dependent on often tenuous and confusing relationships with mentors whose estimations make and break careers; our career requires an enormous amount of personal sacrifice, often one's marriage and friendships, just to stay in the game. Though I was lucky enough to work with extraordinarily kind people and to like my job, I, like most junior faculty members I know, still worked seven days a week in Blacksburg, usually for twelve or more hours per day, perhaps for six or seven on the weekends; I already knew the rules of the game, I work fast, and yet I never caught up. I have heard that people eventually do catch up, but even if I had caught up, I likely would have worked this schedule anyway because there were bound to be two hundred or more unemployed Ph.D.s who wanted my job, which was a temporary contract that paid $45,000 for the 2006–2007 academic year, much of which had to be spent on resources that I needed in order to do my job, but that the university did not provide. Note well that academics still have it better than most people in the world and this is not to say that academic life is bad; it is not bad. I chose which of the twelve hours per day I wanted to work, I chose where I would work them, and I chose the work that I wanted to do, which was work that I enjoyed. That said, academia is not the ideal that we are asked to pretend it is specifically because the stakes are so *perceptibly* high.

Junior academics, and, I suspect, some senior academics, are daily confronted with the expectation that we pretend that we are experiencing academia as something other than what it is. On the one hand, we are expected to present an image of ourselves as working in serene institutions secluded from the calculated demands of the market. We are told that we are valued as scholars and teachers. On the other hand, we are expected to conform to a calculated overemphasis on marketing, promotion and tenure, evaluation, counting, performance, and other management instruments that are tools of control. Hincker's and McNamee's messages expose the inherent tensions that untenured faculty members are confronted with every day; they tell us that we are a family concerned with ideas while simultaneously, if subtly, reminding us that promotion and tenure still count and we must think about our evaluation because it could be the basis for our elimination from the "family." This is not working out well for anyone and it may be working out the worst for those who are coping with it (see Nickel and Eikenberry 2006).

Animate existence certainly is a critical prerequisite for all other experiences that we value, but the hierarchism that distinguishes between physical and intuitive violence eclipses that the day-to-day destruction of life takes place where life is our lived experience in the world. Steger's statement to the Virginia Tech community that "On the surface, things may seem normal, but they're not. Even those among us who seem to be coping well are often struggling internally" could have been honestly spoken on any campus in the United States at any point in the past ten years (or longer). The normality of academia screens that norms in academia are often violent. Indeed, those who are "coping" best may suffer the greatest violence, having so fully internalized the "normal" that they can no longer comprehend that there is an alternative. The reduction of space for thinking is politically problematic, a point recognized by Marcuse (1964): "In the society at large, the mental space for denial and reflection must first be re-created" (12). Yet, on campus, where supposedly we have mental space for denial and reflection, the immediate administrative reaction to things "not being normal" was to collapse the space for thinking under the weight of the Hokie Nation.

Observation Three: From Normative Violence to Performative Violence

> He was found by the Bureau of Statistics to be
> One against whom there was no official complaint.
>
> —W. H. Auden

Academic norms govern the expression of our personal reactions to the everyday experience of academia. When I observed the disciplining of the junior professor in Texas, who made the "mistake" of being visibly vulnerable, I quickly learned that such exposure takes place at great professional expense. I was thus somewhat startled when, if only temporarily, the boundaries of professional norms on the Virginia Tech campus following The Massacre shifted. The pain revealed by this shift is instructive. I did not know, though I may have suspected, that my colleagues were suffering at such a deep level prior to The Massacre and I did not know specifically because they were suffering the normative violence of the academic career which required them to perform as though the everyday life of the academic career were not shot through with normative fictions. Catherine Mills (2007) writes succinctly of Butler's conception of normative violence, "vulnerability—to violence, loss, and dissolution—requires that the question of the human be opened to reflection on normative violence" (133). It is specifically this brief *opening* of an alternative ontology based in the everyday experience of life in academia that the ontological fiction imposed by the media, the Virginia Tech administration, and the "Hokie Nation" prevailed over. Reflection was quickly overtaken by the "official reflection," by the barrage of e-mails demanding attention to new policies and requests for information, by the media presence, and by the fact that one still needed to publish because the tenure clock was still ticking.

A feminist reading of this situation helps us to understand the norms of everyday life in academia as being politically relevant. In his reading of Butler, Samuel A. Chambers (2007) argues that her conception of normative violence is a political theory that reveals the way in which norms *do* violence (44). As I have argued with Angela M. Eikenberry (2006), organizational life, including academia, disguises normative violence as a personal failure. Thus it is possible to frame the junior professor in Texas as a weak individual who is unable to cope rather than recognize that there is a systemic and politically relevant problem, which is that the system in which she finds herself subordinates the personal to the professional (Nickel and Eikenberry 2006:360). The personal internalization of blame, which, not always, but frequently ought to be attributed to the professional norms of academia, results in what Butler (2004) understands as normative violence, which I interpret to be the violence done by the internalization of norms that damage our lives.[3]

The understanding of how norms function as power has been extensively addressed by critical theorists, perhaps most explicitly by Foucault and Sheridan (1995). The disciplinary function of norms in academia has been criticized by Ben Agger (1989a, b, 1993, 1991) and Tim Luke (1999, 2005). In my reading, what is unique about Butler's contribution, especially in the case of the Virginia Tech Massacre, is that she challenges the hierarchy of *violence* in order to demonstrate that it is no less painful to suffer the violence of norms than it is to suffer the violence of "physical" pain: the suffering inherent to everyday life is no less violent than the suffering of *observable* bodily harm. Violence is not as simple as primary and secondary; as Chambers (2007) writes, normative violence "both facilitates typical, physical violence and simultaneously renders such violence invisible" (43).

It is helpful to understand Butler's conception of violence through the lens of Agger's (1993) feminist critique of the hierarchy of the valued over the valueless (production over reproduction). There is a hierarchy of pain at play in Blacksburg, and elsewhere, in which pain that is a reaction to the destruction of the "normal" is valued over pain that results from the norms themselves, Butler's normative violence. In other words, pain suffered as a *loss* of what exists is valued over pain suffered as the *continuation* of what exists, thus forestalling transformation. The administrative assertion of Hokie sovereignty assumed that expressions of pain resulting from damage done *to* the ontology of the Hokie Nation are considered legitimate and thus warrant action, while expressions of pain resulting *from* the ontology of the Hokie Nation, pain that would result in transformation, are illegitimate.

Accordingly, the *value* of grief was assumed to be measurable and instigated a process of assigning zeros and ones to our thoughts, stripping them of any value that did not fit the scale. On Saturday morning, July 7, 2007, I received an e-mail from Faculty/Staff Assessment Research on behalf of two Virginia Tech faculty members. The e-mail informed me that "In two days, you will receive an e-mail invitation to participate in an important survey of the emotional effects of the tragic April 16 events at Virginia Tech on students, staff, and faculty." The e-mail further informs the reader that their compliance with this request will:

- help guide service plans at Virginia Tech to target the counselling needs of students, staff, and faculty;
- to support an application for government financial assistance to expand counselling services at Virginia Tech for students, staff, and faculty; and
- and for data analysis/use by other Virginia Tech researchers in separate studies.

These objectives simply do not make sense together. The informed consent prefacing the survey states that there is an emotional risk associated with viewing the survey and that counseling services are available to those with insurance and a free clinic is available to those without insurance. This indicates that funding already is available and, if it is not, there are people in counseling clinics who are taking account of the demand for their services. If it were true that Virginia Tech needed this specific survey data in order to apply for funding then the task would not have been left to two researchers in need of Institutional Review Board (IRB) approval and the e-mail probably would not have included this last bullet about research. Surveying faculty, staff, and students about their anticipated counseling needs does not require IRB approval; IRB approval is required when the faculty, staff, and students are *denied the authority to anticipate their own needs* and when the research is invasive, ethically risky, and puts the subject at risk. If targeted funding were truly the point of the survey, the surveyors could simply ask, "Do you feel that you will need to use counseling services in the fall? Yes or no?" Do the researchers assume that they have the formula for determining without our *self-determined input* and yet with 93 percent certainty how many of us will be abnormal in 2007? Can they peer into our psyches in order to conquer the unknown number of mentally abnormal people on campus and the associated number of them who will see a counselor? Is this really a case of using any means necessary, even a survey deemed by its authors to be so potentially psychologically damaging that it is accompanied by information on how to obtain counseling? This level of risk—and of knowledge of our most personal thoughts—is necessary in order to apply for federal funding? It would be useful to know whether or not all of us managing to appear normal would have nixed a request for federal funding. Even the titles used are confused about this issue. Microsoft Internet Explorer displays the page title as "Virginia Tech Survey of the Aftermath of the April 16 Events" while the title at the top of the survey page is "Virginia Tech Faculty & Staff Needs Assessment."

Keeping in mind that these data are being collected under the auspices of the respondent's employer, the informed consent also indicates that one's answers are not guaranteed to be confidential:

> Because of ongoing law enforcement investigation, Virginia Tech must comply with federal requirements for preservation of evidence, and thus cannot destroy any data, documents, or records related to 4/16/07. Therefore, should you choose to participate in this study, information that you provide for this study may, with a valid subpoena, be obtained. Based on that remote possibility, strict anonymity and confidentiality in this study cannot be definitely promised.

Without confidentiality, meaning publicly, among other things, the survey asks for the respondent to choose from a fixed list of possible answers:

> During the past two weeks, about how often did you feel Nervous? Hopeless? Restless or fidgety? That everything was an effort? Worthless? So depressed that nothing could cheer you up? How much did the events of April 16 affect you in each of the following ways over the past two weeks. . . . You were less able to handle day-to-day stress; You were less able to have positive feelings or take pleasure in things; Your reactions to the tragedy interfered with your ability to work or carry out

your daily activities; You took less care of your physical needs than usual (e.g., ate poorly, did not get enough rest, smoked or drank more than usual); You took greater care of your physical needs than usual; You engaged in more risky behaviors than usual (e.g., used drugs, had unprotected sex, drove too fast, drove while drunk); You engaged in fewer risky behaviors than usual; You were upset or distressed by memories of the tragedy; You were worried or bothered by your reactions to the tragedy; You had feelings of forgiveness for the person responsible for the shootings. . . . In the aftermath of the April 16 events, have you thought about leaving Virginia Tech permanently? Since April 16, have you received any sort of professional counseling or therapy for problems with your nerves, emotions, or mental health? Since April 16, have you taken a prescription medicine for problems with your emotions, nerves, or mental health? Was there a time since April 16 when you felt that you might need to see a professional because of problems with your emotions, nerves, or mental health? Not counting the time since April 16, did you ever in your life have a month or longer when you felt sad or depressed most of the time? Not counting the time since April 16, did you ever in your life have a month or longer when you were nervous, edgy, anxious, or worried most of the time? Not counting times since April 16, did you ever in your life have anxiety attacks—when all of a sudden you felt very frightened, panicky and you had physical sensations (like pounding heart, shortness of break, dizziness, or feeling like you were going to throw up) that made you feel like you were going to lose control or go crazy or die? Have you ever in your life seriously thought about committing suicide? What is your religious preference? How religious or spiritual are you? When you have problems in your day to day life, how often do you seek comfort in a religious or spiritual way—such as praying, meditating, a religious service, or talking to a spiritual advisor? Do you have medical insurance that covers mental health treatment? What is your marital status? Are you living with someone in a marriage-like relationship? Which of the following best describes your current dating situation? About how many friends and relatives do you have whom you talk to on the phone, e-mail, or socialize with on a regular basis during the school year? (If you have a lot of such people, just give us your best estimate of the number.) About how many people do you have in your personal life that you can really open up to about your most private feelings without having to hold back?

The survey seems to want to take account of the most inner dimension of ourselves. Interrogation of emotions through computerized survey(lance) in order to assess the level of repressively acceptable reaction and then channeling this "knowledge" into administrative action makes no sense except as containment of the emergence of the real issue at hand: something was already wrong in academia. Given the egregious ethical issues and the invasiveness of the survey, both directly acknowledged, first by the IRB review and second by the provision of a phone number and web address for counseling in case one finds oneself emotionally unable to handle their reaction to the survey, there should have been some objection to this strip search. Perhaps there was and I am unaware of it. Or, perhaps just like the millions of people moving through U.S. airports, silently and calmly taking off their belts and shoes, handing over their fluids, and walking past x-ray machines that inventory their body cavities while an anonymous computerized voice tells them over the loud speaker that we need to *know more* because of a heightened security threat, we have simply become resigned to the invasion of our personal privacy in the interest of the unknown. Instead of asking deeper questions about the anonymous computerized voice of the survey inventorying our minds, which, we are told, contain potential evidence, we seem not to have prevailed, but to have given in.

We also seem to have given in to the supposed reality that the survey imposes. Survey questions are typically referred to as "items," but in fact they are authored and thus stances (see Agger 1989a). As Alvin W. Gouldner (1970) explained, the act of gathering information through computerized survey(lance) is itself embedded in a logic of control:

> Stated otherwise, information-gathering systems or research methods always premise the existence and use of some system of social control. It is not only that the information they yield may be used *by* systems of social control, but that they themselves *are* systems of control. Every research method makes some assumptions about how information may be secured from people and what may be done with people, or to them, in order to secure it. (50)

For Gouldner (1970), like Horkheimer and Adorno before him, the attempt to "study" society scientifically is a means of administrative domination: "the conventional methodologies of social research often premise and foster a deep-going authoritarianism, a readiness to lie to and manipulate people: they betray a bureaucratic numbness" (50). Despite the researchers' appeal to our (imposed) desire for federal funding (in order to care for us) and the provision of phone numbers to call in order to reach counselors (who will care for us in the researchers' absence), the survey does not care about us. The survey wants to *know* us in the most productive way possible.

The survey takes control of our patterns of thought, bringing them in line with questions and answers that are normatively and productively mapped out in order to secure funding, research output, and a population under the "care" of federally funded experts. Each question takes a specific stance about the appropriateness of the respondent's answers by delimiting the possible response to predefined categories of possibility, by which the range of human emotion and experience are circumscribed. In this way, the list of possible answers are themselves normalizing and productive. In its limitation of response to a prescripted list of possible and acceptable reactions, the survey takes a stance on the subject—the "victim"—inscribing on her a label that is a basis for intervention and a limit to what she is permitted to react to. In order to answer the questions, the subject is forced to isolate how she experienced the tragedy into a single event, unrelated to the normative violence of the months prior; she is forced to define her experience in Blacksburg only in terms of the event. The months of victimization prior to The Massacre are isolated and the only person held responsible for the infliction of pain is Cho: the blight that we, for our own protection, would prefer to is considered external to the system (Ryan 1982:127).

The message of the survey is that our grief must perform in ways that are marketable and thus our grief must be normal; were our grief to result in political resistance it most certainly would not result in federal funding. The normative violence of academia becomes performative as we proceed to click on the buttons that will allow researchers to draw from a set of predetermined possible conclusions about our experience in the world, which will then produce research outputs that have sanitized our responses as being from "Multiple Recipients" who think only in terms of the questions. First, we take our cues from the survey and perform the scripted path of our emotions, as Butler (1999, 2004) observed of our performance of norms. Then, we perform for funding and research output, as Lyotard (1997) observed of the norms of our academic careers. In both senses of performativity—Butler's understanding of how we perform norms and Lyotard's understanding of the emphasis on performance optimality in academia—the assumption of the survey is that we must know what is proper to know (Foucault and Gordon 1980), discover any risky mentalities that we do not have knowledge of (Beck 1986), and that our knowledge must perform optimally as a means to obtain funding (Lyotard 1997).

The survey and its associated funding for the *management of grief* robs us of the chance to realize that the tragedy is that we *already lived* in a world in which a student bought a gun and killed thirty-two people and himself, just as much as the tragedy is that we live in a world *after* a student bought a gun and killed thirty-two people and himself. Expert grief managers are trained to get us back to a functional normal, not to help us to understand that normal was not at all functional to begin with: management of our mentality is healthy only for the system that resulted in our grief. Butler (2004) reminds us of the need to pause and refuse the demand to make our grief perform: "Is there something to be gained from grieving, from tarrying with grief, remaining exposed to its apparent tolerability and not endeavoring to seek a resolution for grief through violence?" (23). Grief would have involved refusing to immediately prevail over the abnormal before we came to realize that the normal was not anymore an ideal than was its result an exogenous aberration.

Conclusion: Proceed as "Normal"(ized)

> Lecturing on navigation
> While the ship is going down
>
> —W. H. Auden

It seems trite to say that I adored my students at Virginia Tech, but I did. The students in my courses were pursuing graduate degrees in public and international affairs and many of them were there because they wanted to make the world a better place; even those students who sometimes seemed like they were not interested in making a difference, let alone interested in making an A, were generally kind and thoughtful. In many ways, my students set a better example of how to understand the Virginia Tech Massacre than the administration did, and a better example than I did. Many of them reserved judgment and questioned the ontological fiction that was being imposed upon them. Not yet caught up in what Agger (1991) calls the economic calculus of the academic career, they were better at creating genuine community than were the official "Hokie Nation" narrators. At least they knew each other as something other than unnamed "recipients." After a week of e-mail after e-mail after e-mail from the administration instructing me on what to think and feel and then attendance at an "emergency meeting" during which counselors who did not know me or my students advised me and everyone else "just like me" on our strongly recommended classroom personalities, I felt administratively paralyzed and consumed by trying to recall what the official response was. I probably already intuitively knew what to do, but given my overexposure to the ontological fiction of the Hokie Nation imposed by the Virginia Tech administration, when people were hurting in my classroom I found myself relying on my students' more organic sensibilities, not as damaged by the administration of their interaction with one another.

By the time I went to my second class on Tuesday I had heard repeatedly from faculty members and administrators about how students were getting confused, we needed to stick to the expert narrative, we needed to keep teaching, keep grading, keep going, all while remaining sensitive. On Tuesday I stupidly "lectured while the ship went down" because I internalized the message that I heard. I sat at the front of the classroom discussing an article while a student sitting to my right had tears running down her face and until another student started crying uncontrollably. I stopped and immediately dispensed with my instructions. Exposing myself to Virginia Tech's administration of who I would be and what I would feel and what I would remember was an unwise thing to do. I did not feel like lecturing toward "normality," but I felt pressured by the administration and its grief scientists to do so. Students had not come to class to interact with the official Virginia Tech policy; they had come to class to see each other and me. I had done exactly what I was told to do when I returned to class the week after thirty-two students were murdered:

1. Take a few minutes to acknowledge the event.
2. Proceed with lectures as normal.

And then I apologized and changed course. Lecturing is the wrong thing to do when the ship is sinking under the weight of the Captain and crew's insistence that: "we will be defined not by an event that happened to us, but by WHO and WHAT WE ARE.... We are Hokies. We will prevail."[4]

Notes

1. Thanks to Tim Luke and Chamsy el-Ojeili for their comments on an earlier draft of this chaper.

2. Hokies United Memorial T-Shirt
T-shirts will be AVAILABLE August 19, 2007 thru September 9, 2007
Available in stores at:
University Bookstore On-Campus
Volume Two Bookstore Off-Campus
Dietrick General Store
Also available ONLINE by clicking here
Sizes: Youth Large
Adult Small—Adult XXL
Proceeds will benefit "A Concert for Virginia Tech"
Price: $10.00
  Please note that the price increase has been necessary in order to allow Hokies United to best meet the potential demand and to support "A Concert for Virginia

Tech" as much as possible. We apologize for any inconvenience that may result from the increase. www.hokiesunited.org.vt.edu (Retrieved September 11, 2007).

3. See Chambers (2007) and Mills (2007) on the evolution of normative violence in Butler's *oeuvre*.

4. Larry Hincker, "personal" communication. Monday, April 23, 2007, *Message to the Virginia Tech Community*.

References

Agger, Ben. 1989a. *Socio(onto)logy*. Urbana: University of Illinois Press.
———. 1989b. *Fast Capitalism: A Critical Theory of Significance*. Urbana: University of Illinois Press.
———. 1991. *A Critical Theory of Public Life: Knowledge, Discourse, and Politics in an Age of Decline*. New York: Routledge Falmer.
———. 1993. *Gender, Culture, Power: Toward a Feminist Postmodern Critical Theory*. London and Westport, CT: Praeger.
———. 2007. "Cho, Not Che?: Positioning Blacksburg in the Political." *Fast Capitalism* 3.1.
Beck, Ulrich. 1992. *Risk Society: Towards a New Modernity*. London: Sage.
Butler, Judith. 1999. *Gender Trouble: Feminism and the Subversion of Identity*. London and New York: Routledge.
———. 2004. *Undoing Gender*. London and New York: Routledge.
———. 2006. *Precarious Life: The Powers of Mourning and Violence*. London and New York: Verso.
Chambers, Samuel A. 2007. "Normative Violence after 9/11: Rereading the Politics of *Gender Trouble*." *New Political Science* 29: 43–60.
Foucault, Michel, and Colin Gordon (ed.). 1980. *Power/Knowledge: Selected Interviews and Other Writings, 1972–1977*. L. Marshal, J. Mepham, and K. Sopher, trans. New York: Pantheon Books.
Foucault, Michel, and Alan Sheridan, trans. 1995. *Discipline and Punish: The Birth of the Prison*. New York: Vintage.
Gouldner, Alvin W. 1970. *The Coming Crisis of Western Sociology*. New York: Basic Books.
Luke, Timothy W. 1999. "The Discipline as Disciplinary Normalization: Networks of Research." *New Political Science* 21: 345–63.
———. 2005. "From Pedagogy to Performativity: The Crisis of Research Universities, Intellectuals, and Scholarly Communication" *Telos* 131: 13–32.
———. 2007. "April 16, 2007 at Virginia Tech—To: Multiple Recipients: 'There is a Gunman on Campus. . . .' *Fast Capitalism* 3.1.
Lyotard, Jean-Francois. 1997. *The Postmodern Condition: A Report on Knowledge*. G. Bennington and Brian Massumi, trans. Minneapolis: University of Minnesota Press.
Marcuse, Herbert. 1964. *One-Dimensional Man: Studies in the Ideology of Advanced Industrial Society*. Boston, MA: Beacon Press.

Mills, Catherine. 2007. "Normative Violence, Vulnerability, and Responsibility." *Differences: A Journal of Feminist Cultural Studies* 18 (2): 133–56.
Nickel, Patricia Mooney, and Angela M. Eikenberry. 2006. "Beyond Public vs. Private Management: The Transformative Potential of Democratic Feminist Management." *Administrative Theory and Praxis* 28 (3): 359–80.
Passavant, Paul. 2004. *Empire's New Clothes: Reading Hardt and Negri*. New York: Routledge.
Ryan, Michael. 1982. *Marxism and Deconstruction: A Critical Articulation*. Baltimore and London: Johns Hopkins University Press.

CHAPTER Eleven

THE APRIL 16 ARCHIVE:
Collecting and Preserving Memories of the Virginia Tech Tragedy

Brent K. Jesiek and Jeremy Hunsinger[1]

> I was wondering whether the memory bank app that has been used for some of the CHNM sites ... is ready and available for new projects. A colleague and I were talking tonight about how we could use a central memory bank for the VT tragedy to begin recording and archiving materials from this terrible event. Most of the things I've seen so far have been simple memorial walls. There are countless accounts, images, videos, etc. spread out all over the place, at risk of being lost since there is no centralized long-term archiving being done (at least that I know of).... Let me know what you think. I'm still not 100 percent sure I want to get myself into this, but after speaking with friends tonight I'm feeling increasingly sympathetic with getting such a project started.
>
> —E-mail from Brent Jesiek to a colleague affiliated with George Mason University's Center for History and New Media (CHNM), sent Thursday, April 19, 2007, 12:45 AM

Memory preserved is the preservation of identity, and thus the preservation of shared sense-making and shared becoming. Memories provide trajectories and foundations for our futures. For countless thousands worldwide, the plurality of trajectories surrounding the events of

April 16, 2007, at Virginia Tech was a break from the everyday, from normality. The shock of the tragedy required new ways of sense-making and negotiating common understandings. Performing this negotiation required memory, but more than a formalized archival memory. Memory had to be memorial. The event demanded memorial for the community and memory found in colleagues, friends, and global community. The tragedy demanded a shared memory on which to build new knowledges and imagine new futures.

Just two days after the April 16 tragedy at Virginia Tech, tending to still-fresh emotional wounds and trying to nurture a sense of community, a conversation occurred that would lead to the digitization of memory, the inscription of shared grief, and the emergence of new pathways for reimagining past events. Conversation over beers in a pub in downtown Blacksburg, Virginia, gradually wandered to the idea of preserving and sharing memories. In that collegial atmosphere an urgent need was recognized, namely a set of tactics and tools that could capture memories, allowing anyone to commit memories to the public whole. It was agreed that a new website should be launched, to collect the many digital artifacts qua memories created in the wake of the tragedy.

Among the many stimuli for this early conversation and subsequent developments, one particular sequence of events stands out. In part, the idea for a memory bank came from one of the coauthor's (Brent's) experience of the event:

> On the evening of Monday, April 16, 2007—exhausted from an arduous and painful day—I forced myself to sit down and document my experiences of the tragedy as it unfolded on the Virginia Tech campus. Early that fateful Monday, and following initial reports of a "shooting incident" in West Ambler Johnston Hall, I found myself in the midst of a campus lockdown. In fact, I was with some of my students in a classroom and building within shouting distance from the now infamous Norris Hall. The burden of the day fell heavily on me, and I felt a desire to record my memories while still fresh. But after I wrote and posted a blog entry late that night, I started to think about what would happen to my testimonial, as well as to the thousands of others that were being produced by so many other bloggers, facebookers, amateur photographers, artists, and citizen journalists.
>
> This line of thought eventually dovetailed with our conversation at the pub a few nights later, where we came around to discussing the work of George Mason University's Center for History and New Media (CHNM) in the area of digital memory banks. Recognizing the deeply personal, public, and ephemeral character of the knowledges surround-

ing the events and aftermath of April 16, we felt a strong desire to preserve what others might share—and what we might collect.

Gradually warming to the idea of launching a memory bank—and realizing we might leverage our pre-existing relationships with GMU—I sent a message to a CHMN affiliate after I got home from the pub. Part of that message is excerpted above. This colleague relayed my inquiry to appropriate others, who responded quickly and favorably. After providing me with some basic information about what it would take to make their software run, I started to prepare the web servers at the Center for Digital Discourse and Culture (CDDC) to handle their application. After some further brainstorming with colleagues, I also registered a domain name that we agreed was suitable and appropriate for this project.[2]

By Monday, April 23, a version of the memory bank application from GMU appeared in my inbox. When I got the software running the following day, I was immediately surprised by the extent to which the CHNM staff had customized the system for us, including in terms of design and functionality. Surely, our prior relationship, geographical proximity, and many shared connections helped motivate their efforts. But I also soon learned that one of the main web developers who pitched in to help was a M.A. graduate of Virginia Tech's History department. His work humbled and motivated me, as it truly represented a labor of love and sharing in the wake of a terrible tragedy.

Over the next few days, we tentatively started to spread word about the project and sought volunteers to help with curation and administration. I received some favorable responses from around campus, which helped buoy both our spirits and commitment to the project. We collected our first items from the general public on April 24, and over the next few days more memories trickled in. Confident with the stability and functionality of the system, on Monday April 30 both the CDDC and Virginia Tech's College of Liberal Arts and Human Sciences did formal press releases announcing the launch of the April 16 Archive (Elliot 2007). Within less than two weeks of the tragedy, a new digital memory bank was live.

Technologies of Memory: From Physical to Digital

The memory bank takes its place amongst a plurality of technologies of memory that are being used in relation to the events of April 16. More traditional archival practitioners are building physical collections from the

FIGURE 11.1 Detail of memorial board at Virginia Tech's Squires Student Center. Photo taken April 19, 2007 by Jinfeng (Jenny) Jiao.

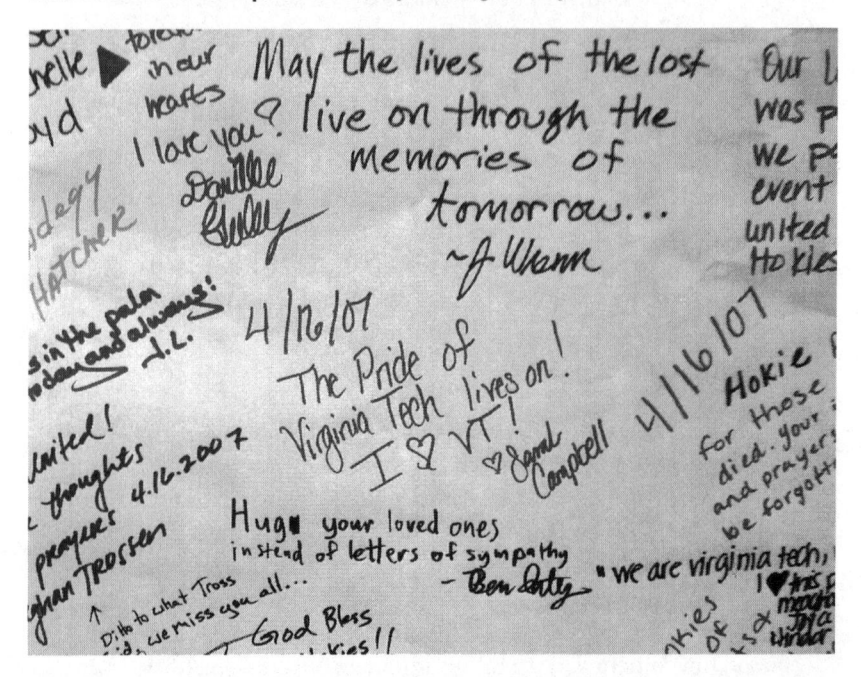

countless memorial items and gifts that arrived on campus after the event (Hutkin 2007; Vargas 2007). The university has built a memorial to remember the victims (Owczarski 2007). The reconstruction of the events after the media frenzy has been manifested in both the pluralization and concretization of various memorial approaches and systems. The functions of the memorials and archives vary widely, especially as they attempt to capture some plurality of emotional and political positions (Craig 1994; Curtis 2004). However, as archives of the event are constructed and finalized, they also become less an active remembrance of events and more a concretization of positionalities. And these positions in turn become less inscriptions of memory, especially as they become recognized as official markers and begin to provide mediated (re)interpretations of events to various publics.

Like all movements toward the cocreation of historical memories, archivists are keenly aware of capturing primary sources, those groundworks of fundamental narratives and their respective majoritarian positions. Capturing and writing these positions is determined by the intrinsic limits of memorials and archives, limits which are often built into physical containers of meaning and physical representations of events. Such physical archives cannot reflect the whole. Nor are they ideal for capturing the ephemeral, because principles of accession often focus on gathering the documents that stand behind the types of primary narratives that archivists and memorialists most readily recognize and value. Minoritarian positions and memories tend to remain largely invisible and marginalized by comparison, more likely to be lost with passing time.

Bound by a limitation of space and design, archivists cannot encapsulate everything about a given event or subject. Quite simply, they cannot totalize the experience. Hence, they do their best within preexisting frameworks and constraints. Normally, there are only so many shelf-feet available to store the material, only so many square feet to build a new memorial, only so much money in the budget for hiring help or creating and outfitting new structures. The physical and economic limits of archives and memorials frame the politics of accession (Cook 1999; Ernst 1999).

FIGURE 11.2 Memorial items on display in a tent, set up on Virginia Tech's drillfield in the wake of the tragedy. Photo taken May 1, 2007 by Brent K. Jesiek.

As spring transitioned to summer at Virginia Tech, these types of constraints were already well recognized by those who were making decisions about how to preserve and archive countless tragedy-related mementos (Hutkin 2007). By mid-August, workers at Tech had logged more than sixty thousand items related to the events of April 16, but admitted they were not yet done counting (Vargas 2007). One library administrator added that she had "probably just seen 1 percent of what there is." By August, the school had provided a scant 800 cubic feet for storing archived goods. Such limitations suggested that archiving even 5 percent of all physical objects collected and received in the wake of the tragedy would be very difficult to achieve, even though this was the target that consultants from the Library of Congress had recommended to Tech officials.

Yet in the digital age, the archivist's traditional physical frame of reference begins to disappear, replaced by the metaphorical space of bytes and bits. The boundlessness of digital expression is predicated in part on the nearly infinite space through which we live and archive our digital inscriptions. Admittedly, we are limited by the physical limits of storage inherent in digital devices such as hard drives. But the capacity to collect and preserve ever-more expansive arrays of digital information breaks the spatial metaphor of the archive and transcends the structures that previously informed accession policies.[3]

Without the physical frame of the archive, the politics of archival preservation—and thus public memory—becomes partially unbound. In the past, debates about inclusion led archivists to either pursue principles of universal inclusion or restrict collections in ways that simply ignored digital information or willfully allowed it to gradually fade and disappear. The debates surrounding what to include in any given archive are transformed by the politics surrounding the underlying technologies of memory, even as these debates are simultaneously reconstructed by and through these same technologies.

We sought to limit our subjection to these ongoing debates in order to focus on the immediacy of memory and transient sentiment, on the expression of personal knowledges and experiences related to the events in question. We sought to allow and assume the archival value of the great plurality of public expression to be collected and preserved in the digital realm. In principle, the maximal scope of the archive was only limited by the principle that any given item should in some way be related to the events and aftermath of April 16, 2007.

Having a memory bank that encompasses every related expression of memory that the public wishes to commit—and that our curators and collectors elect to gather—provides a very different constitution of the public memory of an event, especially when compared to what can be provided by those archival missions constructed in a top-down manner and constrained accordingly. The technology that was selected for our project matched digital ethos to digital archive, thereby motivating and informing how we approached the building and ongoing management of our memory bank.

Memory Bank Infrastructures

The larger trend exemplified by the April 16 Archive is the "digital memory bank." This type of web application is being used to preserve the richness of the present as it transitions to the past, thereby ensuring that digital records related to a given historical event, period, actor, and/or group are readily accessible and carefully preserved for future access. While many early memory bank projects were based on custom code built from scratch, the launch of the April 16 Archive depended crucially on a software platform under development by CHNM and its partners.

Extensively informed by the work of numerous archivists, technical experts, historians, and other scholars, this particular application is the product of numerous years of experience and many iterations of software development (Cohen and Rosenzweig 2005). In fact, the software has been refined through a much larger and longer series of projects, including the September 11 Digital Archive,[4] which in 2003 became the first digital acquisition of the Library of Congress (Library of Congress 2003), and the Hurricane Digital Memory Bank,[5] which collects stories and digital objects related to hurricanes Rita and Katrina.[6]

From the start, this software was built with scholarly and archival considerations in mind. It will also soon be available for much wider use. Supported with a grant from the Institute of Museum and Library Services (IMLS) and developed through a partnership between CHMN and the Minnesota Historical Society, the first public release of the open source software platform dubbed "Omeka" is planned for late fall 2007.[7] It stands as an important harbinger of change in an ongoing shift in archiving praxis from traditional to new media, in no small part because of how this technology pushes us to reconceptualize our individual and collective relations to memory.

Phenomenal Memories

Funes the Memorious, a character from Borges's classic story on the nature of memory, had the problem of perfect living memory (Borges 1999). He could not act, because whenever he would seek to remember how to do something, every context and detail would become immanent in his mind, taking up the time that would be required to accomplish the task in question. Machinic memory, or digital memory from a perfect recorder, would act much the same way, absorbing the whole of the time of experience and reordering our personal narratives in relation to it. In absorbing and reordering time, perfect memory can be a totalization of life, where the story takes longer to tell than the lives actually lived.

In contrast, capturing memory by digital contribution collects people's memories and thus their sentiments and their expressions. The gross weight of the individual differences inherent in a multiplicity of contributions problematizes the experiences of time and space through which we tell our narratives. In reading the contributed memories, one gets a sense of space and time as plural, yet shared, in relation to the materials contributed. This reading gives people a new way to make sense of how they relate to their memories, their spaces, and their senses of time. The materials in the memory bank neither unify or totalize. The shared memories create aporetic spaces and times, where people can get fruitfully and beneficially lost in the relations between their own memories and the contents of the archive. As a result, one's own personal narrative of events is to some extent displaced. Relating to the contributed memories of others, our memories are reconstituted with a new sense of being, with a different narrative, with an expanded sense of the significance of an event.

The question of the personal significance of the contributions should not be overlooked, as it is central to the idea of a memory bank. Memory banks contain the ephemeral, which is one of the most difficult types of content to capture, and ephemerality is given meaning by the lives and contexts that surround it (Unsworth, et al. 2006, 27–28). Ephemeral memories are subjectively experienced and frequently forgotten unless they are shared. In sharing memory, one can commit memory to the public, such as by contributing to a memory bank. Alternatively, one can keep one's memories to him or herself, or maintain them among a closed and thus private community. There is a tendency in archives work to address these individuals and closed communities as constituents that become likely contributors and audiences for the archival materials. Archives can then develop to become specialized resources for those that hold the materials in common, but that is not the intention of a memory bank. Contributions to memory banks help break down the subjective experience of closed memories. The sharing of memories allows people to perform their significance publicly, thus breaking the confines of their immediate community and personal experience in preference to the memorial act of public contribution.

This focus on contributor's significance can cause tensions in memory bank projects, because the audience is often imagined as similar or homogeneous, as possessing similar needs for memorials and memory systems. Yet the constituency for such systems is often quite plural, involving assortments of individuals, communities, organizations, and institutions that are frequently diverse, differentiated, and unequal. When faced with these inequalities and differences, archives tend to normalize toward the standard narratives based on their mission. Memory bank missions, on the other hand, tend strongly toward inclusivity, which allows people to create multiple and differential relationships to a given archive. These relationships are the foundations of multiple and overlapping narratives. As the memory bank becomes a repository for ephemeral yet personally significant memories, the relations between the memory bank and the contributors do not simply involve a separation of memories from their point of origination, but rather the memories enroll their contributors as part of the whole. This whole is not only broader and richer, it is also more accessible and relatable. Contributors can feel the acceptance of their own significance.

Memory bank architectures thus replicate less of a repository culture and its relationships to memories found in physical archives and objects. Instead, they embody the relationships of participatory cultures and communal memories that are being constructed through next-generation Internet technologies such as Second Life, blogs, wikis, and social network sites like Facebook and MySpace. The memories of these sites are frequently shared with those with whom you participate. And while the items in a digital memory bank are not mutable like the text in a wiki, they do allow recontextualization through tagging individual items with keywords, and this type of functionality enables the construction of new relationships of knowledge and memory. Memory bank developers are also exploring other possibilities for recontextualization and social interaction, such as rating and commenting add-ons. But even without such features, the types of participatory contribution and reconstruction of memories enabled by even a simple memory bank can help people make sense of the importance of their own narratives, as well as those of others.

As we have discussed, perfect memory is not the goal of a memory bank. The problem of Funes's inaction is not a problem for the creators or participants in memory banks, as the memories that are shared leave adequate spaces for continued action and participation. Rather than paralysis, these shared memories provide a basis for discussion, experience, and action. The public memory that an emergent memory bank community constitutes is thus not the cause of inaction, but rather an inspiration for action, for creating new identities and trajectories. The memory bank provides for living our lives in the context of memories.

FIGURE 11.3 Virginia Tech memorial on Info Island in Second Life®. Image captured April 17, 2007 by Wagner James Au.

As this line of inquiry suggests, preserving memory relates not just to the formation of individual identities, but also to the collaborative and subjective construction of organizations, institutions, and social structures. The role that shared memory projects play in constructing and sustaining memories of events enables people to reflect on their relation to an event, as well as to other individuals and groups. In fact, participating in communal memorial activities allows some people to assign some of their memories to the memorial, as a reminder, thus enabling them to forget. This ability to forget can be a vital part of experiencing and creating knowledge about an event (Augé 2004). But in other cases forgetting may be neither possible nor desirable, so these activities may instead help individuals screen memories from immediate recollection.

We must therefore be able to particularize the specific information that is important to us, and then assign the rest of the information to other categories. The memorial function of the April 16 Archive enables people to assign things to the archive that they want to remember, but do not want to internalize indefinitely. By externalizing those parts of the event into the archive, the community assigns it a new register, a public register, and in that they might allow themselves to forget. Public memory projects enable forgetting through processes of memorialization, and forgetting is important for identity creation and continued existence (Bowker 1997). Quite crucially, digital memory projects open up new online spaces where these processes can unfold.

Building the April 16 Archive

Omeka represents the democratization of the online archive, lowering the barriers that have historically hampered the ability of committed individuals or small groups to establish their own digital memory banks. With an early version of the software and a little help from our friends at the CHMN, we were able to use our preexisting systems and technical expertise at the CDDC to respond rapidly in the face of tragedy. To the confusion and chagrin of some Virginia Tech faculty who are more accustomed to the slow-moving bureaucracy characteristic of a large state university, the April 16 Archive was launched in less than two weeks and without a single formal meeting. The project was also conceptualized as being exclusively dedicated to collecting and archiving materials. This placed it outside the purview of Institutional Review Board (IRB) requirements, which only apply to directed research projects involving human subjects.[8] Coordinating with other formative initiatives and projects was temporarily overlooked while we focused on our main priority, namely making available a space for the public to share memories with one another in a time of need.

We still feel that our fast implementation strategy was appropriate, effective, and beneficial. In fact, the scope and scale of all archival-related tasks that have followed in the wake of April 16 are truly staggering. As noted above, they include documenting on-campus memorials and events, tracking the massive quantities of memorial and gift items that have streamed into the university, preparing to conduct follow-up surveys and oral histories, and creating permanent physical and digital repositories for artifacts and objects related to the events of April 16. Other ambitious memorial and archiving projects that were started early failed, while others moved along at a slow pace. Our memory bank fills an important niche within a larger ecology of projects, and ongoing communication and coordination efforts have helped minimize overlap and improve coordination within this network.

As for the site itself, in our first six months of operation we have recorded more than 11,000 unique visits to the site and 85,000 page views. Since the end of April, the site has been mentioned or profiled by more than thirty major online and traditional media outlets, including radio, TV, newspapers, and high profile blogs (Grant 2007; Haegele 2007; Hutkin 2007; Vargas 2007).

FIGURE 11.4 Main entry/index page for the April 16 Archive. Captured by Brent K. Jesiek on November 26, 2007.

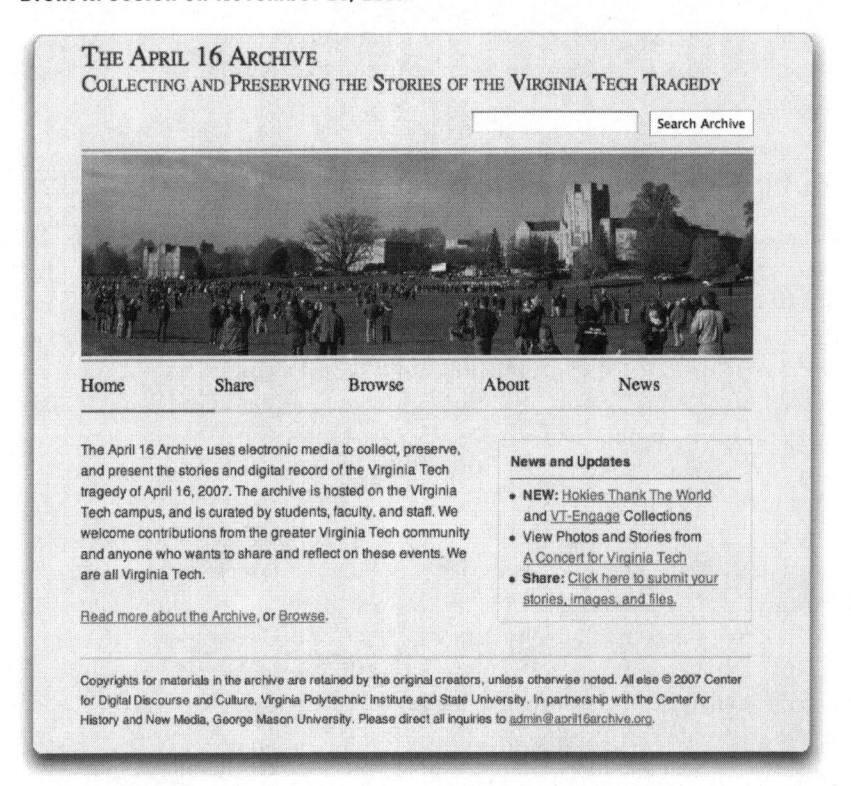

By mid-August the archive consisted of more than one thousand discrete digital objects, and by mid-November the count had reached fourteen hundred. Our staff collected a large share of these items, but a sizable number were submitted directly to the site by the public. The archive includes numerous stories, images, poems, and tributes that are available nowhere else. Our accession policy for items submitted to the site has been as inclusive as possible—we have rejected only a handful of items. We also remain largely agnostic with regard to what types of views we archive.

To provide further perspective on this wide array of content, the archive now features:

- A collection of the official university e-mails that were sent on April 16.[9]
- Hundreds of photos and stories documenting memorial and other related events at Virginia Tech and beyond, including collections for the

FIGURE 11.5 Pile of memento items on the drillfield at Virginia Tech during construction of a new intermediate memorial. Photo taken July 6, 2007 by Brent K. Jesiek.

April 16 Memorial Dedication, a Concert for Virginia Tech, and the Hokies Thank the World project.
- Relevant articles and editorials from more than sixty college and university newspapers and media outlets, mainly in North America.
- Commentaries and reflections on topics as diverse as gun control, violent culture, Asian American and Korean American identity, mainstream media coverage of the event, the role of new media and citizen journalists, privacy laws, and mental health.
- Documentation of memorial structures and events in the Second Life® virtual world.
- Numerous audio files, including talk show excerpts, musical tributes, and podcasts.
- Many pieces of digital artwork and poetry.

We continue to actively collect materials for the archive, including through the efforts of five part-time workers who assisted with the project during summer 2007 and a smaller number of assistants hired for the

2007–2008 academic year. For the most part, we have focused our collecting efforts on materials that: 1) are most likely to get lost with the passage of time; 2) provide unique, local, and/or original viewpoints rather than repeating widely known facts or knowledge; and 3) are not well-indexed or preserved elsewhere. We have also cast a wide net by looking for commentaries and reactions from outside the United States. In fact, the archive now includes materials in native languages as diverse as Romanian, Spanish, Korean, Chinese, and French that highlight reactions to April 16 from more than a dozen countries all over the globe.

Some of our work has also focused on Creative Commons (CC) licensed content, whether text, images, audio, etc. Given the nature of our site, we can archive this material without having to obtain author/creator permission, so long as we follow and reproduce the license provisions. To date, more than 20 percent of the items in our archive (or nearly 300 of 1,400 total objects) are archived under CC licenses. We have also had significant success in getting permission to archive copyrighted items, in no small part due to the nature of both the tragedy and our project.

Yet it is worth emphasizing that ownership and copyright issues pose significant barriers to preservation in many memory projects. Copyrights in the United States lie with the people who originally write the memories, and not necessarily with either the originators of the memories or those who run memory banks or archives. We have sought to include as much material as we can within the constraints of law, but by necessity this means that some materials cannot be submitted to the memory bank because copyright owners do not wish to participate. For some, issues of profit and ownership are very significant. While we understand these concerns, the recontextualization of memories in a digital memory bank comes with significant benefits, especially in terms of externally preserving relevant materials and promoting the communal sharing of memory. Thus, there remain questions about how the economic construction of copyright that overlay memories of tragedy stand in tension with the possible public good that comes with freely and openly sharing memories.

CC licensing is one way to overcome some of these assumptions about private goods, but there are other licenses that perform the same or similar functions. For instance, the artistic license (Open Source Initiative 2006)—which provides for uses and mutability so long as there is no profit—would be equally beneficial for archival purposes, as could be the GNU Free Documentation License (Free Software Foundation, Inc. 2002). Both of these approaches recognize the value of having an open and accessible public sphere, much like the open access movement (Suber 2007) as exemplified by the Public Library of Science[10] and the Access2Knowledge project.[11] Memory bank systems can use and promote the use of these licenses, especially in order to increase knowledge and awareness about both their availability and the movements to which they relate. Memories, as writable, are copyrightable, but they need not be copyrighted. Public knowledge could as well be committed to the public domain, rather than being copyrighted or licensed. Since the legal status of the written memory can take many forms, managing these forms is one complication among many for those who curate and maintain digital memory banks.

Memory Bank Limits and Challenges

We also recognize the many other limits of both our project and our labors. For instance, our software platform is ideally suited for collecting individual digital objects or small collections of objects. When we received more than six hundred photos from a local photographer, for example, we decided that a manageable approach to this material would involve placing about one hundred exemplary images in the archive. The full collection will be given to our library staff, although they, under their own resource constraints, may do little more than file away a copy of the DVD. The choice to not archive this whole collection of images was not a choice of exclusion, but rather a choice of inclusion of exemplary material that recognizes the realpolitik of labor that constrains our work.

Our archive is also not designed to capture or display entire websites, but then few systems actually do, and none do it perfectly (Brügger 2005). On a closely related note, we face major challenges with regard to large collections of commercial/copyrighted content, including from big media outlets. In light of these issues, we were fortunately able to partner with the Internet Archive,[12] who gave us free access to their Archive-It service[13] for one month. This allowed us to "scrape" other relevant content from the web.

Featured for a period on the archive-it.org homepage, this complementary collection includes content from more than forty memorial and tribute sites, commercial and noncommercial media outlets, and other relevant web-based materials.[14] This archive supplements and complements our memory bank and other projects underway at Virginia Tech. But it is also important to recognize that collaborating with outside organizations to preserve content does take more commitment from all parties. Creating an external online archive necessarily brings a new set of constituencies into the archival mission, and thus transforms relationships among the stakeholders in the university, which were already stressed.

It is also worth highlighting some of the other hurdles that we have encountered with this project. With regard to labor, for example, virtually no unpaid volunteers came through to help curate or collect materials, despite many early expressions of interest. This problem was likely exacerbated by the end-of-semester lull, continued emotional fall-out from the tragedy, and a desire among faculty and graduate students to get back to neglected work. Similar reasons likely promoted the rapid decline of other promising initiatives, such as the student-led Hokies 4/16: A Memorial Project.[15]

Having paid full-time staff (in the form of coauthor Brent Jesiek) and summer workers was therefore extremely valuable for growing our archive, although many were challenged by the emotional impact of this work. For some, helping on the archive served as a coping mechanism. For others, it was simply traumatic. Yet the diversity of emotional responses in the workers and collaborators helps us realize the purpose of the archive with respect to sense-making and creating a common understanding. As noted above, the process of forgetting is an important part of overcoming trauma. And forgetting, like remembering, takes work (Olick and Robbins 1998). Both forms of memorial work are important for recovery from traumatic events. Inasmuch as our labors were both constituting new sets of memories and causing the reprisal of forgotten ones, one can clearly see that working on a memory bank is emotionally charged labor.

This issue is particularly acute for those who work locally to archive traumatic events. In the past, many memory banks have been created at locations and institutions that were geographically remote from the incident, and this has arguably provided emotional buffers. But our memory bank is located on Virginia Tech's Blacksburg campus, which largely eliminated the buffer between the immediate memories of the workers and the materials being submitted. Many of us responded by developing our own coping strategies—such as skimming text, working quickly, taking frequent breaks, playing music in the background—to help keep us from getting too tangled up in the mass of memories that we encountered through our work.

This project also forcefully revealed some of the politics related to the location of our Center within a competitive, grant-driven research university. On one hand, our relationship with GMU helped reduce the internal collaborative politics that can hamper such a project. But as word about our work spread on our own campus, concerns were expressed about our lack of engagement with relevant faculty in other departments, the possible encroachment of our project onto the turf of other university units and research groups, and the extent to which we were exploiting the tragedy for financial gain. One faculty member even alleged in an e-mail that our motivations were mainly instrumental and financial, going so far as to suggest that we were "practically jumping over the graves of the victims to get first in line for money." Even though our only funding sources for the project were our normal operating budget and a small allotment of funds from the Dean of our College, these exchanges took their own emotional toll, especially given our feeling that we had worked selflessly and tirelessly on the project from the very beginning. Fortunately these concerns eventually faded, especially as our colleagues came to see both the value of our project and our dedication to it.

Publicity has also proved a continuing challenge. While our initial press release and the ensuing media coverage greatly boosted both overall traffic and the quantity of materials submitted to the public website, our statistics have ebbed and flowed in the months since. We hope that continuing to add content to the archive will drive more traffic to the site and encourage submissions. We are also planning further promotional efforts, including another press release and publicity campaign in early 2008. On the other hand, we respect that normal processes of forgetting tragedy may mean that the site's objectives and audiences will evolve considerably in coming months and years. In fact, over time we expect that our collection will become more a site for archival research and less a place for members of the public to visit, share, and reflect.

Another related type of difficulty has centered on maintaining an appropriate balance between our public memory and archival missions. While first and foremost framed and positioned as an archive, such a site is also necessarily a memorial. In fact, we explicitly noted this aspect of the project in our initial press release, which explained: "Through this archive, we aim to leave a positive legacy for the larger community and contribute to a collective process of healing, especially as those affected by this tragedy tell their stories in their own words." To date, we have received two complaints about materials in the archive that visitors found offensive. One of these items—a graphic yet realistic comic-style drawing of the perpetrator opening fire in a classroom—was temporarily removed from public view, as we decided that it could evoke feelings among visitors that were simply too visceral and immediate. But we decided that the other troubling object—an anonymous "confession" from a self-described "loner" who expressed some sympathies with Seung-Hui Cho's actions—should remain online. Our decision was strongly informed by our commitment to make visible minoritarian perspectives that are frequently marginalized, made invisible, and disappeared by mainstream media, traditional archives, and dominant public discourses.

In more pragmatic terms, questions also remain about the long-term future of the archive. We recognize that valuable submissions can trickle into such sites for years and even decades. We recently heard, for example, that new materials are still being collected related to the 1970 Kent State shootings. We also feel that the materials on the site should be readily available to scholars, researchers, and the general public for the indefinite future. Our university library and archives is one possible long-term home for this site, but whether they will have the appropriate technical and financial resources to support it on an ongoing basis remains an open question.

These issues and challenges are primarily practical, political, and economic. The motivations of preserving a public memory outside of normal archival institutions and practices have helped move the archive forward to the next stages of development, which involve more routine types of maintenance, curation, and promotion. But the materiality of digital memories, the servers and disk drives, are not permanent devices and will eventually need upgrading or replacement. The foresight of pursuing a project as quickly as we did should not be foregone, because it is by establishing early access to the sharing of memory that we constituted the actuality and thus the value of the contributions to the memory bank. It is now clear that the value of the archive is self-legitimizing, as reflected in the value of the memories, knowledges, and sentiments it now contains.

Conclusion

The phenomenal experience of memory grounds the motivations for building the April 16 Archive. We cannot escape the history of the event, nor the memories that were created as a result of that event. We can forget some things, but we should strive to preserve memories worthy of collecting and preserving. Doing so has demanded that we grapple with or move beyond a range of difficult issues, including as related to accession and deaccession, balancing our archival and memorial missions, and grappling with institutional and organizational politics.

Work on the archive continues, albeit at a slower pace given our limited resources and other active projects. We are pleased, however, to be planning a major upgrade to the archive's underlying software platform, which promises additional features. A new plug-in structure, for example, will likely enable the development and installation of modules that allow greater interactivity on the site, such as via commenting and/or rating features. New versions of Omeka may also improve our ability to develop curated, virtual exhibits dedicated to particular themes.

And then there are the countless items that remain unarchived, some scattered about on the web, others hidden away on phonecams and hard drives, memory sticks and CDs. Surely, items will continue to trickle into the site in coming months and years. Yet very early on, we were forced to come to terms with an important reality of our undertaking: namely, that we would only ever capture a small fraction of the digital ephemera related to the events of April 16. Even if we aspired to a machinic memory of April 16, this goal remains a practical impossibility. Yet if the items we have archived provide some measure of healing and recovery for those touched by the violence of that fateful day, if they stand as an appropriate memorial to the victims, if they provide insights for future researchers, then this project will be a success. And by these measures, perhaps we have already succeeded.

When Brent first chronicled the events of April 16 on his blog, he closed with the following:

> The remainder of the semester will not be easy here. I know not what lies ahead, but hope that this community can come together and find some way forward, out of this mess. For those outside of the

FIGURE 11.6
An attendee at an April 17, 2007 vigil on the Virginia Tech campus raises a candle in the air. Photo by David J. Franusich.

community, please be thinking of us. We need all of the positive energy you can spare.

For us, the archive represents one way forward—among many ways—out of the mess of April 16, 2007.

But it is also more than that. Creating the future from the past is a process of creating and shaping identities and trajectories. We become lines of flight, transversal operants in a field of others. Reforging our identities through a continual process that has been diverted by the tragedy of April 16, our collective constructions can matter more in their memorialization and their communal sharing than the ephemera of our lives that we frequently and quickly forget. Memories and memory banks provide a field of interconnections through which we can relate and reform our collective identity into something greater than atomic, anomic individuals. By creating the April 16 Archive, a certain moment of identity in creation occurred. In continuing the archive, we hope more people will find inspiration to enact similar projects in the future.

Acknowledgments

This chapter is dedicated to all who have been touched by the April 16 tragedy at Virginia Tech. We also extended our appreciation to the organizers of the 2007 Forty-Eighth Annual RBMS (Rare Books and Manuscripts Section of the American Library Association) Preconference, who invited us to speak about the April 16 Archive in one of their seminar sessions. The presentation developed for that event was the initial basis for this paper. And finally, thanks to all who so graciously contributed to and/or otherwise helped out with the April 16 Archive. Without your support and encouragement, this project would never have gotten off the ground.

Notes

1. Equal coauthors on this paper.
2. See www.april16archive.org.
3. It is telling, for example, that the current size of the April 16 Archive—which consists of more than fourteen hundred digital objects—represents less than 1.5 gigabytes (GB) of data. By contrast, the web server on which the archive is hosted has a total storage capacity that is nearly one thousand times larger (about 1.4 terabytes).
4. See www.911digitalarchive.org/.
5. See www.hurricanearchive.org/.
6. Other innovative sites based on this platform include the *Mozilla Digital Memory Bank* (www.mozillamemory.org/), which aims to preserve the history of

the Mozilla open source software community, and *Mason Basketball Digital Memory Bank* (www.hoops.gmu.edu/), which collected memories of the underdog successes of the GMU men's basketball team at the 2005–2006 NCAA basketball tournament. More recently, this software was used to create *Thanks, Roy* (www.thanksroy.org/), a website dedicated to collecting memories of Roy Rosenzweig, the recently deceased founding director of GMU's CHNM. For still more examples, see the Omeka showcase page (omeka.org/showcase/).

7. See www.omeka.org/.

8. However, Institutional Review Boards at many institutions are starting to pay closer attention to oral history and other types of research that are common in the humanities but have traditionally been unregulated (Howard 2006). This trend could have a chilling effect, including on the development of future online memory banks.

9. See www.april16archive.org/object/62.
10. See www.plos.org/.
11. See www.access2knowledge.org/cs/.
12. See www.archive.org.
13. See www.archive-it.org.
14. See www.archive-it.org/collections/694.
15. See hokies416.wordpress.com/.

References

Augé, Marc. 2004. *Oblivion*. Minneapolis: University of Minnesota Press.

Borges, Jorge Luis. 1999. *Borges: Collected Fictions*. A. Hurley, trans. New York: Penguin.

Bowker, Geoffrey. C. 1997. "Lest We Remember: Organizational Forgetting and the Production of Knowledge." *Accounting, Management and Information Systems* 73: 113–38.

Brügger, Niels. 2005. "Archiving Websites. General Considerations and Strategies." (January) Århus, Denmark: Centre for Internet Research. Retrieved 11/27/07 from www.cfi.au.dk/publikationer/archiving/guide.pdf.

Cohen, Daniel J., and Roy Rosenzweig. 2005. *A Guide to Gathering, Preserving, and Presenting the Past on the Web*. Philadelphia: University of Pennsylvania Press. Also available at chnm.gmu.edu/digitalhistory/.

Cook, Terry. 1993. "The Concept of the Archival Fonds in the Post-Custodial Era: Theory, Problems and Solutions." *Archivaria* 35 (Spring).

Craig, Barbara L. 1994. "Memories and the Memorial: Developing and Managing Nursing Archives for Canada." *Canadian Bulletin of Medical History/Bulletin canadien d'histoire de la médecine* 11 (1): 237–48.

Curtis, Neal. 2004. "Art and the Immemorial." *Space and Culture* 73: 302–12.

Elliot, Jean. 2007. "Center for Digital Discourse and Culture Launches April 16 Archive." *Virginia Tech News* (May 1). Retrieved 11/29/07 from www.vtnews.vt.edu/story.php?relyear=2007&itemno=261.

Ernst, Wolfgang. 1999. "Archival Action: The Archive as ROM and Its Political Instrumentalization under National Socialism." *History of the Human Sciences* 122: 13–34.
Free Software Foundation, Inc. 2002. "GNU Free Documentation License." Retrieved November 27, 2007 from www.gnu.org/licenses/fdl.html.
Grant, Elisabeth. 2007. "Archiving Tragedy, Promoting Healing." *American Historical Association Blog* (May 2). Retrieved November 29, 2007 from blog.historians.org/resources/208/archiving-tragedy-promoting-healing.
Haegele, Katie. 2007. "The April 16 Archive Tells a New Kind of Virginia Tech Story." *Philadelphia Inquirer* (May 6). Retrieved November 29, 2007 from www.thelalatheory.com/dig7.html.
Howard, Jennifer. 2006. "Oral History under Review." *The Chronicle of Higher Education* 5312 (November 10): A14. Retrieved November 27, 2007 from chronicle.com/free/v53/i12/12a01401.htm.
Hutkin, Erinn. 2007. "Tech to Archive Shooting Mementos." *Roanoke Times* (June 24). Retrieved November 29, 2007 from www.roanoke.com/vtmemorials/wb/121923.
Library of Congress. 2003. "Library Accepts September 11 Digital Archive, Holds Symposium News Release" (August 15). Retrieved November 21, 2007 from www.loc.gov/today/pr/2003/03-142.html.
Olick, Jeffrey K., and Joyce Robbins. 1998. "Social Memory Studies: From 'Collective Memory' to the Historical Sociology of Mnemonic Practices." *Annual Review of Sociology* 24: 105–41.
Open Source Initiative. 2006. "The Artistic License." Retrieved November 27, 2007 from www.opensource.org/licenses/artistic-license.php.
Owczarski, Mark. 2007. "Virginia Tech to Dedicate April 16 Memorial on Sunday, August 19." *Virginia Tech News*. Retrieved November 21, 2007 from www.vtnews.vt.edu/story.php?relyear=2007&itemno=450.
Suber, Peter. 2007. "Open Access Overview" (June 19). Retrieved November 27, 2007 from www.earlham.edu/~peters/fos/overview.htm.
Unsworth, John., et al. 2006. *Our Cultural Commonwealth: The Report of the ACLS [American Council of Learned Societies] Commission on Cyberinfrastructure for the Humanities and Social Sciences*. New York: American Council of Learned Societies. Retrieved November 29, 2007 from www.acls.org/cyberinfrastructure/acls.ci.report.pdf.
Vargas, Theresa. 2007. "Preserving the Outpouring of Grief: Va. Tech Archives 60,000 Condolences." *Washington Post* (August 19): A1. Retrieved November 29, 2007, from http://www.washingtonpost.com/wp-dyn/content/article/2007/08/18/AR2007081801200.html.

CHAPTER Twelve

COLONIZATION AND MASSACRES:
Virginia Tech, Jamestown, Korea, and Iraq

Roxanne Dunbar-Ortiz

What does it mean, if anything, that a student, child of Korean immigrants, killed thirty-two classmates and faculty at a Virginia university while nearby celebrations of the onset of colonialism were taking place?

In April 2007, all the news seemed to be coming from Virginia and was about mass murder, occurring yesterday (four hundred years ago in Jamestown) and today. I heard no commentary on the coincidence of those bookends of colonialism. Maybe I noticed because I was working on the first chapter of a history of the United States and had colonialism and massacres on my mind.

Jamestown famously was the first permanent settlement that gave birth to the Commonwealth of Virginia, the colonial epicenter of what became the United States of America nearly two centuries later, the colony that in turn gave the United States its national capitol on the Potomac River up the coast. A few years after Jamestown was established, the more familiar and historically revered Plymouth colony was planted by English religious dissidents, but still under the auspices of private investors with royal licenses, accompanied by massacres of the indigenous farmers, just as Jamestown was.

This was the beginning of British overseas colonialism, which led to its eventually far more powerful spawn.

Some 343 years after ragged mercenaries set foot on Powhatan territory at Jamestown and began massacring the indigenous farmers and stealing their food crops, the United States invaded Korea, a half-million troops strong, with thirty thousand remaining more than a half-century later.

The Virginia Tech killings were heralded as the worst "mass killing," and "worst massacre," in the United States. Descendants of massacred ancestors—indigenous peoples, African Americans, Mexicanos, Chinese—took exception to that designation. But, we know what those headlines meant; they meant the largest number of innocents killed by one armed civilian, although even that's probably not accurate either, so they really mean with guns and in the last half-century or so, maybe beginning in 1958 with nineteen-year-old Charles Starkweather, and his even younger girlfriend Caril Fugate, who killed eleven in Nebraska and Wyoming. Then, in 1966, there was Charles Whitman up on top of the University of Texas tower, sniping and killing thirteen, wounding thirty-one others before being shot by police. Twenty years later, the post office killings began in the quiet town of Edmond, Oklahoma, a few miles from where I grew up, giving rise to a new term, "going postal." Other workplace killings followed, with around fifty deaths up to now. More recently, school killings have prevailed, some twenty-two incidents since 1989 in the United States.

Having lived through all of them, I have been interested in the mass response to each one, ever since Starkweather, who was my age at the time. Each mass killing is followed by an orgiastic chorus of proclamations about a bubble of normality punctured by a sole evildoer. Perhaps the incidents play a role in U.S. society somewhat as Dostoevsky had his character, the "idiot," play as the member of the family who is weird or evil so that the rest of the family can be perceived or perceive themselves as "normal." With all the anger and tension we experience and observe daily, it's a wonder mass killings don't happen more often, but maybe the mass killer speaks for many and is a preventative.

The Dostoevskian "idiot" is a universal archetype under the patriarchal Western family and the triad of family, church, and state. But, there's more to it than that in the United States. This can be seen from how we react. Some say we react so massively because it's the 24/7 television and Internet that causes us to dwell on such events. But, I recall the Starkweather crime spree from my youth in rural Oklahoma with no television at all and only local papers and local radio, and it didn't even happen in Oklahoma. Everyone knew about it, following the news of the killers' evasion of the massive law enforcement pursuit, fearing the killers' arrival at their homes.

At the same time the news repelled and terrified me, I harbored curiosity about and perhaps admiration for the teen killer and his girlfriend. I was already successfully "the idiot" in my family, as an invalid with chronic asthma. Sickliness still was considered a character flaw and a weakness in that post frontier rural setting. As well, my childhood bedtime stories were about heroic outlaws—Jesse James, Billy the Kid, Pretty Boy Floyd, Belle Starr, Bonnie and Clyde. They were heroes to many who were inspired by their deeds. I can understand how Cho might be secretly admired. Cho stated in his suicide message, "I die like Jesus Christ to inspire generations of the weak and defenseless people."

Then there's the factor of the continual reincarnation of the Anglo-Scots outlaw, so pervasive on the North American frontier, often erroneously referred to as a "cowboy." But, I think we have to go back to that yesterday in another part of Virginia, Jamestown, the site of the British queen's visit in April to celebrate the first permanent English colony in the Western Hemisphere; Vice-President Dick Cheney, in his Jamestown speech commemorating the four-hundred-year anniversary called the birthplace of the United States. Indeed it is, a bloody birth at that.

When Cho went on his killing spree, there was a great deal of news about the four-hundred-year commemoration, especially in Virginia, highly publicized planning for which had been ongoing for a year. Was Cho curious enough to do a search on the Internet about Jamestown? (Maybe the FBI knows from studying Cho's hard drive, but they most likely wouldn't "get it.") Or maybe Cho just looked at a book, or had taken a history course. Perhaps he saw some pictures of drawings of the Powhatan Indians who were killed by Captain John Smith and his soldiers. Perhaps Cho saw a reflection of his own features in those Powhatan faces, and was reminded of what had happened to his own people, the multiple massacres of Korean civilians in the 1950s U.S. invasion and occupation of his parents' homeland, the occupation and humiliation continuing today. (I recall stories from Native American vets returning from Vietnam, how they could not bring themselves to shoot when they could see the faces of the people who looked like their relatives.)

Much was made in the press about Cho being Asian, then specifically, Korean, surely touching on those mystic chords of memory of "yellow peril" and Asian wars "lost" by the United States, or not "won" militarily. Yet, there was nothing about the Korean War, 1950–1953, and the ongoing U.S. military presence. Uncountable millions of Korean civilians were killed in the war, many in U.S. military massacres of refugees. Millions of children were left without parents. Cho was not a child of those Korean war orphans stolen by U.S. religious groups, children who grew up in white, middle-American communities not knowing their real names or birth dates or families or villages.

Cho's parents had immigrated in 1992, when he was eight years old, settling in a Virginia suburb of Washington, D.C., where they started a dry cleaning business, sending Cho and his older sister to the best schools. That may sound like the "American Dream" realized, but only if one has never taken notice of the toxic, backbreaking work involved in a family owned and run dry-cleaning operation, with the immigrant parents working themselves to death so their children might have a crack at that putrid dream of consumerism. Cho and his sister were beneficiaries of their parents' labor to pay for their elite educations.

In his video rant, Cho expressed hatred for the "rich kids" who surrounded him. In U.S. society we are not allowed to hate anyone or anything not designated by the State as the enemy. We are jumped on and accused of "playing the class card" or "playing the race card."

"The rich are not like you and me." "The poor will always be with us." Get real and accept it we are told. It's toxic thinking. Why should we have to swallow and internalize our righteous hatred of the rich? Hate, yes. The language can be dressed up by calling it rage or outrage, but, hate is a concept underrated. Everyone does it, but no one wants to admit it. We are held back and diminished by the claim that hating is bad for us, bad for everyone. We are told that it's all right to hate the act but not hate the person. We are allowed to hate wealth or capitalism but not the purveyors. Even in the postmodern intellectual world where "agency" is bestowed upon the poor and oppressed (they are responsible for their actions), the rich remain an abstraction. It's a ridiculous logic that keeps us hating and blaming ourselves for not being rich and powerful, literally driving people crazy.

Who are the rich? We have to be careful about that, living in a country that does not admit to class relations, and class is subject to little analysis. It's not a matter of income per se. High income can certainly make a person delusional, and most U.S. citizens who live on high fixed or hourly incomes due to circumstances of a good trade union or a professional degree have no idea that they aren't rich. In polls they say they are in the top fifth of the income ladder, and they aren't. A majority of U.S. citizens don't want to tax the rich more, because they think they will be rich one day. They won't. The rich own not just a mortgaged house and a car, maybe a boat or a cabin in the woods or a beach house to boot; rather they own us. Even the cash and luxury soaked entertainment and sports stars are not the rich; they certainly deserve contempt and disgust, but not hatred. Don't go for scapegoats—Jews, Oprah, Martha Stewart, or random kids on campus as Cho did. Hatred should be reserved for those who own us, that is, those who own the banks, the oil companies, the war industry, the land (for corporate agriculture), the private universities and prep schools, and who own the foundations that dole out worthy projects for the poor, for public institutions—their opera, their ballet, their symphony, that you are allowed to attend after opening night, and they own the government. My oldest brother, who like me grew up dirt poor in rural Oklahoma, landless farmers and farm workers, rebuts my arguments by saying that no poor man ever gave him a job. That says it all. The rich own you and me.

In all the arguments about the crimes of the Judeo-Christian-Muslim religions, rarely is their greatest crime ever discussed—the leveling of class, rich and poor are the same in god's sight. What a handy ideology for the rich! The same with U.S. democracy with its "equal opportunity" and "level playing fields," absurd claims under capitalism, but ones held dear, even by liberals.

When rampages such as Cho's occur, my first thought is not why, rather why not more often. What do we do with the anger, the rage? Violence in the United States is usually associated with the narrative of the frontier having hardened the society, creating the killer, the "cowboy," all that is bad, a direction taken away from the rational Puritans and the wise Virginians who did all they could to get along with the Indians. But, that's a lie; the killing began at the beginning and the purpose was to eradicate the inhabitants of North America, to take their land, and to replace them. There is no redemption in exorcising the "cowboy" or firearms.

Such probing as this is said by some to justify or rationalize individual violent behavior, and in a way it does. But, the alternative, to name it evil, is not helpful, nor is blaming guns, freedom, lack of mental health counseling. Why not seize the opportunity to explore what we have in common with the culprit, explore his humanity, rather than vilify him? Some say that any time or effort spent trying to understand does a disservice to the victims and their families. That kind of thinking has strangled and suppressed even studies of history, such as the Holocaust. Whose interest is served by shutting down discussion of motives and circumstances, and, particularly, history? One is not alleging lack of criminal intent or behavior, but what made it possible? Wouldn't this be an appropriate moment at least to acknowledge the pathological celebration of colonization in Virginia at the time of the shootings, and the war and continuing occupation of Korea as possible causes for Cho's decision?

As a child during the Korean War, I sold Veterans of Foreign Wars crepe paper roses. Several young men in our rural farming community were drafted and came home wounded or not quite right in the mind. One of the boys who returned sat with my brother and me and our cousins and told us about Korea. He told us, poor as we were, how lucky we were in comparison with the Koreans. "They're lucky to eat a spoonful of rice once a day," he said. Then he told us about going through a small village and seeing an old man die of starvation right in front of him, and said a tapeworm came out of his mouth. His story made us feel lucky to be free Americans fighting communism, proud of our country for helping others. He later blew his brains out with a shotgun, but he didn't take anyone with him. Maybe he had a conscience.

Video games portraying violence and casual killing are blamed for leading young men like Cho to act out in reality. But what about the virtual real war that has saturated the brains of everyone since the invasion of Afghanistan in October 2001, and subsequent war in Iraq? From age seventeen to his death at twenty-three, Cho, like the rest of us, had a head full of pictures of licensed killing and torture. His highly functional sister, a Princeton graduate, works as a contractor for the U.S. State Department's management of the Iraq War. Which of the actions of the two were more destructive?

CHAPTER Thirteen

ALL THE RAGE:
Digital Bodies and Deadly Play in the Age of the Suicide Bomber

Carolyn Guertin

"Violence is viral..." Jean Baudrillard says in *The Spirit of Terrorism*. "It operates by contagion, by chain reaction, and it gradually destroys all our immunities and our powers to resist" (94). Seung-Hui Cho succumbed to those powers at Virginia Tech, as did Kimveer Gill at Dawson College in Montreal, and Eric Harris and Dylan Klebold at Columbine, and too, too many others to mention. Meanwhile, half the world away, young men and women in the grip of a spiritual agenda enact similar acts of suicidal revenge to answer their own need for salvation, a sense of entitlement, and a retaliatory yearning to set right real or imagined wrongs. As much as these killers' acts are incomprehensible, they are simultaneously sanctioned by our own news media and entertainment industry. If these lost souls do not know where to draw the line, it is surely because our culture makes no distinction. In fact, the infamous psychedelia professor Timothy Leary, who performed his own death as a fashion statement and online signature media event in "designed dying," said "The most important thing you can do in your life is to die." We are immersed in visual violence of all kinds on a daily basis as entertainment. Suicide, especially murder-suicide, has become commonplace, yes, but more to the point it is now both fashionable and newsworthy. We are bombarded by popular culture forms that require ever worse—bigger and more dramatic events—to feed its massive hunger. These symbolic acts (and to say they are symbolic is not to suggest that they do not cause very real carnage) of blowing up bridges and markets in Baghdad, twin towers in Manhattan, or performing enactments of resentment against those Cho claimed had trust funds and drank cognac are happenings made real and more powerful because of their dramatization as carefully staged events for the media.

Serial killers, mass murderers, and suicide bombers appropriate the tools of the powerful (from planes to cameras to the World Wide Web) to spread terror far more effectually than their considerable death counts do, for the fear they cause is a viral weapon that spreads like a pandemic via our own addiction to networked communication. In "Packaging the Suicide Bomber," Hal Niedzviecki notes that "the attraction of becoming a suicide bomber is not the fantasy of being rewarded with virgins in heaven, but the intense feeling of being noticed in a world where being noticed—preferably on video—has somehow become the sole crowning achievement in and of itself" (68; quoted in Murray 2005). Murder-suicide is the quickest road to celebrity, and the latest incarnation of Andy Warhol's fifteen minutes of fame.

The special, grisly weapon that the suicide bomber has that increases his terror quotient above the others is his body. In the essay "Thanatopolitics: On the Use of Death for Mobilizing Political Life," Stuart Murray calls this phenomenon "biopolitics" where the body of the terrorist actually becomes a weapon of destruction, where his shattered body parts become destructive projectiles, just like the ensuing broadcast images of the violent event do. Murray (2006) observes that "The attacker's body is literally weaponized. Shards of bone become human shrapnel" (207). Similarly, in "McLuhan, Rhetoric, Politics," Murray says, the media guru Marshall:

> McLuhan warns us that "every separatist group of the future will have an educated—and therefore skilled—terrorist fringe" (*Global Village*:115). With uncanny premonition, he prophesied that "The satellite will distribute terrorist paranoia around the world in living color to match each accelerating disruptive event" (*Global Village*:115; Murray 2005).

McLuhan continues, "TV, as a maker of fantasy, reinforces that feeling of disembodiment.... A terrorist will kill you to see if you are real" (McLuhan:115). What would he have made of the far more pervasive and unsettling World Wide Web where anonymity can even tempt adults into cyberbullying the young and defenseless. (I am referring specifically to the suicide of thirteen-year-old Megan Meier in October 2007 after a friend's mother posed as a boy who liked her on the online community MySpace. In some senseless act of "revenge" after Meier and the unnamed woman's daughter had a falling out, "he" viciously and publicly dumped her after a month. Meier hung herself.)

McLuhan saw the media as extensions of our bodies. Media act in effect as networked, externalized nervous systems. This phenomenon is equal parts symptom and manifestation of McLuhan's prophetic vision of a global village: the violent, conflict-ridden, media-saturated world that is the twenty-first century. Media ecologist Lance Strate observes that, as McLuhan clearly saw in *Understanding Media*, "Guns and cameras are both media of communication" with guns acting as extensions of the "fist and fingernail" and cameras as instruments of voyeuristic violence (Strate 2007):

> Guns and cameras are both methods by which people communicate, sending messages to their target, and to bystanders alike.... Guns and cameras are both weapons, both used to attack and cause harm ... both used to control and imprison—that is why we talk about cameras using words like shoot, snapshot, load (the film), capture (the subject, the moment), that is—this is a deep metaphor that reveals an often-unconscious understanding of the link between the two technologies.
>
> We can therefore understand that the video and stills prepared by the Virginia Tech killer, and sent to NBC, was an assault by other means, another violent act prepared and perpetrated by a mass murderer. The intent, clearly, was not only to justify his actions, but to incite more violence by others. The model that he was imitating was not so much fiction films, as some commentators have suggested, but the video recordings made by suicide bombers coming out of the Arab world. (Strate 2007)

We see these parallels at suicide bombers recruitment sites and in the executions of prisoners broadcast by Iraqis over the Web. The roles such images play in our culture are highly ambiguous. As terrorism spreads messages of fear, we simultaneously revel in their instantaneous global broadcast and are appalled by their content. In reality these attacks come from the inside out for they mirror Western culture's violence as they incite and recruit us to do more harm against each other and ourselves.

Seeds of Terrorism

Jean Baudrillard argues that the seeds of terrorism were planted with the collapse of Soviet Communism, and that, previously, that balanced symmetry of two global powers had kept the forces for good and the forces for evil at a standoff. As the military might of the United States has grown ever more powerful in the interim since that collapse, there has come to be no possible military challengers, and so the only remaining forms of attack against the most powerful nation in the world (for the most powerful always must have challengers) can be symbolic attacks through guerrilla methods.

While all major religions condemn suicide, acts of violence on the enemies of Islam have come to be seen as acceptable means of performing extreme religious devotion, secular desires for revenge, and acts of cruelty. Encouraged by unscrupulous recruiters in person, in the media, and at special Websites, suicide bombers aim for critical mass in human casualties and media spectacle. Campus killers similarly derive their power from delusions of grandeur and an obsession for celebrity among the ranks of this dubious genealogy. Cho aligned himself with Christ and his suffering, and Gill saw himself as the Angel of Death. It is the media that render these brief reigns of terror as a performance to be consumed and it is us who cannot look away. Saddam Hussein was similarly and pornographically paraded before us first as a docile medical prisoner subject to dissection, and then as a subject of raw documentary footage, simultaneously real and unbelievable, with his final moments performed and "filtered through cell phones and YouTube, passing through Sky News and CNN and Al Jazeera" for our viewing pleasure (Burgess).

The danger of the media, Baudrillard warns in *Spirit of Terrorism*, is that the "image consumes the event," that is, absorbs it and gives it back as an object of consumption (Baudrillard 2002:27). NBC got considerably richer by showing Cho's images, and he knew they would show them when he mailed them his terrible "multimedia manifesto" between attacks. Then, predictably, twelve hours later NBC expressed crocodile tears of remorse, saying in the future they would "strictly limit" their use of these images—not, you will notice, cease using them (Mikkelsen 2007). Initially, NBC claimed, Cho's packet was news, but "[o]nce you've seen it, its repetition is little more than pornography," one news executive claimed (Mikkelsen 2007). How convenient for them. How sad for us that "the fascination of the attack is primarily a fascination with the image" (Baudrillard 2002:28). That these images are real adds another thrill: a layer of terror. Terrorism is a media event. Such acts become unforgivable and unforgettable once broadcast. But even that is illusory, for there is no good usage of the media in these cases. The media are an integral part of the event itself—and all of the Virginia Tech families' pleas to remember the dead instead of the murderer only remind us of the bizarre and vicious performances of the perpetrator. The media are a part of that terror and a part of the game. They unite the "white magic of the cinema and the black magic of terrorism" (Baudrillard 2002: 29–30), for, as Baudrillard says, the spectacle of terrorism imposes the terrorism of the spectacle (Baudrillard 2002:30).

Computer Game Violence

Like flies in ointment, we are stuck in this conundrum. What is the distance between a Texas Chainsaw Massacre and a brutal sniper attack at the University of Texas at Austin campus in 1966? How far removed are digital bodies executed by religious extremists, blown apart for so-called fun in Mortal Kombat, Soldier of Fortune, or Gears of War from the images of a first person shooter gunning for Virginia Tech students and staff? Computer and video games get singled out as the culprits of these homegrown attackers by right-wing critic Jack Thompson and others (Benedetti 2007), even though study after study has shown that these games are dangerous only to the kind of people who already have difficulties distinguishing between the fictional and the real (Majendie 2007). Kimveer Gill was, to be sure, a serious gamer as were the Columbine killers; Cho on the other hand was not. Not a single game was found on his computer in his dorm. But what is real and what is virtual in a digital age? Does violence not cross these boundaries precisely by the way it harnesses our fears and spreads terror, just as the suicide bomber's ultimate weapon is his body? In order to explore these connections, I will take a look at three different kinds of digital games and activities that purposely trouble the boundaries between real and fictional worlds.

Pay-Per-View-Slaughter

Early in 2005, a San Antonio rancher named John Lockwood set up a website for hunters all over the world. With high-speed access and a fee, they could shoot deer, antelope, wild boar, and other game on his property using a webcam and a remote-controlled rifle. Lockwood planned to send them the head as a trophy. Before his venture got off the ground though, hunters and sportsman cried foul and Texas lawmakers moved in to declare his business illegal. It gave the animal no chance critics said, and there was no challenge for the hunter either (in fact, even during the initial demonstration the hunter only wounded the pig and Lockwood had to go and finish the job). Other states have since moved to outlaw the practice elsewhere, including it under provisions that make hunting big game in captivity illegal. Why all the hoopla? Hunting an animal with a high-powered weapon even in the flesh is hardly a fair contest in the first place. Arkansas State Senator Ruth Whitaker summed it up like this:

> The animal has no chance.... There's no challenge for you—except knowing how to use a computer and push a button. You never left your tufted sofa. What's sportsmanlike about that?" So far a couple dozen states have blocked the practice, which the Humane Society calls "pay-per-view slaughter." (Associated Press 2007)

Digital bodies litter the Internet. Virtual killing is a major industry. I found dozens of so-called games online in which one can torture or kill or humiliate

Osama Bin Laden when I was researching this essay. Clearly this exceeds acceptable ethical boundaries. Other spaces online have no such plain demarcations.

Terrorism in Second Life

Second Life (SL) is not a game. "[I]t does not have points, scores, winners or losers, levels, an end-strategy, or most of the other characteristics of games" (Wikipedia). What it does have is the first online economy, more than 20 million registered accounts (as of February 2008, Wikipedia) and the promise of a social new world with user-generated content that you can shape to meet your imaginative dreams. Based on Neal Stephenson's metaverse from the novel *Snow Crash*, Second Life is a virtual world software created by the company Linden Labs that has become something of an addiction for its most fervent users: it is a gathering space for residents with unique avatars or cartoon-like online personas to meet, converse, socialize, form alliances, trade, and do business. Since residents control their own copyright on SL creations, own land and make money (in Linden dollars) within the world, there has been a strong movement to establish civil rights and freedoms. Former Democratic presidential candidate John Edwards was the first politician to set up shop there, an occurrence that is now commonplace. Multinational corporations, including Reebok and American Apparel, have also opened stores within SL.

When the first multinationals arrived, and Linden Labs altered some of the basic programming within the world to accommodate them, a handful of residents became alarmed about their in-world future if they were to be subject to the whims of the parent corporation. As a result, the Second Life Liberation Army (SLLA) was formed in April 2006 with a primary goal of universal suffrage. Comprised of a very small number of people (probably less than a dozen members), the SLLA conducts military operations to win rights for their virtual selves. (See images of so-called acts of terrorism in SL here.) Their first attack was against the clothing store, American Apparel. They shot "white balls," a visual effect, which obscured areas of the screen temporarily, and interfered with people's ability to see merchandise and to shop. Sometimes these effects actually pushed customers out of the store. This led to the SLLA being dubbed "terrorists" by the outer world media when they learned of the events and the same media lighted on the phenomenon with a near-hysterical fervor. "An article published by Agence France-Presse even claimed that 'virtual-world banes now mirror the havoc of the real one, as terrorists have launched a bombing campaign in Second Life'" (McCarthy). This is a grievous misrepresentation of these events. Even when SLLA detonated so-called atomic bombs at Reebok and American Apparel's virtual stores, there was no damage committed. These attacks are simply visual pyrotechnics. "Some can temporarily freeze avatars, and [at their worst some] graphics-heavy attacks can crash residents' computers or Linden Lab's servers" (McCarthy).

In-world since the media hype happened, the SLLA themselves have been subject to attacks called "griefings" (griefers are people who annoy other people in cyberspace) including having their headquarters painted with Nazi symbols and being bombarded by Super Marios. In-worlders take the issue of avatar rights seriously, especially since Homeland Security has started a SL experiment. Griefings can take the form of a blitz of exploding pink pigs or an alien invasion. One anonymous griefer draped the American Apparel store with large pink penises, and in February 2007 political protest took up real world issues as a group wearing Bush '08 badges attacked the John Edwards campaign office, blotting it with images of dinosaurs, obscenities, and an image of Edwards sporting blackface (McCarthy).

Hacktivism

Political protest and the Internet have gone hand-in-hand for a long time. The first hacktivist, computer engineer Carmin Karasic, started out using similar methods. She uses the Internet to implement a strategy called hacktivism. The term was first coined in 1998 to describe an emerging hybrid form that unites the best attributes of peaceful social protest—activism—and tech-savvy online civil disobedience—hackerism. It should not be confused with its adolescent and illegal cousins, cracktivism—code cracking, vandalism, data blockades and the loss of digital data—or cyberterrorism—acts and agents of wanton destruction including worms and viruses.

Hacktivism as an artistic praxis was born in December 1997 when Carmin Karasic was so appalled by the events of the Acteal Massacre—forty-five Zapatistas were murdered at the hands of the Mexican government—that she set out to create a Web interface that would perform political protest as an aesthetic act. Her electronic civil disobedience engine (run by a collective called Electronic Disturbance Theatre) is named FloodNet; it is Karasic's brainchild in her war against injustice. Filling the browser page with the names of the dead, this activism tool "would access [for example] the page for Mexico's President Zedillo seeking bogus addresses," so the browser would return messages like "human rights not found on this server" (Cassell 2000). Unlike the attacks launched by cracktivists, no damage is done by this software agent, but political points are made.

When the Electronic Disturbance Theatre would alert its online activists to launch a protest they visit the group's website and click on FloodNet's icon. Given Karasic's politics, it is no accident that FloodNet must function as a community-based performance: "It was only actualized through thousands and thousands of participants," she remembers. "It was meaningless without the masses." Popular support transforms a random act of vandalism into a show of presence, she argues (quoted in Cassell 2000). Karasic sees her collectivity interface as something more closely akin to "conceptual art" than to cyberterrorism (Harmon 1998). No one and no data are harmed in these "attacks," but websites are effectively shut down while the protest is being transmitted. While the SLLA has no such clear agenda or broad-based sanctioning as yet, other kinds of social protest are growing in-world. When the ultra-right wing French nationalist group the Front National (who have been likened to the Ku Klux Klan) set up a SL headquarters for instance, the response from griefers was swift, adorning their site with Nazi symbols and endowing their leader's images with Hitler mustaches.

Super Columbine Massacre RPG!

A considerably more controversial usage of computing technology is Danny Ledonne's (2005b) Super Columbine Massacre RPG![1] Styled as a video game set at Columbine High School, Ledonne's critical perspective requires us to step into the shoes of either Eric Harris or Dylan Klebold, in order to kill students, try to blow up the school, commit suicide, and ascend to hell where we must battle more demons. Shocking in its choice of subject matter and ruthlessly documentary in its material, Ledonne said that the events at Columbine were such a wake-up call for him—for he feared that he had been heading down the same road himself—that he wanted to create a forum for the disaffected to discuss their feelings. Turning to art to find a medium to express his own anger at having been ferociously bullied, he has reclaimed his life and become a film and video game maker.

He sees his free, downloadable game as a cautionary tale, educating damaged souls against the dangers of violent behavior. Ledonne (2005a) says in his artist's statement:

> Eric Harris and Dylan Klebold, through their furious words and malevolent actions, can be understood as the canaries in the mine—foretelling of an "apocalypse soon" for those remaining to ponder their deeds. With "Super Columbine Massacre RPG!," I present to you one of the darkest days in modern history and ask, "Are we willing to look in the mirror?"

You would expect a game like this that is so carefully documentary in nature, being stitched together from Harris and Klebold's journals, writings, and videotapes, to be realistic. Instead Ledonne creates a cartoony, Nintendo-like game with cheesy music that takes the horror (but not the message) out of the events. Dead students (who are scored as types—Jock Boy, Preppy Girl, Sheltered Girl) turn into red squares, which do nothing to satisfy a taste for gore, blood, or destruction. Instead stepping into the killers' shoes means that you must watch clips of movies that the pair found inspirational, retrace their steps, and listen to their bombastic, twisted philosophies on the world. Reducing their victims to types, despite Harris and Klebold complaining so bitterly about being pigeonholed by others, makes their hypocrisy palpable. Harris and Klebold did not just want to be the worst school killers ever. They wanted to be the worst mass murderers ever. If their bombs had worked the way they had planned, they had hoped to kill six hundred people with the first blast alone. Similarly, in this game, every killing is a choice. In order to succeed in Hell and overcome the DOOM-derived demons there, you have to kill virtually every student in the school to acquire enough power to survive the so-called next level (Thompson 2007).

Cybercidal Games

Denounced as a "monstrosity" by many and recently dropped from the edgy and previously unapologetic Slamdance "Guerrilla Gamemaker Competition" when sponsors threatened to pull out, Super Columbine Massacre is so misunderstood precisely because it uses the conventions of games—their visual and interactive language—to deal with these very real issues. The outraged opposition to this game demonstrates how little games are understood or taken seriously, which is one reason why they get blamed as a cause in so many of these violent attacks.

Ledonne would probably argue that games are a symptom of the disease of our spectacle-loving times, not the cause. It is easy to see the links, for instance, between Kevin Klerck's suicide as media event and Timothy Leary's celebration of death as dramatic events—styled, in their own minds, as both heroic and tragic theater. Klerck was a notorious hacker (Kevin Early was his real name) who posted a suicide note to *LiveJournal*, continued to chat online for a time, and then put a shotgun to his own head and fired. Timothy Leary likewise hoped to Webcast his own death (instead his death was videotaped and will only be shown in a forthcoming documentary). They are not alone. Kimveer Gill posted pictures of himself posing with guns before he made the trek to Dawson College, and, cybercides—group suicide pacts made in chatrooms and carried out collectively in RL—are an escalating phenomenon, especially in Japan, which has the highest suicide rate in the world.[2]

While splatter and twitch games are certainly not harmless, these bloody images are commonplace everywhere. They saturate our media, our advertising, and our entertainment on a daily basis. It is the action-based nature of games, however, that seems to make them favored targets for criticism and censorship. It was even assumed and misreported by newspapers after the Dawson College shooting that Gill must have played Super Columbine Massacre. While Gill was a big video game player and included among his favorite games a number of the most violent ones ever created (including Grand Theft Auto, The Punisher, and Soldier of Fortune II), one has to wonder if events might have played out differently for him if Gill had in fact ever tried on Super Columbine Massacre for size.

Rage

This virulent sickness that is so insidious in our society is rage. Rage is very different from anger, which arrives quickly in the moment in the presence of its cause and then is gone. Rage festers and burns slowly under the skin, often fed for years by feelings of indignation, entitlement, and superiority, until it explodes with brief but catastrophic force. Rage is a product of abuse and is a disease of the dysfunctional ego.

The more we live connected in virtual worlds (in our minds or online) and disconnected from the real world the greater the potential mismatch between our egos and ourselves, between who we are and who we think we are. In March, "a report by American psychologists, [called] Inflated Egos over Time, suggested that social-network sites such as MySpace and YouTube were promoting damagingly high—and illusory—levels of self-esteem among teenagers" (Appleyard 2007). The user-generated content revolution of Web 2.0, which includes blogging and other social network lifestyles, is in short fostering a new kind of egomania.

At their best blogs can uncover stories ignored by the mainstream media and expose deception or cover-ups, but at their worst blogs are notorious for encouraging a particular kind of opinionated aggressor who will use any form of abuse to pump themselves up or to "win" a point. Furthermore, since blogs mostly recycle material from one site to another, they produce a kind of shark-like feeding frenzy or emotional contagion that spreads from blog to blog. Oliver Kamm of the *London Times* thinks that bloggers are parasites that bully and poison debate (quoted in Appleyard 2007):

> In *The Guardian*, Jonathan Freedland pointed out that the abusive, vitriolic nature of many blogs had turned the blogosphere into a "claustrophobic environment, appealing chiefly to a certain kind of aggressive, point-scoring male—and utterly off-putting to everyone else." (Appleyard 2007)
>
> Freedland believes the defining feature in this phenomenon is the anonymity factor on the Web. People more frequently behave badly if no one knows who they are and there are no reprisals for doing so.

Freedom to Abuse

Early Internet culture was steeped in Libertarian values, and hackers lived by the motto that information wants to be free:

> But simple libertarianism is a meaningless and easy creed. It takes little or no account of Isaiah Berlin's crucial distinction between "freedom to" and "freedom from", the latter requiring external controls of the individual. Or, as Kris Kristofferson put it, rather more resonantly, "Freedom's just another word for nothing left to lose." (Appleyard 2007)

As the World Wide Web emerged and sprouted from that earlier infrastructure, it has incorporated all kinds of loopholes that make space for unrestricted harassing, abusive spamming and hacking behavior (Appleyard). And the potential for anonymity ensures that there are no reprisals. As the emotional bile builds at blog sites, it often evolves to dangerous levels allowing rage to become the reason for commenting, as blogger Kathy Sierra discovered in March 2007. The author of a popular blog, she is ranked among the top fifty technorati on the Web. When, however, she deleted some offensive postings at her site, she was shocked at the violent responses she received (Stone). She has since been driven into police protected hiding on account of rape and death threats at her own and other blogs (Sierra 2007).

In one of the last entries at her blog site, Sierra reflects on the phenomenon of emotional contagion. "Anger and resentment are the most contagious of emotions," according to an expert on road rage, she tells us. The anger and resentment that precedes road rage in particular is something that is easily passed from one driver to another, as one further provokes and imitates another that is near the breaking point (Sierra 2007). Road rage in the flesh is accompanied by a sense of entitlement and superiority over other drivers. Like bloggers and other bullies at their worst, ragers "feel it is their duty to punish bad drivers and teach them 'lessons'" (Kolton 2007). Emotional contagion is the ultimate in mob mentality, and we all feel it to some extent in particular situations: when in the presence of someone who is angry, depressed or ill or happy, or of a team that is winning, we easily become infected by those extreme emotions.

The Contagion Spreads

This epidemic of deep psychopathological emotions seems to be spreading. Dave Grossman's book *On Killing* documents how profoundly difficult it has been to train people to kill each other in the history of warfare. Examining changing technologies in conditioning from World War II until the Vietnam War, Grossman's findings are terrifying. In World War II, even when faced with a direct attack by the enemy, no more than 15 percent of soldiers would fire their weapons. By the Vietnam War, 95 percent of soldiers were firing (quoted in Millner 2000:65). Now, as our entertainment applies many of these "stimulus discriminator" techniques to the population at large, Millner fears that we may be creating a generation of psychopaths (Millner 2000:66).

While our children and our students may be the most susceptible to catching and transmitting these negative undercurrents, our society as a whole is experiencing this epidemic on a vast scale. Misogyny, homophobia, and racism seem to be the most powerful catalysts for these outbursts of societal forms of road rage as witnessed recently in highly visible incidents with Mel Gibson, Michael Richards, and Don Imus. In Imus's case, hip-hop was immediately deemed by many (just like computer games in the wake of campus shootings) to be the real villain responsible for the racist and sexist language that is gaining cultural currency in the mainstream. It is telling too that in computer games, as Sherry Millner notes, the possibility for empathizing with other characters is never an option (73).

Clearly boundaries are coming down and more raw, unrestrained, and disrespectful modes of expression are becoming commonplace, if still not officially acceptable. But, once more, this seems to be only a symptom of this sweeping disease that plagues us, with rage sending out shockwaves like tsunamis in a time when moral, cultural, economic, and political values are undergoing violent change on a global scale. The more the United States engages in aggressive and bullying behavior—warranted or not—around the world, flexing its military muscles, the more we feel the backlash on the Home Front in the West (and not just in the United States). The Home Front used to be the purview of the civilian population in wartime. Now, we have lost sight of boundaries, sides, and enemies. In an age of user-generated culture, we run the risk of living in a culture filled with homicidal/suicidal "Armies of One," each puffed up with a sense of his own self-importance, where everyone's concern is only for themselves.

Notes

1. View the trailer at: youtube.com/watch?v=Xr1oWtfFhiw.
2. Ninety-one people in thirty-four separate events are known to have killed themselves in Japan in 2005 (McCurry 2007).

References

Alter, Lloyd. 2006. "Road Rage Live: Bikes, Beef Patties and Blogs." *Treehugger* (February 2). Retrieved October 11, 2007 from www.treehugger.com/files/2006/02/road_rage_live_1.php.

Appleyard, Bryan. 2007. "The Web Is Dead: Long Live the Web." *Sunday Times Online* (April 22). Retrieved October 11, 2007 from technology.timesonline.co.uk/tol/news/tech_and_web/the_web/article1673425.ece.

Associated Press, comp. 2007. "Should Killing Merely Be a Mouse Click Away?" *New York Times Online* (March 11). Retrieved October 11, 2007 from www.nytimes.com/2007/03/11/sports/othersports/11hunt.html?ex=1331355600&en=dd5b6bd5aa2a5faa&ei=5124&partner=permalink&exprod=permalink.

Baudrillard, Jean. 2002. *Spirit of Terrorism*. Chris Turner, trans. London and New York: Verso.

Benedetti, Winda. 2007. "Were Video Games Responsible for the Massacre?" *MSNBC*. (April 20). NBC. Retrieved October 11, 2007 from www.msnbc.msn.com/id/18220228.

Broadband. 2007. "Top 10 Most Violent Video Games." *DX Gaming* (April 2). Retrieved October 11, 2007 from www.dxgaming.com/?p=14.

Carter, Bill. 2007a. "NBC Defends Its Use of Material Sent by Killer." *New York Times Online* (April 20). Retrieved October 11, 2007 from www.nytimes.com/2007/04/20/us/20nbc.html?th&emc=th.

———. 2007b. "Package Forced NBC to Make Tough Decisions." *New York Times Online* (April 19). Retrieved October 11, 2007 from www.nytimes.com/2007/04/19/us/19nbc.html?th&emc=th.

Cassel, David. 2000. "Hacktivism in the Cyberstreets." *AlterNet* (May 30). Retrieved October 11, 2007 from www.alternet.org/story/9223.

Crescente, Brian D. 2006. "Gamer Was on Deadly Road." *RockyMountainNews.Com* (May 24). Retrieved October 11, 2007 from www.rockymountainnews.com/drmn/local/article/0,1299,DRMN_15_4722344,00.html.

———. 2007. "Exclusive: Columbine Game Kicked from Competition." *Kotaku.Com* (January 5). Retrieved October 11, 2007 from kotaku.com/gaming/top/exclusive-columbine-game-kicked-from-competition-226272.php.

Cullen, Dave. 2004. "The Depressive and the Psychopath: At Last We Know Why the Columbine Killers Did It." *Slate.Com* (April 20). Retrieved October 11, 2007 from www.slate.com/id/2099203/.

Fox, Spider. 2007. "Top 10 Lists: Top 10 Most Violent Video Games Ever." *Gamespot GameFacts*. Retrieved October 11, 2007 from www.gamefaqs.com/features/top10/909.html.

Guertin, Carolyn. 2007. "All the Rage: Digital Bodies and Deadly Play in the Age of the Suicide Bomber." *Fast Capitalism* 3 (1). Retrieved October 11, 2007 from www.fastcapitalism.com.

Gumbel, Andrew. 2007. "Stop Using All This Bad Language, Says Hip-Hop Pioneer." *The Independent* (April 25). Retrieved October 11, 2007 from www.independent.co.uk/arts/music/news/article2483858.ece.

Harmon, Amy. 1998. "Hacktivists of All Persuasions Take Their Struggle to the Web." *New York Times Online* (October 31). Retrieved October 11, 2007 from query.nytimes.com/gst/fullpage.html?res=9807E4D6143FF932A05753C1A96E958260.

"In Pictures: Saddam in Custody." *BBC Photo Gallery*. December 15, 2003). BBC Online. Retrieved October 11, 2007 from news.bbc.co.uk/2/hi/in_depth/photo_gallery/3318041.stm.

Kaitlin. 2007. "Terrorists Attack Second Life." *New Public* 26 (February). Retrieved October 11, 2007 from www.nowpublic.com/terrorists_attack_second_life.

Kolton, Tara. 2007. "Tackling Road Rage." *DoItYourself.Com*. Retrieved October 11, 2007 from www.doityourself.com/stry/roadrage.

Kuchera, Ben. 2007. "Super Columbine Massacre RPG! Pulled from Game Competition." *Opposable Thumbs* (January 9). Retrieved October 11, 2007 from arstechnica.com/journals/thumbs.ars/2007/1/9/6534.

Leary, Timothy, and R. U. Sirius. *Design for Dying*. New York: HarperCollins, 1998.

Ledonne, Danny. 2005a. "Artist's Statement." *Columbinegame.Com*. Retrieved October 11, 2007 from columbinegame.com/statement.htm.

———. 2005b. "Super Columbine Massacre RPG! Trailer." *Google Video*. Retrieved February 5, 2008 from youtube/watch?v=Xrlowtffhiw.

———. 2005c. "Welcome to the World of Super Columbine Massacre RPG!" *Columbinegame.Com*. Retrieved October 11, 2007 from www.columbinegame.com/.

Linden Labs. 2003. "Second Life: Your World. Your Imagination." *Second Life*. Retrieved October 11, 2007 from www.secondlife.com.

Maccloud, Scott. 2007. "Saddam's Hanging Reverberates Throughout the Middle East." *Time Online* (January 3). Retrieved October 11, 2007 from www.time.com/time/world/article/0,8599,1573593,00.html.

Majende, Paul. 2007. "Violent Video 'Exhilarating Escapism.'" *Reuters* (April 18). Retrieved October 11, 2007 from www.reuters.com/articlePrint?articleId=USL1840949320070418.

McCarthy, Caroline. 2007a. "Griefing in Second Life." *CNETnews.com* (March 5). Retrieved October 11, 2007 from www.news.com/2300-1043_3-6163932-4.html?tag=ne.gall.pg.

———. 2007b. "In Second Life the Ring of Revolution." *CNETnews.com* (March 5). Retrieved October 11, 2007 from news.com.com/In+Second+Life,+the+ring+of+revolution/2100- 1043_3-6163917.html?tag=sas.email.

McCurry, Justin. 2007. "Nine Bodies Found as Japan Fails to Curb Suicide Pact." *Guardian Unlimited* (March 11). Retrieved October 11, 2007 from www.guardian.co.uk/japan/story/0,,1728698,00.html?gusrc=rss.

McLuhan, Marshall, and Bruce R. Powers. 1992. *The Global Village: Transformations in World Life and Media in the 21st Century*. London: Oxford University Press.

McLuhan, Marshall. 1964. *Understanding Media: The Extensions of Man*. New York: Signet.

McLuhan, Marshall, and Quentin Fiore. 2001. *War and Peace in the Global Village*. Corte Madera, CA: Gingko Press.

Mikkelsen, Randall. 2007. "U.S. Networks Limit Use of Va. Tech Gunman Video." *Reuters* (April 19). Retrieved October 11, 2007 from www.reuters.com/article/latestCrisis/idUSN19400335.

Millner, Sherry. 2000. "Wired for Violence." *Digital Desires: Language, Identity and New Technologies*. Ed. Cutting Edge. New York and London: I. B. Tauris Co. 61–77.

Murray, Stuart. 2005. *McLuhan, Rhetoric, Philosophy*. Ms. By Permission of the Author. Toronto, Canada.

———. 2006. "Thanatopolitics: On the Use of Death for Mobilizing Political Life." *Polygraph: An International Journal of Politics and Culture* 18: 191–215.

Porter, Wayne. 2006. "Exclusive Interview with the Leader of the Second Life Liberation Army." *Wayne Porter on Attention Revenue* (December 4). Retrieved October 11, 2007 from www.wayneporter.com/2006/12/04/exclusive-interview-with-second-life-liberation-army-reflections-on-snow.

"Prince's Weapon Is a Camera-Gun." *Modern Mechanix* (June 1950). Retrieved December 12, 2006 from blog.modernmechanix.com/2006/12/12/princes-weapon-is-a-camera-gun/.

Sanneh, Kelefa. 2007. "Don't Blame Hip-Hop." *New York Times Online* (April 25). Retrieved October 11, 2007 from www.nytimes.com/2007/04/25/arts/music/25hiph.html?pagewanted=1&_r=1&th&emc=th.

"Second Life." *Wikipedia*. Retrieved October 11, 2007 from en.wikipedia.org/wiki/Second_Life.

Sierra, Kathy. 2007. "Angry/Negative People Can Be Bad for Your Brain." (April 17). Passionate: Creating Passionate Users. Retrieved October 11, 2007 from headrush.typepad.com/creating_passionate_users/2006/04/angrynegative_p.html.

Stone, Brad. 2007. "A Call for Manners in the World of Nasty Blogs." *New York Times Online* (April 9). Retrieved October 11, 2007 from www.nytimes.com/2007/04/09/technology/09blog.html?ref=technology.

Strate, Lance. 2007. "Guns and Cameras." *Lance Strate's Blog Time Passing* (April 20). Retrieved October 11, 2007 fromlancestrate.blogspot.com/2007/04/guns-and-cameras.html.

Thompson, Clive. 2007. "I, Columbine Killer." *Wired Online* (January 15). Retrieved October 11, 2007 from www.wired.com/gaming/gamingreviews/commentary/games/2007/01/72491.

Turner, Jeremy O. 2007. "Terrorism is Temporary in Second Life." *NowPublic* (February 26). Retrieved October 11, 2007 from www.nowpublic.com/terrorism_is_temporary_in_second_life.

Walsh, Tony. 2006. "Politico Grabs Second Life Publicity." *Clickable Culture* (August 31). Retrieved October 11, 2007 from www.secretlair.com/index.php?/clickableculture/entry/politico_grabs_second_life_publicity/.

CHAPTER Fourteen

IS VIRGINIA TECH AN EXCEPTION?

Stanley Aronowitz

Columbine, Kansas City, Virginia Tech, Omaha.... The scenario is eerily similar. One or more young men, classified by the media and psychology experts as deranged, isolates, singular in an otherwise calm, contented population suddenly, and apparently without warning, enter a room or a mall-space and start shooting randomly. As reports of the dead and severely wounded climb to the double digits the entire country begins a very brief period of self-examination, sometimes recriminations, and solemnly declares—at least for a nanosecond—that we will take seriously what has happened, delve to the root causes of violence, and most important, dedicate ourself to mobilize moral and security resources to make sure it does not happen again. Executive authorities appoint commissions, the police assure the public that the perps will be duly rounded up and punished. The incident becomes an occasion for renewed calls for stricter gun control (as if legal prohibition will significantly restrict access to weapons); teachers and administrators defend themselves by claiming they tried to address the severe alienation that lay at the root of the crime: for example, at Virginia Tech they knew the student was disturbed but, after all, there are limits to what counseling can achieve. If suicide follows the killings, as was the case in Virginia Tech and Columbine, we are certainly relieved because the moral, symbolic order is preserved by the self-condemnation of the shooter(s). Days and sometimes weeks later everything returns to "normal" but little has been done except to tighten security to make sure the school, the mall, the streets are safe. Having persuaded ourselves that "these kids" who perpetrated the killings are mentally ill, it is relatively easy to classify the incident as an anomaly, in which case the "community" holds itself largely blameless for what occurred. Of course, there are always a few clergy who call attention to the moral decrepitude of a materialistic, Godless civilization but, they too, are mostly ignored.

Let us stipulate at the outset that we are not witness to a new crime wave, and the country is not overrun by violent, irrational outbursts by otherwise nice, middle-class youth. In contrast to "riots" in the Paris suburbs, for example, these are not signs of rebellion born of discrimination and economic hardship, yet these events have been precipitated precisely by the discontent of well-mannered young people from affluent or relatively secure middle-class environments. Many recognize that violence is an important aspect of everyday life in poor, working-class neighborhoods and we know that while thousands are murdered every year in the United States most, thankfully, are perpetrated among family members, friends, and neighbors, and a good number connected to the drug trade, but killings rarely occur in clean suburban or upscale urban precincts where most of the professional/managerial class (PMC) live. The "public" coded as members of the PMC and the outright ruling class must be safely removed from the more sordid aspects of our collective life; after all if wealth cannot buy safety, what's the point. Thus, the occasional murders in white affluent communities—remember Ms. Harris and Klaus Von Bulow?—are, for most of us, grist for the scandal sheets we surreptitiously consult at supermarket check-out counters and some eventually find their way to the silver screen or become television specials that whet our prurient interest. These crimes are the stuff of popular culture, not the frenzy associated with random mass killings. And they partake of a long, and honorable tradition among the upper reaches of society; jealousy and intrigue are as much the stuff of upper-class life as, say, gang warfare is of the ghettoes of large cities.

Of course, the PMC does not really care whether the poor kill each other. Gang violence, often the consequence of the still flourishing drug trade and of other types of turf wars between organized groups, although not rare, rarely spills over to the suburbs or to the more affluent neighborhoods of the cities. Let the police take care of that kind of violence. But it becomes alarmed when their own children become the objects of lethal violence. What disturbs the PMC is that most of the recent "Virginia Tech" types of killing sprees have come home to their own spaces and the culprits as much as the victims are not outsiders, but their own children. Of course, we could regard the young Korean-born student who let loose on his fellow students and teachers at Virginia Tech as an outsider, but this only works at the margins. To all appearances he was good at schoolwork, kept to himself, and only "made trouble" rather late in the months leading up to the drama and typifies the striving immigrant population seeking professional and business status.

The question that requires consideration is not why Virginia Tech, but why such incidents do not occur more often? The shooting at Virginia Tech and by the boys of Columbine whose aggression first stunned us and enflamed long suppressed fear and trembling, are recurrent symptoms of a malaise among middle-class young people who find themselves trapped, not in the Brechtian "jungle of the cities," the site of many a story and song from John Gay to Dickens to Brecht, but in the profound and scary environments of affluent suburbs and of colleges and universities that often inhabit a portion of their spaces. On one level, these events serve to remind us of a deep flaw in the American Dream. As articulated by its protagonists the Dream has clear and almost exclusive economic dimensions. After World War II the goal of economic security was attained by millions at a time when the United States was virtually the only global economic superpower. In this context going to college and, among a smaller coterie, to graduate school where one could acquire a profession or a credential in business or public administration, was sufficient to find a job that paid well enough to buy a single or two family home and pay down a mortgage, to assist their kids to acquire the cultural capital needed for admission to an elite or mid-range university, sometimes by paying private school fees they could barely afford and then to pay university tuition.

The price of achieving the American dream for many is that work, which starts out as a means to obtain its rewards, becomes an end. Absent fathers are an old story: If the male leaves for the office, construction site, or the factory at seven in the morning and returns at seven in the evening, having traveled two hours or more to and from work, there was always the mother and sometimes a grandparent or two to raise the children. But the advent of consumer society has been accompanied by a steep rise, not only in living standards, but the costs of maintaining the way of life commensurate with the cultural norms of middle-class life. From the late 1960s we have seen a progressive rise of paid employment among women. During the industrializing era about 30 percent of women were engaged in paid work, most of them young women. But for the past forty years the proportion of married women, and not only single parents, who have entered the paid labor force has risen dramatically to over 70 percent. The new story is that what neighborhoods existed in many urban and suburban communities are in the process of disappearing. PTAs, civic groups, and charitable organizations complain that citizen participation has disappeared, that they are forced to restrict their activities or employ paid staff to perform the tasks once performed by volunteers. It may be argued that civil society owes its demise to the cultural ideals that equate the Good Life with economic goods.

After the war when the cities were no longer sites of population growth and did not supply adequate housing for upwardly mobile families, the Federal government came up with a solution: instead of building urban multiple dwellings for middle income as well as low income residents, it entered into an alliance with private builders to build single family houses in the suburbs. What followed were the myriad of malls and shopping centers that litter the highways that were built, instead of adequate mass transit, to carry tens of millions into the cities where most of the jobs reside. The phenomenon we call suburban "sprawl" had by the 1960s dominated many regions. States like Connecticut and Virginia, for example, witnessed the precipitous decline of its main cities as consumers chose to venture to the "burbs" to do their shopping. If the characteristic teenage hangout of the 1950s was the diner, it has largely been replaced by the mall. In time, in the absence of streets, recreational centers, organized youth groups, the malls became social centers, not only for business meetings and civil organizations, but for young people who hang out mainly at the multiplex cinema that plays the main Hollywood fare, in the record and DVD stores, and in the inevitable food court that offers every possible variety of fast food—greasy tacos, hot dogs, Asian food, and even sushi of doubtful origin that kids and their families eat on plastic cafeteria furniture. In short everyday life in the suburbs is a circuit of buying, eating, and movie-going.

And the kids travel in packs, adopt fashion conventions, rules of behavior, aesthetic standards, and criteria for admission to their various groups. In many instances, "deviants" whether racial, ethnic, sexual, emotional, or intellectual, live a lonely life, often constituting a minority of one or, if they are lucky, manage to find sympathetic souls, which doesn't exempt them from the contempt in which they are held by the majority. They often suffer the abuse that minorities in this culture are wont to endure for, in the main, young people are increasingly self-raised, their references are not to the "family" but to each other and to the commercial environment within which they live their actual lives. Even when they go to college, schooling is viewed chiefly as a site of social life, secondarily as a means to the end of obtaining a credential and often as a prison whose invisible bars hold them they know not why.

It may be that for those fortunate to have been accepted by a group the teeth-grinding boredom of schooling and of suburban culture saves them from suicide, from dropping out, or from committing acts of violence they cannot control. Of course, we must acknowledge that one of the conditions of survival in these precincts is that young people in great numbers are self-medicated; the statistics on drinking and drugs among young people continue to alarm educators, law enforcement officials, and the absent parents. Do the social costs of fulfilling the American Dream outweigh its benefits? For young people, having become accustomed to a certain level of material well-being, now face the emptiness of spiritual life under late capitalism. Moreover, as this is part of the mosaic, many can no longer expect to attain the level of prosperity that their parents enjoyed. For they are coming of age at a moment when uncertainties dominate the economic landscape, when even the affluent face a future of contingent and temporary jobs, when the concept of "career," recently extended from law, clergy, and medicine to teaching, social work, retail, and wholesale, and to administration, is being shredded by almost daily announcements of mass layoffs in the financial services sector, manufacturing, and retailing.

To which must be added the fragmentation and virtual disappearance of the political, social, and cultural opposition. The left, never strong in electoral terms, once did offer a haven for thousands of what Kenneth Kenniston once termed "alienated youth," written at a time when the New Left was at its zenith. The New Left, perhaps the most vital youth movement in U.S. history, has all but disappeared, leaving behind the shards of altered cultural mores against which conservatism still rails and prospers as a political movement. But with the collapse of the Soviet Union and the erosion of the socialist alternative as a global phenomenon, the Old Left is, for most intents, defunct. Perhaps equally important, the counterculture, which exploded in the wake of the civil rights and antiwar rebellions of the 1960s, and which has changed our lives in many ways, not the least of which is alimentary, has succumbed to the same real estate boom that engulfed the PMC. And, of course, bohemia is no longer a refuge for the outsider for the same reasons. What young people have to look forward to is graduate school, a temporary respite in the inevitable march toward professionalization. As we know professionalism is the enemy of the imagination, disdains creativity, dissent, and difference.

Under the circumstances we should not be shocked and surprised that the inheritors of American exceptionalism, the middle-class young, resist conformity in desperate, futile, and destructive forms. It is not the shattering of the family romance to which we should turn for explanations for the empirical bourgeois family has been dead for decades and even its symbolic existence is under erasure. It is the economic ideal of the American dream that is finally being questioned, even as it enjoys something of a revival among recent immigrants. For if all young people have to look forward to is more of the same, in the absence of the shelters that dissident communities sometimes provide, we can expect violence to escalate, for it's not the economy, but the culture, stupid.

CHAPTER
Fifteen

BAUDRILLARD (1929–2007) AND MAO:
A History of Normal Violence

Charles Lemert

When Annie and I arrived in Beijing, it had been two virtual days since we left New York for what turned out to be a thirty-hour trip that erased March 7, 2007, from our lives. We were met at the airport by my friend and colleague in sociology who, by the end of our stay, Annie came to be called Auntie Ming. After greetings and inquiries as to the trip, her first question to me was, "How is this day being celebrated in the States?" The day was March 8, International Women's Day, which of course was not being celebrated at all back home. If in China, and much of the sane world, it was not exactly being celebrated, the Day was a holiday. So much for globalization in the fast-fading core. Time is very fast these days. Still some global spaces can pick and chose at will.

Not only that but, in some places, space makes for slow. It is nearly impossible to get anywhere fast when the place through or around which you must get is New York City. Annie and I started our impossibly long trip on a fast plane a good ten hours before take off. This just to get from New Haven, where we live, to JFK—a real distance of about 80 miles; hence, waiting, traffic, and security lines included, the speed of our airport trip was around 10 miles per hour or, not that much faster than it took Henry David Thoreau to walk the same journey in 1843. Real space can grind virtual velocity to a halt, occasionally with real consequences. In our case, the unbearable slowness of fast time meant that my daughter and I were out of this world for the better part of three calendrical days. So far as news was concerned, we also missed March 6, 2007. For Annie, age nine, this meant little in particular. For me, it meant that in the time lost getting to China I also missed the day Jean Baudrillard died.

Actually, in real historical time, if there is such a thing, I had missed a good bit of Baudrillard. I had never met him, nor bothered to read many of his later books, which were, even when I was younger, a little too cool. My time diverged from his sometime after the famous *Simulacra and Simulation* (1983 [1981]) essay in 1981—just when, on the plane of my personal life, divorce and related troubles made books like *Cool Memories* (1990 [1987]) dispensable. From the tiny window I afforded myself I could see his plane speeding off on a tangent I could not, then, pursue. I did not begin to catch up until my personal life had broken new ground to enter its own new time. Yet, Baudrillard's death, like his life, is an event, so to speak, that is hard to outrun, impossible to ignore.

The end of Baudrillard may well have signified the end of the infamously important French tradition of post-something-hard-to-say-what— a *whatever-it-was* that many in this world wished would never have been.

It has been my fate, if such a term applies to this world, to work in a field, sociology, that stirs the heart and mind with provocations so rich as to be too much for those encamped in the field's center ground. Though Baudrillard taught sociology at Nanterre, many of the profession abhorred his ideas which, when left unread, can indeed be overstimulating. The very idea that Disneyland and such like are the only reliable realities is unnerving to those who stake their sense of personal worth on hard realities that have rewarded them. The most memorable of these types, in my experience, was a lesser French sociologist whose academic post owed more to his bourgeois credits than to any real accomplishment. When invited to join an editorial project, he agreed on one condition: that Jean Baudrillard be excluded. Baudrillard sped on; this one sank of his own dead weight.

Baudrillard, in *The Illusion of the End* (1994 [1992]), one of the books I caught up with, put the issue of our time just right: "The illusion of our history opens onto the *greatly more radical illusion of the world*." This was 1992, when he was among the first to appreciate the true importance of the events of 1989–1991 for Europe and the world.

> Now we have closed the eyelids of the Revolution, closed our eyes on the Revolution, now we have broken down the Wall of Shame, now that the lips of protest are closed (with the sugar of history which melts on the tongue), now Europe—and memories—are no longer haunted by the specter of communism, nor even by that of power, now the aris-

tocratic illusion of the origin and the democratic illusion of the end are increasingly receding, we no longer have the choice of advancing, of persevering in the present destruction, or of retreating—but only of facing up to this radical illusion.

As Baudrillard's earliest books were written in the wake of the events of 1968, his later ones were of the events of 1989.

What the queasy never quite understood is that the French social theorists who came into their own around 1968 were clear about what history was and was not. The French, after all, had invented History in the sense of the tragedy of 1789 and the farce of 1848. Europeans of the short twentieth century lived quotidian history with a sober intensity that even the Americans who died and suffered in the world wars had not. The Americans have always believed that History was on their side. This is an arrogance that can be justified only by an inexcusable abstraction from the surrealities of war. The Europeans lived with the violence of capital-H History—the tragedies and farces, the chambers and the saturation bombings, and all the rest that carried over with ever more sinister inventiveness from the failures of the nineteenth-century ideal of History's purposeful End.

If lower-case history has anything good to say about the pathetic George W. Bush it might be that his time as the administrator of modern values exposed them for what they always had been—a phantasmagoria of moving pictures projecting the illusion of progressive History as more real than any true story could ever be. The Greatest Story Ever Told is that History triumphs, when in fact (so to speak) history just is what it is, without beginning or ending, save those supplied by popular fictions.

Modernity's bourgeois revolution was—referring to one of Baudrillard's early theories—a system of consumption created by necessity at one and the same time as the system of production. Already in *The System of Objects* (1996 [1968]), "There are no limits to consumption." If the capitalist mode of production is to *be* history, then even Marx's all-too-neat, if all-too-prescient, idea that production determines everything of value planted the seed of its own revision. Consumption is not an end, but a resource. Thus, as Baudrillard made clear, use-value must be analytically cut from exchange-value in order to insert the ownership of desire. Without the manufacture of need, there can be no surplus value. Production, in the end, such as it is, does not produce value-seeking subjects but consuming humanoids—reifications of the real beings ground down by the avarice of modernity. "The system of needs is the product of the system of production."

Thus, later, from the notoriously wonderful essay, *Simulacra and Simulation*:

In this passage to a space whose curvature is no longer that of the real, nor of truth, the age of simulation thus begins with a liquidation of all referentials—worse: by their artificial resurrection in systems of signs, which are a more ductile material than meaning, in that they lend themselves to all systems of equivalence, all binary oppositions and all combinatory algebra. It is no longer a question of imitation, nor of reduplication, nor even of parody. It is rather a question of substituting signs of the real for the real itself; that is, an operation to deter every real process by its operational double, a metastable, programmatic, perfect descriptive machine which provides all the signs of the real and short-circuits all its entire vicissitudes. Never again will the real have to be produced: this is the vital function of the model in a system of death, or rather of anticipated resurrection which no longer leaves any chance even in the event of death. A hyperreal henceforth sheltered from the imaginary, and from any distinction between the real and the imaginary, leaving room only for the orbital recurrence of models and the simulated generation of difference.

In lines that would make Žižek blush, Baudrillard lends specific gravity to his semiotic theory of consumption as a theory of history as the reality of History. When need is the only product of the modern system, then the fetishism of commodities is more than a moral error. It exhausts the meaning of historical reality, in the modern sense, as a fog of fungible references without referents—a system beyond systems that renders impractical the very idea of discernible values, whether material or ideal; hence, the hyper reality of all things—a universe without end in which social things disclose their perfect instability.

Beijing on March 8, 2007, was just the place to be forced to meditate on Baudrillard's passing into a time that never ends. On that day, in a city where many wear masks to protect what lung tissue remains, the air was uncommonly clear. The sun was bright. Tiananmen Square was crowded with tourists from the provinces. The Great Hall of the People was hosting the National Party Congress (an institution so illusory as to meet but every five years). Party flags were flapping in the brisk wind. Mao's Tomb, just across the Square from the Great Hall, was beset, I thought, by an unusually long line of visitors waiting to gape at the Chairman's remains.

Even on a bad weather day, Tiananmen is a sight to behold. Few places on earth, in my experience, better suit Baudrillard's theory of consumable objects. It is a Disneyland in which Mao is the ubiquitous Mickey Mouse. An enormous mug shot of the Chairman is mounted over the South Gate of the Forbidden City. His visage is plainly visible from any point in Tiananmen's 4.3 million square feet wide open space; or, better put, he, in death, stares far along the ancient axis of the city he meant to modernize.

The Forbidden City was the Imperial Palace of the Ming and Qing dynasties (1368–1912). The Palace occupied an enormous center ground of the ancient walled city. From the Imperial Palace looking to the South, Tiananmen Square is framed to the East by Mao's Tomb and to the West by the Great Hall of the People. Beyond the Square, on the same meridian, the eye can make out in the distance the delicate outline of the Temple of Heaven—the Taoist temple built in the fifteenth century under the Ming dynasty. Each year on the winter solstice, the emperors processed from the Imperial Palace to the Temple where they paid homage to the Heavenly powers. Just beyond, still to the South, on the 700-acre Temple grounds that dwarfed both today's Square and the Forbidden City, stand the remnants of the Southern Gate of the once-walled city. The Communists had torn down most of the ancient walls, as they are destroying the remaining urban villages that carry on much as they did in the days of the emperors.

The empires were overthrown in 1912 by the nationalist revolution. Mao was then a young student in Changsha in Hunan Province. He served perfunctorily for six months in the Republican army. His studies were under local provincial scholars who taught rudimentary philosophy based on Confucian classics. Mao quickly soured on the nationalists and their enlightened politics that turned out to be as cruel as were the feudal ones they overthrew.

By 1927, then in his midthirties, Mao had risen in the ranks of the Communist Party and begun to organize the peasants in eastern Hunan. They were the peasants who lent force to the army of the romanticized Long March. The Communist revolution suffered many defeats by the Kuomintang before Chiang Kai-shek was vanquished in 1949. After the Korean War ended in 1953, the Party under Mao began a Soviet-style "reconstruction" program.

Jonathan Spence, in *Mao Zedong: A Life* (1999), said of Mao:

> Both the Hundred Flowers movement and the launching of the Great Leap show Mao more and more divorced from any true reality check.... And he himself seemed to care less and less for the consequences that might spring from his own erratic utterances.... For the strange fact was that Mao had created a world in which things could hardly be otherwise.

Hence, even if Spence exaggerates, the Cultural Revolution of 1966 proves the point that Mao's vision for China was defiantly trapped in the traditional China of the imperial dynasties—a world cut off from the outside, a world organized around what turned out to be Disneyland principles. The enduring suffering of the Chinese people, most notably the peasantry that formed the political foundation of Mao's revolution, continued until the Chairman's death in 1976, and continues still. The Tiananmen slaughter in 1989 was but the most visible sign of the system that killed so many for so long, violating the moral grammar Mao had imposed, then destroyed in his own unreal system of human consumption.

Baudrillard and Mao were not of the same worlds, nor of like mind. Yet, in a weird way, both were caught up, to differing ends, in the two most symbolic of late modern years: 1968 and 1989. Baudrillard flourished in the events of 1968, which were in Paris a street theater replaying modernity's unfinished revolutions—1789, 1848, 1871, 1968. That year must also have brought Mao to his senses, to a degree. In 1969, he declared the Cultural Revolution over. But it had already taken on a life of its own. He could not end what he had begun. He died in 1976 still swimming up river against the violence he had wrought out of the reality he had made after his own illusions. In Beijing, 1989 was a Prague springtime—an oddly deferred revelation of the force of popular rebellion against the power of a state gone mad on its own ideological opiate. In Europe, as Baudrillard said, the End of the Revolution exposed the illusion of all the epiphanies of all of modernity's insistences on the reality of its own systems—communist, aristocratic, democratic. In Beijing as well as Europe, 1989 established, as Baudrillard said, "a system of death, or rather of anticipated resurrection which no longer leaves any chance even in the event of death."

Beijing today is a magic kingdom. Mao looks out in death over Tiananmen Square, guarding the Forbidden City modernity meant to tear down. Tourists from the countryside stream through the Palace gates under the overblown image of the dead Chairman. They are the fortunate ones who can afford the price of admission, even perhaps a cup of Starbucks once sold at the coffee shop deep within the once forbidden Palace. They, the younger generations, are among the descendents of the same rural poor Mao championed before he became a surreal fact of his own imagination. Their distant cousins at several removes suffer in the remote provinces, some stealing into the capital city to work for scant pay, with irregular sleep and meager rations, to build the new, pseudo-modern buildings that will sell Buicks and Audis, Kentucky Fried Chicken, and other Western poisons. They kill our dogs; we kill their children.

In the end, so to speak, the Magic Kingdom is everywhere. The postmodern China that Mao made possible is itself an imitation of the Western idea of the Good. Beijing is not yet Mumbai, but lord knows it is trying; and, if this, then Dubai cannot be far behind—the world as indoor mall, reality as shopping, truth as denial of the suffering one can see from the hotels late at night as peasants, chilled to the bone, work on pouring the foundations of the Kingdom.

It is not easy to get to Blacksburg, Virginia. Flying requires a series of hub connects. Driving is through the mountains. Blacksburg is a remote oasis on the wrong side of the mountains that separate the Blue Ridge playground from Appalachian poverty.

What made the slaughter of so many students and faculty at Virginia Tech so senseless was, in part, that it happened here. For a time, the world moved to Blacksburg to gawk at the terrible pain. In time, the dead will be forgotten in the system of death that moves on inexorably without ending.

I have lost a child to another kind of violence. I do not minimize the suffering of parents who lost children that terrible day. But in time's slow progress, life triumphs, for what that may be worth. Those who get through the pain will allow their dead to find their places in a time the living cannot, and must not, understand. Fast time or slow, all time, as Levinas and Heidegger taught, is the time of nonbeing. The dead measure what progress there might be.

Blacksburg shocks, still now and for a while longer, because it is so remote in a world where the well-connected believe everything is connected. The rural poverty of the western Virginias is Appalachian, which in turn is a comparable to Eastern Hunan where Mao started out with the best of intentions and few clues as to what was and was not real History.

The rage that pushed a boy from Korea to murder innocents who, to him, no doubt, looked like all the faceless others who had, in his mind, tormented him is like unto the rage in all human beings. The normals hold it in. The paranormals pretend it is not there. The abnormals succumb to it. Normal violence is a terrible thing. It is the lifeblood of the modern world. Once it pours out of open wounds it drowns the pain.

Today, as for several centuries, normal violence is done in the name of class, ideals, values, and all the rest of the purported realities by which this world has been organized since, say, 1500 or so, when the Iberians sailed for their India and the Mings built their Forbidden City. What were they escaping? Who were they sheltering themselves from? What makes them so different from the rest of us who have been invented in the wake of the modern illusion?

Blacksburg is not terrorism. It is not even murder. It is but one of the realities of a world that Baudrillard, among many others, saw dimly in 1968 and Mao, among many others, must have dimly figured out when he tried, in 1969, to stop the violence he had begun. Time moves, ever more now than then, at odd, tangential ways and speeds. It may even be reversible, but it certainly cannot be taken back. A thousand mile march may begin with a single step. But if its drummer beats too hard, the march will not end well.

Mao looks out on us as the reminder of what moderns wanted—a republic of peoples the world over. It is, instead, a state of continuous violence. If, as Baudrillard put it, we accept this world as a radical illusion, then, who knows—might we begin to live as people can?

References

Baudrillard, Jean. 1983 [1981]. *Simulacra and Simulation*. Paris: Semiotext(e).
———. 1994 [1992]. *The Illusion of the End*. London: Polity.
———. 1990 [1987]. *Cool Memories*. London: Verso.
———. 1996 [1968]. *The System of Objects*. London: Verso.
Spence, Jonathan. 1999. *Mao Zedong: A Life*. London: Penguin.

CHAPTER
Sixteen

CHO, NOT CHE?:
Positioning Blacksburg in the Political

Ben Agger

The power of our media culture was demonstrated in the week or so after the killing of thirty-three people (including the gunman Seung-Hui Cho) on the Virginia Tech campus in Blacksburg, Virginia, on April 16, 2007. Day and night coverage of the event, and its aftermath, blanketed the airwaves, especially on the cable television channels such as CNN and MSNBC. These media framed the event and in so doing produced a viewership which held certain common assumptions and perceptions. The event was portrayed as somehow *outside the political*, an account that I want to challenge here. This is not to provide an alternative reductionism, which positions Cho and his victims entirely inside the political. The personal and political interpenetrate but they do not overlap entirely. In no way am I suggesting that Cho is a latter-day version of Che, in spite of his meandering messianism in which he defends his scorched-earth policy (replicating Columbine) on behalf of lost souls everywhere. But to view Blacksburg as occurring outside the political, merely as a human tragedy without social and political echoes and underpinnings, is to miss the point: Cho led a "damaged life," as Adorno termed it. And some of the damage was done by the world. Critical theory needs a social psychology in order to understand events such as those that occurred at Blacksburg.

How was Blacksburg framed as somehow outside the political?

Waves of psychologists and psychiatrists, some of whom were designated as hired hands of the networks themselves, were recruited to tell us that Cho was insane, implying or stating that his apparent mental illness (psychosis, sociopathy, etc.) was the result of organic causes. That might be partially true, but certainly no one could know this so quickly (or ever, given that he is dead).

The event was framed as a universal human tragedy and the dead were honored and remembered in collective vigils and demonstrations and by the wearing of Virginia Tech-themed and -colored apparel. By week's end, Hokie pride was on display. In this sense, the Blacksburg events were unifying themes supposedly cutting across political and party lines and thus preempting debate about the social causes and consequences of "damaged life." Virginia Tech became the latest version of the Indonesian tsunami or Hurricane Katrina, although, again, these events, although seemingly "natural," were heavily influenced by social and political decisions and indecision. Nature, since the Frankfurt School's writings in the 1940s, is squarely within the realm of the political; and I am suggesting that human nature should be as well.

The Second Amendment of the U.S. Constitution, which enables citizens to form armed militias in face of government tyranny, was assumed as a given framework not subject to debate. Although gun control was discussed in some quarters, that was matched by the idea that students and faculty should arm themselves in order to prevent further massacres. I heard no one suggest repealing the Second Amendment, which allows individuals to own Uzis and other automatic weapons as a basic Constitutional right. I am not of the view that America was built on violence, that violence is as American as apple pie; rather, America was built on the possibility of revolutionary insurrection, which is a much more progressive reading of the Second Amendment than is offered by the NRA.

The psychologism discussed above drowned out consideration of Cho's immigrant status and his marginalization in his suburban Washington, D.C., high school, where he struggled to fit in. And most of the Virginia Tech students interviewed were Anglo and not Asian, suggesting that Cho felt equally marginalized in his university years. The two shooters at Columbine were also estranged from their fellow students and sometimes bullied. Although marginality need not lead to murder, it is important that these so-called mass murders involved young men with access to weaponry who experienced what Durkheim called anomie.

Any generationally inflected cultural/political reading of Blacksburg and Columbine cannot blithely ignore the penchant among young men for violent video games. Cause/effect are difficult to disentangle, just as the psychic and the social/political do not sort neatly. However, solving existential problems by blowing people away is certainly prefigured by violent video games, especially those in which the young players actually simulate shooting. I am not saying that video games "caused" Blacksburg but that people who like violent video games are alienated and that alienation—the damaged life—is what led to Blacksburg. Doug Kellner in his piece in this symposium analyzes Cho's video for its cultural influences.

The deaths at Blacksburg are no greater in number than the deaths in Iraq over a few days. We chose death in Iraq, a political decision. And yet the Blacksburg dead attract much greater attention, largely because we can position Cho outside of the political and thus create a narrative of undeserved death. A demography of death is sometimes betrayed by the media attention given them. From smallest to largest death counts: Columbine, Blacksburg, Hurricane Katrina, 9/11, U.S. casualties in Iraq.

The Virginia Tech administration has been faulted for reacting slowly to the first shootings, in one of their dormitories. That shooting occurred at about 7:15 AM. It is suggested that they could have prevented the slaughter some two hours later if they had immediately called off classes. However, the local Blacksburg police led the Tech administrators to believe that the first shooting involved a "domestic" situation and not a large-scale murderous rampage. They focused on the boyfriend of the girlfriend killed in the dormitory and kept him in custody all day until they realized that Cho was the shooter. They focused, mistakenly, on the boyfriend because he was a gun enthusiast. Again, the Second Amendment issue, this time leading tragically to many deaths.

Most so-called mass murderers are men. If we reject biologism, we must conclude that social and political influences predispose young men to commit these deeds, whereas women deal with their alienation in other ways.

Psychologism, the reduction of human problems to intrapsychic processes, is tempting because it leads us away from the political. Mass murderers are evil monsters, deformed by inherited madness. This explanation allows us to avoid the more challenging project, which is to trace the social in the psychic while refusing to reduce individuality to social structure—explaining away Blacksburg and Columbine.

Psychologism—reading Cho as mentally ill—misses the political and social dimensions of this tragedy which surely interact with his so-called state of mind. It is telling that Cho had no history of violence but suffered his wounds silently and privately. To be sure, he was accused of stalking a couple of women students, and briefly institutionalized for this. But many men stalk without killing. More telling is that Cho was invisible, a "question mark" even to himself (as he called himself in his self-describing screen name). The only adult who really picked up on Cho's damaged selfhood was Giovanni, the poetry professor who refused to teach him because she said he was "mean." She had begun to read him politically as damaged; that is, she situated him in the interpersonal politics of the classroom in which his anger and self-loathing percolated.

One of my theses is that Cho does not occupy a different world from the rest of us but we belong to his world, in which many of us suffer agony, anxiety, and isolation that could, given the right circumstances and crises, lead us down his path. To say he was evil, a rare demonic property, ignores the two, three, many Chos who make up what David Riesman years ago called the lonely crowd. We are not as lonely as Cho, nor as indignant, nor as likely to obtain small-caliber weapons. Perhaps we buffer our suffering with alcohol or drugs or entertainment. But we live in his world, eternally angry. Perhaps we do our violence by acting it out in perverted fantasy lives, allowing us otherwise to appear to function.

My other thesis is that the damaged life, as I am describing it and as Adorno termed it, is not a human inevitability but a product of particular social arrangements in which privatization and the lack of intimacy and community are endemic. Many choose to view people like Cho as evil or mad. I view them as damaged, perhaps even right out of the box. But for most people, the damage comes later, as they are mishandled by the world. Hannah Arendt's (1994) *Eichmann in Jerusalem* is a signature work of the time: She argues that Adolf Eichmann, architect of Hitler's final solution to the Jewish problem, was not mad at all, nor evil, nor demonic, nor possessed. He was "banal," an ordinary guy carrying out orders. And he had a hand in killing over six million, not the thirty-two murdered at Blacksburg. Arendt makes it clear, as did the Frankfurt School in the study of "authoritarian personality," that powerlessness mixed with scapegoating can produce monstrous outcomes.

We await Cho's written "manifesto," carefully guarded by federal authorities. I suspect he names names of people at Tech against whom he bore ill will. The video we have seen is sophomoric; he acknowledges his debt to the Columbine killers, Eric Harris and Dylan Klebold, not to Regis Debray or the Unabomber or Lenin.

When I heard Cho speak on his death-day video, I thought he sounded like a person locked away in solitary confinement who was finding his voice after years of silence. He sounded strange to himself, spewing forth his childish manifesto with a voice that he had rarely heard. Astonishingly, people objected to the airing of this video, claiming that this "gave him what he wanted"—a platform. But the video was fascinating, showing a person possessed by his own words, which made no sense. No one who listened could possibly understand the roots of Cho's alienation, lacking information about his particular background and sensibility. But everyone could understand that he was angry about something—the damaged life shadowing him.

It is important to position Blacksburg inside the political in order to resist the spectacular psychologism that turned Cho into an evil madman and not a person who suffered the world perhaps more intensely than the rest of us. This is not to deny organic causes and consequences of his behavior but to observe that these organic issues interact with the social and political in ways that produce variable outcomes. Not everyone who is bullied in school, or marginalized, picks up the gun. And in some societies, there are no guns to pick up. And just because some tried to help does not mean that mere helpers could penetrate Cho's psyche to its core after years of isolation that emerged as self-hatred. His murderous behavior, pumping over one hundred bullets into the bodies of his victims, led to his own self-inflicted demise. He committed suicide, which lay on the far side of his rampage. He could not differentiate himself sufficiently from the world in order to avoid bringing everyone down, murder/suicide blending to the point of indistinguishability.

The kids trapped in the classrooms of Norris Hall on the Tech campus were huddled behind desks and pretending to be dead, struggling to survive. They describe the eerie silence that followed Cho's suicide. Most of the kids still alive did not realize he had killed himself; his own mortal wounding sounded exactly like all the others. The disturbing video taken by the student outside of Norris Hall whose soundtrack is punctuated by those echoing gun shots stands with the Zapruder film of the Kennedy assassination as a video chronicle of our times. Kennedy's death, it could be said, ended the sixties before they got going and issued in decades of right-wing hegemony. This hegemony has deepened a culture of violence in which anyone can acquire automatic weapons (and bullets) by eBay. And it could be said that Zapruder and Walter Cronkite, who broadcast the assassination weekend, initiated a media culture in which Cho copied Columbine and CNN positioned Blacksburg outside of the political, accompanied by the meaningless gestures of Americans wearing Virginia Tech colors in solidarity.

We should be worried about two, three, many Chos, souls so damaged that they cannot understand themselves in relation to the world. That Cho took the innocent down with him is literally correct: nearly all of the college kids interviewed during massacre week were sympathetic and caring. It was left to the Fox pundits, abetted by their dime-store psychiatrists, to spin the narrative of Cho's irreducible insanity, thus distinguishing him from the rest of us.

We want him to occupy a different space from the rest of us. He must lie on the far side of civilization, as its Other. But he is borne of this society; he is the "question mark" produced by alienation (Marx's word) or anomie (Durkheim's word). By that they meant people who lack social connection, community, intimacy, love, friends. To say that Cho became who he was (which we will never fully fathom, except via his deed) "because" of the crushing aloneness that he seemed to suffer risks sociologism, the opposite mistake of psychologism. Self and society interpenetrate, intermingle, overlap to near identity. Adorno's point was that the self is also "objective," frequently object-like, in a society in which people's inner recesses are occupied by social, economic, and cultural imperatives. Kids play videos games because they lack social connections. When I was a kid we went outside to play after school. Today kids either have too much homework or, if they don't, there is no one outside when they seek playmates.

Imagine how bad this must be for petite bourgeois Koreans in an affluent D.C. suburb. This is not to deny that Cho probably had serious issues before he came to America. But his probably already damaged self became more damaged at Virginia Tech, a virtual small town of thousands of other students, none of whom connected with him, nor he with them.

The only rescue for damaged selves—and we are all damaged in our various ways, some hiding it better than others—are the nucleic utopian moments when we occasionally count for something. We are cherished, befriended, celebrated, sheltered. But in this atomized, individualistic world in which no one plays outside anymore only a lucky few achieve these utopian moments that prefigure larger political and social movements. During my childhood and then adolescence, we had an ample politics of everyday life in which young people could seek and find community and even move beyond into a humane politics. Our role models were Tom Hayden, Bob Moses, Martin Luther King, Bobby Kennedy, Betty Friedan. These people embodied utopia, an otherness achievable by small changes that accumulate into a new politics. The New Left, both black and white, was a politics of small gestures, both kindnesses and protests, that remade selves and reshaped national agendas. Today kids such as Cho identify with the Columbine killers; they lack utopian icons and ideas. They have no heroes.

Much of my argument about the objectivity of subjectivity that led to Cho's damaged life is drawn from Adorno's critical theory. But I depart from Adorno where he proposed only a "negative utopia," a utopia defined by what it is not. His argument was compelling: the total society damages almost everything and everyone. Simply to gain distance affords room to move. But Marcuse, more grounded in early Marx and a certain reading of Freud, argues for a positive utopia, which in his 1955 book *Eros and Civilization* he calls a "rationality of gratification" and in his 1969 *Essay on Liberation* he terms the "new sensibility."

Today, with no progressive social movements and a clannish society of fraternities and football, the Marcusean imagery seems overly abstract. My wife and I just finished a book, *Fast Families, Virtual Children* (Agger and

Shelton 2007), in which we argue that family and school can become radical ideas if we understand family as convivial intimacy to be sought in public as well as in private and if we understand school to be a lifelong Chautauqua in which schools occupy a meso level in between private and public—a town meeting and a site of continuing education. Today, families, like childhood, are attenuated, and schools are prisons blending adult authoritarianism and rote learning. I have thought more than once about the Tech students who decided to attend morning class on that chilly April day instead of sleeping in and staying home. Perhaps they were called by the life of the mind and classroom conviviality, or perhaps they were worried about their GPAs. We will never know.

Cho had no such luck, either in high school, where he was marginalized, nor in college, where his marginality deepened and became malignant. To be sure, we should worry that there could be two, three, many Chos. But for every Cho who erupts, no longer able to accept his own agony, there are many more who suffer in silence. On a prepatriotic school spirit campus such as Virginia Tech, in which Hokie-ism must be suffocating for skeptics and outsiders, kids like Cho are ticking bombs. But the damage of alienation/anomie/aloneness is much more general in an individualistic society in which "community" is equivalent to collegiate sports fandom, remininscent, of course, of the mass rallies captured by Riefenstahl during the Third Reich.

I hated school spirit from the beginning of my school days, perhaps recognizing that this was a form of prepatriotism and an augur of the martial state, in which support of football teams suggests the support of armies. Watching the relentless Hokie-ism in the week after the deaths in Blacksburg gave me the creeps; I would have been on the outside looking in, not wearing orange and purple nor attending pep rallies. Few in America had heard of Hokie Nation before Cho, and I predicted to a friend of mine that high-school student applications to attend Tech will actually rise now that the nation has witnessed the *Gemeinschaft* demonstrated on the drill field on which Norris Hall sits. People will be drawn to the hallowed ground of the Tech campus, as the media spectacle of the ensuing weeks suggests to them their own participation in the group psychology of fascism, which is what big-time football schools are all about. The word "hokie" already decides in favor of a sham—as in "hokey," make-believe.

Psychologism is an evasion. Cho wasn't evil; he was damaged. I am enough of an antipsychiatry person to have grave doubts about posits of individual psychopathology as if the flimsy boundary between psychic health and social pathology is in fact firm and obvious to trained professionals. The fact is that Cho wandered around aimlessly, with his indignation fermenting.

During the sixties, utopia abounded as a possibility, even if COINTELPRO, the White House, the police, the Klan beat back the New Left and presaged decades of mounting right-wing hegemony, which endures to the present. Kids could affiliate to causes and in communal projects in which their mortal aloneness would be buffered. Could a Korean American kid have found meaning in the hectic fraternity life at Virginia Tech or in the stands at football games? Imagine how he felt walking the halls of his preppy white high school. Perhaps his parents applied relentless pressure on him to duplicate the academic successes of his Princeton-bound sister. I know an Asian girl in my daughter's high school class who is not allowed to recreate, having to keep her nose to the academic grindstone. She is "grounded" if her grades sink below 95. She experiences America as a series of hurdles; she is old before her time.

We did damage to Cho by ignoring him. I have had problematic, angry students for whom I didn't do enough. We are ourselves damaged by the same social forces at play in his life. To be sure, we did not pump three bullets per victim into their agonizing bodies, as he did. Most of us are too bound in, or we have everyday opportunities for utopia—friends, hobbies, exercise, creative outlets, perhaps even a restorative politics.

One day we may piece together Cho's sad life. We may triangulate the interaction of his mental illness and his social isolation that led to April 16, 2007. In the meantime, we must not ignore the social and political as if Cho came from another planet and walked among the Hokie Nation, which has only sane and decent citizens. Although no one reading these words is close to planning a murderous rage and videotaped confession, there are times when we want to lash out at enemies real and imagined. In the same way, we must recognize the Eichmann in all of us, the diligent engineer who does what he is told. More important than recognizing Cho and Eichmann in ourselves is recognizing them in others, who we can help or redirect. This redirection amounts to political action of a sort—acknowledging, even reaching out to, those who suffer a world we recognize as our own.

References

Agger, Ben, and Beth Anne Shelton. 2007. *Fast Families, Virtual Children: A Critical Sociology of Families and Schooling*. Boulder, CO: Paradigm.

Arendt, Hannah. 1994. *Eichmann in Jerusalem: A Report on the Banality of Evil*. New York: Penguin.

Marcuse, Herbert. 1955. *Eros and Civilization: A Philosophical Inquiry into Freud*. New York: Vintage.

———. 1969. *An Essay on Liberation*. Boston: Beacon.

ABOUT THE CONTRIBUTORS

Ben Agger is professor of sociology and humanities at the University of Texas at Arlington, where he also directs the Center for Theory. He has published widely in critical theory and cultural/media studies, including *Fast Capitalism*; *Public Sociology*; *Critical Social Theories*; and *Cultural Studies as Critical Theory*. His most recent book (with Beth Anne Shelton) is *Fast Families, Virtual Children*, a book about schooling, family, childhood and utopia. He is completing a book called *The Sixties at Forty: Radicals Remember and Look Forward*.

Stanley Aronowitz is Distinguished Professor of Sociology at the Graduate Center of City University of New York. He is author or editor of twenty-five books. His latest is *Against Schooling* (2008). He is working on an intellectual and political study of the work of C.Wright Mills.

William Ayers, Distinguished Professor of Education and Senior University Scholar at the University of Illinois at Chicago, and founder of both the Small Schools Workshop and the Center for Youth and Society, teaches courses in interpretive and qualitative research, urban school change, and teaching and the modern predicament. A graduate of the University of Michigan, the Bank Street College of Education, and Teachers College, Columbia University, Ayers has written extensively about social justice, democracy and education, the political and cultural contexts of schooling, and the meaning-making and ethical purposes of students and families and teachers. His articles have appeared in many journals including the *Harvard Educational Review*, the *Journal of Teacher Education*, *Teachers College Record*, *Rethinking Schools*, the *Nation*, the *New York Times*, and the *Cambridge Journal of Education*. His books include *A Kind and Just Parent: The Children of Juvenile Court* (1997), *The Good Preschool Teacher: Six Teachers Reflect on Their Lives*, (1989), and *To Teach: The Journey of a Teacher*, (1993) which was named Book of the Year in 1993 by Kappa Delta Pi, and won the Witten Award for Distinguished Work in Biography and Autobiography in 1995.

Tara Brabazon is professor of media at the University of Brighton, having previously taught and lived in Australia and Aotearoa/New Zealand. A former national teaching award winner, she is the author of nine books, including *The University of Google: Education in a (post) Information Age*, *The Revolution Will Not Be Downloaded: Dissent in the Digital Age*, *Digital Hemlock* and *From Revolution to Revelation: Generation X, Popular Culture and Popular Memory*.

Roxanne Dunbar-Ortiz is a writer, historian, university professor, and red state rebel from Oklahoma. Her most recent work is a trilogy of historical memoir: *Red Dirt: Growing Up Okie*; *Outlaw Woman: A Memoir of the War Years, 1960–1975*; and *Blood on the Border: A Memoir of the Contra War*.

Carolyn Guertin is director of the eCreate Lab and assistant professor of digital media in the Department of English at the University of Texas at Arlington, as well as a graduate faculty member in the summer MFA program at Transart Institute in Austria. She is curator of the celebrated collection *Assemblage: The Online Women's New Media Gallery* out of the U.K., and is Senior McLuhan Fellow at the McLuhan Program in Culture and Technology at the University of Toronto, where she was SSHRC postdoctoral fellow from 2004 to 2006. She has exhibited and published internationally.

Gwen Hunnicutt is an assistant professor of sociology at the University of North Carolina at Greensboro. Her research interests include exploring the connection between gender, age, and victimization, studying masculinity, aggression, and empathy in social context and building theory to explain gender specific violence and nonviolence. Her most recent paper is titled, "Varieties of Patriarchy and Violence Against Women: Resurrecting 'Patriarchy' as a Theoretical Tool."

Jeremy Hunsinger is an ethics fellow at the Center for Information Policy Research at the University of Wisconsin, Milwaukee, and is a visiting assistant professor in communications at the University of Illinois at Chicago. He is completing his Ph.D. in Science and Technology in Society at Virginia Tech. His research centers on the transformations of the modes of production in the information age. At Virginia Tech, he was one of the founders of the Center for Digital Discourse and Culture and a 2006 scholar fellow.

Brent K. Jesiek is manager of Virginia Tech's Center for Digital Discourse and Culture. In addition, he is a postdoctoral research associate in the school's Department of Science and Technology in Society and is an instructor in the Department of Political Science. Dr. Jesiek holds a B.S. in Electrical Engineering from Michigan Tech and M.S. and Ph.D. degrees in Science and Technology Studies from Virginia Tech. Much of his academic work is focused on the historical and social dimensions of engineering and computing. He also performs research in the field of engineering education.

Douglas Kellner is George Kneller Chair in the Philosophy of Education at UCLA and is author of many books on social theory, politics, history, and culture, including *Camera Politica: The Politics and Ideology of Contemporary Hollywood Film*, coauthored with Michael Ryan; *Critical Theory, Marxism, and Modernity*; *Jean Baudrillard: From Marxism to Postmodernism and Beyond*; works in cultural studies such as *Media Culture* and *Media Spectacle*; a trilogy of books on postmodern theory with Steve Best; and a trilogy of books on the media and the Bush administration, encompassing *Grand Theft 2000*, *From 9/11 to Terror War*, and *Media Spectacle and the Crisis of Democracy*. Author of *Herbert Marcuse and the Crisis of Marxism*, Kellner is editing collected papers of Herbert Marcuse, four volumes of which have appeared with Routledge. Kellner's latest book *is Guys and Guns Amok: Domestic Terrorism and School Shootings from the Oklahoma City Bombings to the Virginia Tech Massacre*. His website is www.gseis.ucla.edu/faculty/kellner/kellner.html.

Michael Kimmel is professor of sociology at State University of New York at Stony Brook. His newest book, *Guyland: The Social World of Young Men between Adolescence and Adulthood* will be published by HarperCollins.

Neal King is associate professor of interdisciplinary studies at Virginia Tech. He is author of *Heroes in Hard Times*, coeditor of *Reel Knockouts*, and has published articles on inequality and culture in such journals as *Journal of Film and Video*, *Gender & Society*, and *Men and Masculinities*. Research interests include controversies over media violence, the masculinity of old men, and social theories of agency and empowerment.

Steve Kroll-Smith is professor of sociology at the University of North Carolina at Greensboro and editor of *Sociological Inquiry*. His latest book, with Valerie Gunter, *Volatile Places*, was published in 2007. His research interests include the sociologies of disasters, environments, and sleep. He is currently working on two Katrina related projects: a comparative study of the 1906 San Francisco earthquake and fire and the 2005 flooding of New Orleans and a comparative neighborhood study of post-flood recovery in New Orleans.

Charles Lemert is the John C. Andrus Professor of Sociology at Wesleyan University. His recent books include *Thinking the Unthinkable* (2007) and the fourth edition of *Social Things* (Rowman & Littlefield, 2008).

Matthew Levy teaches writing in the First Year Experience Program and English Department at Pacific Lutheran University. Previously, he served as writing program administrator at the University of Texas at Arlington and as a writing center instructor at Texas Christian University. His research focuses primarily on cynicism as a political issue that impacts college writing instruction.

Timothy W. Luke is University Distinguished Professor of Political Science at Virginia Polytechnic Institute and State University in Blacksburg, Virginia. He also is the program chair for Government and International Affairs in the School of Public and International Affairs, director of the Center for Digital Discourse and Culture in the College of Liberal Arts and Human Sciences at Virginia Tech, and university senior fellow for the Arts, Humanities, and Social Sciences. His research focuses on critical theory, environmental politics, and public culture.

Patricia Mooney Nickel is a lecturer in the School of Social and Cultural Studies at Victoria University of Wellington. Her research interests include critical social theory, epistemological hierarchy, philanthropy and the nonprofit sector, public sociology, social policy, the sociology of public administration and governance, and critical theories of the state.

Stephen Pfohl is a professor of sociology at Boston College where he teaches courses on social theory; postmodern culture; crime, deviance and social control; images and power; and sociology and psychoanalysis. Stephen is the author of numerous books and articles including *Left Behind: Religion, Technology and Flight from the Flesh* (2007); *Death at the Parasite Café*; *Images of Deviance and Social Control*; *Predicting Dangerousness*, and the forthcoming volumes *Venus in Video* and *Magic and the Machine*. A past-president of the Society for the Study of Social Problems and a founding member of Sit-Com International, a Boston-area collective of activists and artists, Pfohl is also co-editor of the 2006 book *Culture, Power, and History: Studies in Critical Sociology*.

INDEX

academia, culture of normative violence in, 160, 170–75
academia, university curriculum: changing, 145–46; cultural studies in, 127; life adjustment movement, 153–54; writing instruction, history of, 146–54; writing instruction, integrated first-year programs, 157–58
academia, university faculty: boundaries of professional norms, 170–75; isolation of, 123; lock down training, 142; promotion and tenure process, 171–73; student relationships, 119–22; *See also* Virginia Tech faculty
Acteal Massacre, 219
Addams, Jane, 83
Adorno, 179, 243, 246, 248
African-Americans, at Virginia Tech, 20–21
Agger, Ben, 74, 137, 167, 175–76, 181, 243–50
Albarghouti, Jamal, 33, 130
the American dream, 231, 233
Anderson, Laurie, 157
Applebee, Arthur N., 153
Arendt, Hannah, 246
Aronowitz, Stanley, 229–33
Auden, W. H., 159

Auvinen, Pekka-Eric, 25, 77
Ayers, William, 79–93

Barber, Tiki, 8
Baron, Jeff, 83–86
Baron, Mr. and Mrs., 84–86
Basic Communications Course (University of Denver), 146–54
Bath, Michigan, 13, 15
Baudrillard, Jean, 213, 216, 235–42
Beijing, China, 238–41
Berkowitz, David, 110
Berlin, James, 143, 146–47, 152, 154–55
Blacksburg, Virginia, 3, 9–10, 13–15, 160–68, 241
Blindness (Saramago), 89–90
blogs and bloggers, 222–23
"Body Ritual among the Nacirema" (Miner), 109
Boone, Daniel, 108
Boortz, Neal, 43–44
Borges, J., 191–92
Boston College, 93–94
Bowling for Columbine, 47
"Boy Breaking Glass" (Brooks), 92
Brabazon, Tara, 119–39
Brauer, Ralph, 7
Brecht, Bertolt, 90, 231
Brennan, Teresa, 99–100

255

Brooks, Gwendolyn, 92
Brzonkala, Christy, 75
Bush (George W.) administration, 30–31, 37, 89, 99
Bush, George W., 10, 30, 37–38, 237
Butler, J., 166–68, 175–76

cameras, as weapons, 214–15
cellular phones, shootings captured on, 33, 130
Center for History and New Media (CHNM), George Mason University, 186–87, 191
Cermak, Mike, 95
Chambers, Samuel A., 175
Chandler, Daniel, 127
Che Guevara, 243
Cheney, Dick, 209
China, history of, 238–41
Cho Seung-Hui: background, 17–18, 36, 210; Columbine shooters and, 17, 18, 38, 41, 44, 47; gun culture and, 47–48; influences on, 44, 47–48, 102, 212, 246; marginalization/social isolation of, 24, 36, 73, 95–98, 137, 244, 246, 248–50; memorial stone for, 21; political ideology, 44; rage of, 243, 248–49; self-image, 17–18, 39, 96, 245–47; suicide of, 6, 247; weapons used, 7, 10
Cho Seung-Hui, media portrayal of: by conservatives, 45–46; ethnic sterotyping, 13–14, 35, 36, 66, 130, 209; as insane, 46, 247; as loner, 35–36; misogynistic/homophobic, 72; in photographs, 36
Cho Seung-Hui, mental health issues: clinical evidence of, 46; court order for treatment, 7, 122; examples of, 7, 98, 122; faculty response to, 36, 74, 145, 245–46
Cho Seung-Hui, motivation: of aggrieved entitlement, 72–77; to create a media spectacle, 36, 38, 41, 216; immortality, 41; media explanations for, 65–66; revenge/class revenge, 39, 41, 73, 94, 97, 122, 210; speculation on, 209, 211–12

Cho Seung-Hui, video narrative: backlash against NBC for releasing, 41–42; content of, 94, 97, 103, 209; intent of, 215; literary expressions, 39–41, 45; mailed to NBC, 6; power of, 16, 142; self-portrayal in, 39
Citadel, 11
Clark, Ryan, 6
Clinton, Bill (William Jefferson), 37–38, 66
College of William and Mary, 9
colonization and massacre, 207–12
Columbine school shooters: Cho inspired by, 17, 18, 38, 41, 44, 47, 246; date, significance to, 37; influences on, 77, 213; marginalization of, 71–72, 74, 76, 244; media stereotyping of, 14; weapons used by, 10; *See also* Harris, Eric; Klebold, Dylan; school shooters
Columbine school shootings: explanations proposed, 46–47, 66; gun control debate post-shooting, 94–95; media commodification of, 8, 245; mentioned, 12, 13, 48; school complicity in, 71–72, 74–75; video game of, 220–21; Virginia Tech shootings compared, 10; *See also* school shootings
communication, guns and cameras for, 214–15
Consolidated School bombing, Bath, Michigan, 13, 14
Constitution of the United States, Second Amendment, 244, 245
Cook County Juvenile Temporary Detention Center, 83
Cool Memories (Baudrillard), 236
Cooper, James Fenimore, 40
Couture-Nowak, Jocelyne, 137
Cronkite, Walter, 247
Crowley, Sharon, 153
cultural lag, 114–15
cultural studies, 31–33, 127
Curtis, Ian, 133–34
cybercides, 221
cyberspace, 218–19

Davids, Chris, 36
Davidson, Levette J., 147–54
death: demography of, 245; as media event, 213, 221
Debord, Guy, 31, 111
DeBray, Regis, 246
DeLay, Tom, 66
Del Rosso, Jared, 96
de Niro, Robert, 39
Dickens, Charles, 231
disaster marathons, 60–61
Dostoevskian idiot, 208
Draper's Meadow massacre, 13, 14
"The Dream Before (for Walter Benjamin)" (Anderson), 157
Duke Lacrosse players rape case, 30
Dunbar-Ortiz, Roxanne, 207–12

Early, Kevin, 221
The Early Show (CBS), 43
Edmond, Oklahoma, 208
education: purpose of, 123–24, 129; web-based, 122, 127, 130, 137; *See also* academia; teaching
educators. *See* academia, university faculty; teachers:
Edwards, John, 218, 219
Eichmann, Adolf, 246, 250
Eichmann in Jerusalem (Arendt), 246
Eikenberry, Angela M., 175
Einstein, Albert, 115
Electronic Disturbance Theatre, 219–20
emotional contagion, 223–24
Engel, Richard, 40, 41
Eros and Civilization (Marcuse), 248
Essay on Liberation (Marcuse), 248
ethics: journalistic, 59–61; social/community, 90–91

Facebook, 42, 95, 130, 193
films, teacher-hero, 143–44, 146, 154–55
Finland, schools shootings in, 25, 77
Flinchum, Wendell, 49n7
FloodNet, 219–20
football, as spectacle, 111–12, 249
Foucault, M., 163, 175

Fox, James Alan, 99
Freedland, Jonathan, 222–23
Freud, Sigmund, 108, 113, 115, 248
Fugate, Caril, 208
Funes the Memorious, 191–92

Garcia, Jerry, 114
Garfinkel, Harold, 115
Gay, John, 231
George Mason University, 9, 186–87, 191
Gibson, Mel, 224
Gill, Kimveer, 213, 216, 217, 221–22
Gilligan, James, 68
Gilmor, Dan, 34
Gingrich, Newt, 66
Giovanni, Nikki, 12, 21, 74, 161, 246
Goetzmann, William H., 40
Goffman, Erving, 74
Goldberg, Jonah, 39–40
Gonzales, Alberto, 30, 37, 38
Gordon, Avery, 61
Goss, Kristin A., 15
Gouldner, Alvin W., 179
Gramsci, Antonio, 91
Granata, Kevin, 137
Greenwood, Glen, 44–45
gridiron gemeinschaft, 24, 76, 249
grief: disaster marathons, 60–61; made spectacle, 56, 60; normative, 180–81; official message regarding, 167; tragedy uniform at Virginia Tech, 161; value of, 176
grief elite, 162
Grossman, Dave, 223–24
Gruwell, Erin, 143–44, 155
Guertin, Carolyn, 213–27
Gulliver's Travels (Swift), 107–8
gun control debate, 11, 15–16, 42–48, 94–95
gun control laws, effectiveness of, 11
gun ownership statistics, 10–11, 110, 130
gun-related deaths, 11, 111
guns: on television, 11; used by Cho, 10; used by Klebold, 10; at Virginia Tech, 11, 130

Hampton Institute, 8
Handler, Nicholas, 141, 156
Hansel and Gretel story, 157
Harris, Eric, 25, 65, 72–73, 135, 213, 220–21; *See also* Columbine school shooters
hauntings, 61
Helmke, Paul, 43
Herbert, Bob, 72
Hilscher, Emily, 6, 33
Hincker, Larry (Lawrence G.), 161, 164–68, 174
Hokie Massacre souvenirs, 162
Hokie Nation, 18, 21–23, 59, 73, 76, 95, 160–68, 249
Hokie Spirit Memorial Fund, 22
Hokies Thank the World happening, 22–24
Hokie Stone memorial markers, 20, 21, 24
Hokies United Memorial T-Shirt, 162, 182n3
Holocaust Remembrance Day, 141, 142
hooks, bell, 123
Horkheimer, 179
human body: biopolitics of, 214; media as an extension of, 214–15
human nature, nature of, 107–8
humans: the bodies of teachers, 121–23, 126; bodies weaponized, 214; the damaged life of, 243–48; species-lag in, 114–15; value of, 90–91
Hunnicutt, Gwen, 104–17
Hunsinger, Jeremy, 185–206
Hunter, Robert, 114
Hunter, Stephen, 39
Hupp, Suzanna, 43
Hussein, Saddam, 216

Iilek, 238
The Illusion of the End (Baudrillard), 236–37
Imus, Don, 30, 224
Ingles, Mary Draper, 14
institutional conflict, 59–61
International Women's Day, 235
Internet: anonymity and violence on the, 222–23; blogs and bloggers, 222–23; group suicide pacts, 221; hacktivism, 219–20; Lucas' use of, 10; memory construction using, 193–94; shooter's use of, 25, 77; shootings reported on, 33; social-networks, 42, 95, 193, 222; virtual killings, 217; *See also* media, new (alternative sources)
Iraq: death statistics, 130; media spectacle in, 30; war in, 38, 98–99, 103, 130, 212
Ismail/Ishmail Ax, 39–40

James Madison University, 9
Jamestown, Virginia, 207–12
Japan, suicide in, 221
Jesiek, Brent K., 185–206
Jesus Christ, cited by Cho, 18, 40–41, 74, 103, 209, 216
Jokela High School, Tuusula, Finland, 25, 77
journalists: citizen, 33–34, 130; role in ritual post-disaster, 59–62; *See also* media
Joy Division, 133

Kaine, Timothy, 16–17, 38, 42, 144
Kamm, Oliver, 222–23
Karasic, Carmin, 219–20
Keilar, Brianna, 35
Kellner, Douglas, 29–53, 245
Kennedy (John F.) assassination, 247
Kenniston, Kenneth, 233
Kerrigan, William, 125–26
The Killer, 39
On Killing (Grossman), 223–24
Kimmel, Michael, 65–78
King, Martin Luther Jr., 90
King, Neal, 55–64
Klebold, Dylan, 10, 65, 72–73, 135, 213, 220–21
Klerck, Kevin, 221
Koch, Andy, 96
Korea, colonization and massacre, 207–12
Korean War, 209, 211–12
Krauthammer, Charles, 44–45
Kroker, Arthur, 100–2
Kroll-Smith, Steve, 104–17

Larkin, Ralph, 71–72
Leary, Timothy, 213, 221
Ledonne, Danny, 220–21
Lemert, Charles, 235–42
Lenin, 246
Levey, Matthew, 140–59
Librescu, Liviu, 44, 137, 141–42
Liebes, Tamar, 60–61
life adjustment movement, 153–54
Limbaugh, Rush, 44
Lindemann, Erika, 141
Linden Labs, 218–19
Linton, Professor, 108–9
Lockwood, John, 217
Lucas, Henry Lee, 9–10
Luke, Timothy, 1–28, 76, 121, 175

Mao Zedong, 238–42
Mao Zedong: A Life (Spence), 239
Marcuse, H., 106, 174, 248
Marvin, Carolyn, 57, 61
Marx, Karl, 237, 248
masculinity: Cho's construction of, 39; United States culture of, 68, 72, 73, 100–1
massacres and colonization, 207–12
Massengill, Gerald, 25
mass killers: characteristics of, 94, 98–99, 208, 245; creating, 223–24, 246, 247–48, 250; influences on, 211, 244–45; motivation, 216; sterotyping, 112; *See also* rampage shootings; terrorism
McCarthy, Carolyn, 43
McLuhan, Marshall, 214
"McLuhan, Rhetoric, Politics" (Murray), 214
McNamee, Mark, 19–20, 161, 171–72, 174
McVeigh, Timothy, 34, 37, 41, 48
Mead, Margaret, 73
media: civil religion through mass, 57–59; as an extension of the body, 214–15; power of, 243
media events, 29–31
media literacy movement, 31, 46
media spectacle: in American culture, 112–13; Cho's construction of, 36, 38, 41, 216; as civil ritual, 57–59; as contested terrain, 31; cultural studies as diagnostic critique, 31–33; football as, 111–12, 249; gun control debate post-massacre, 43; in Iraq, 30, 31; as motivation for violence, 36–37, 41, 216; racialized attribution of killers, 34–35, 39–40; rampage shootings as, 112–13; terrorism as, 215–16; violence and, 213–14
Melville, Herman, 40, 45
memorials: archives of physical items, 189–90; for Cho Seung-Hui, 21; Hokies United Memorial T-Shirt, 162, 182n3; to Virginia Tech dead, 20–22
memory, technologies of, 187–91
memory bank, April 16 Archive: building the content, 195–99; conclusion, 202–4; creating the, 186–87, 191; limits and challenges, 199–202; purpose of, 192, 201
memory banks: architecture, 193; contributor's significance, 191–95; copyright issues, 198; forgetting through participation in, 194–95; infrastructures, 191; technologies of, 187–88
memory preserved, 185
Middlebrook, Samuel, 150–52
Millner, Sherry, 224
Mills, Catherine, 175
Miner, Horace, 108–9
Minnesota Historical Society, 191
Moby Dick (Melville), 40, 45
Molloy, Joanna Rush, 46
Montgomery County, Virginia, 9
Moore, Michael, 47
Morva incident (2006), 3, 9
"Motto" (Brecht), 90
murder-suicide, 214
Murray, Stuart, 214
MySpace, 33, 34, 42, 95, 193, 222

Nacirema, 108–14
Nancy B. Jefferson School, 83
narrative, power of, 142–43
National Military Academies, U.S., 11
"Nation Shocked by Prenatal Shooting" (*Onion*), 79–80

NBC News, 6, 41–42, 94, 216
New River Valley, Virginia, 9
news media: new forms of, 7, 29, 33–34, 130; role in ritual post-disaster, 59–62
news media, the Virginia Tech shootings and the: callousness of/resentment toward, 56–61, 163–66; Cho profiled by, 35–36, 66, 130, 209; commodification and exploitation, 24–25, 43–45, 56–60, 163–66; faculty responses to, 56–61; initial reports, 33; new media used by, 33, 130; oppositional logic in reaction to, 55–57; positioning outside the political, 243–50; positive results of, 30–31; racial dimensions of, 13–14, 39–40; spectacle created by, 30, 33–35; statistics, 34; White House official response, 43, 105–6
news media, traditional: clichéd language of rampage shootings, 79–80, 105–6; commodification of violence, 7–16, 23–24, 216, 245; culture of sterotyping, 33; role in perpetuating violence, 36–38, 41, 63n5, 116, 213–14, 216; tabloidization of in attempt to compete with new forms, 29–30, 60
"New Study Reveals 20 Million American Children Suffering from YTD" (*Onion*), 79–80
Nickel, Patricia Mooney, 160–84
Niedzviecki, Nal, 214
Nietzsche, 106, 115
1960s urban violence, U.S., 44–45
No Child Left Behind Act, 71, 154
Norris Hall, 6, 26, 33

Ogburn, W. F., 114
Oklahoma City bombings, 34, 37, 48
Oldboy, 39
Old Dominion University, 9
Onion, 79–80
Operation Hokie Nation Stabilization, 164–66
O'Reilly, Bill, 35
O'Reilly Factor (Fox TV), 35

"Packaging the Suicide Bomber" (Niedzviecki), 214
pain, hierarchy of, 176
Paula Zahn Now (CNN), 35
Perino, Dana, 43, 105–6
Perlstein, Rick, 156
Pfohl, Stephen, 93–104
Phil, Dr., 53n39
the posteverything generation, 154–58
"The Posteverything Generation" (Handler), 156
The Prairie (Cooper), 40
Pratt, Larry, 43
Precarious Life (Butler), 166–67
Preston, William B., 13
Prison Notebooks (Gramsci), 91
psychologism, 245

racism, media's contribution to, 13–14, 34–35, 66, 130
rage, 222–24, 241, 246–47
rampage shootings: in America, 49n4; dates, significance in, 37, 141; globalization of, 24, 77; history of, 7, 121, 208; shooters in, 24; as spectacle, 112–13; typical responses to, 80, 229–30; why not more often?, 208, 211, 231; *See also* mass killers; school shootings; *specific events*; violence
rampage shootings, the media and: clichéd language in reporting of, 79–80, 105–6; individual shooter narrative, 15–16; myth-making/moralizing fables, 15–16; role in perpetuating, 63n5, 216; stereotyping of, 80, 112
religious intolerance, violence and, 72
Rhetoric and Reality (Berlin), 143–44, 146–47, 154–55
Richards, Michael, 224
Riesman, David:
rituals: civic, 57–59; haunted, 61–62
Robach, Amy, 42
Roy, Lucinda, 36
Rush, George, 46
Rutgers women's basketball team, 30

sacred space, invasion of, 55–57
Samenow, Stanton, 94
Saramago, Jose, 89–90
Sardar, Jam, 35
Schlussel, Debbie, 34–35
schools: counselers available in, 71; guns in, 71
schools, violence in: explanations proposed, 46–47; geography of, 25, 69–70, 77; globalization of, 25, 77; other than gun-related, 13, 15, 80; preventing, 25–26, 77, 145; profiling schools with, 69–73, 80–82; race factor in policing protocols, 14; school funding and, 70–71; statistics, 67, 80–82
school shooters: profiling, 67–69, 71–72, 74, 76; sterotyping, 13–14, 123; *See also* Columbine school shooters
school shootings: history of, 7, 121, 208; pre-1950, 13, 15; preventing, 221–22; race factor in policing protocols, 14; statistics, 13, 67; typical responses to, 229–30; *See also* Columbine school shootings
Scientology, church of, 45–46
Second Life, 193, 194, 218–19, 222
Second Life?Liberation Army (SLLA), 218–19, 220
serial killers of Blacksburg, 9–10
Seung-Hui Cho. *See* Cho Seung-Hui:
Seung-Hui family, 17, 210
Shapiro, Sherry, 125
shootings at Virginia Tech. *See* Virginia Tech massacre:
Sierra, Kathy, 223
Simone, Nina, 87
Simulacra and Simulations (Baudrillard), 236, 237–38
Slotkin, Richard, 73
Smithfield Plantation, 13, 14
Snow Crash, Second Life (Stephenson), 218
Socrates, 115, 120
Sorenson, Frederick, 147–54
Sowell, Thomas, 44–45, 66

species-lag, 114–15
spectacle in U.S. culture, 111–13, 249; *See also* media spectacle
Spence, Jonathan, 239
The Spirit of Terrorism (Baudrillard), 213, 216
Springsteen, Bruce, 76
Stannard, Sylvia, 46
Starkweather, Charles, 208
Steger, Charles W.: counseling e-mail from, 169–70; message of, 174; news conference, 163; Shooting at Virginia Tech e-mail, 5–6; "We Will Prevail" e-mail, 160–61
Stephenson, Neal, 218
Strate, Lance, 214–15
students: anger of, 124, 130; characteristics of, 120, 156–57; e-mail to Brabazon, 124–25, 128–29, 130–32, 133–36; faculty relationships, 119–22; with mental health problems, responding to, 71, 133, 135–37; percent carrying weapons, 82; the posteverything generation, 154–58; teachers responsibility toward, 124, 129, 133–34; *See also* youth
suicide: of Cho Seung-Hui, 6, 247; Internet group pacts, 221; as media event, 221; by rampage shooters, 25; youth, 74, 82, 119, 133–36
suicide bombers, 214–16
Super Columbine Massacre RPG!, 220–22
Swank, Hillary, 143
Swift, Jonathan, 107–8, 115
The System of Objects (Baudrillard), 237

"A Tale of a Tub" (Swift), 107
Taxi Driver, 39
teacher-knowledge-student relationship, 126, 127
teachers: the bodies of, 121–23, 126, 130; ethos and wisdom in, 142; as heros, 44, 137, 141–42, 143–46, 154–55; responsibilities of, 91, 124, 129, 133, 135, 145

teacher-student relationship: Brabazon's experiences, 119–20, 124–26, 128–32; importance to students, 124–25; Kerrigan's involvement in, 125–26; troubling, example of, 119–20

teaching: online/non-corporeal, 122, 127, 130, 137; as passion vs. profession, 144, 146, 155; students with behavioral and emotional problems, 71

teenagers. *See* youth:

terrorism: in cyberspace, 218–19, 220; dates, significance in, 37, 141; seeds of, 215–16; *See also* mass killers; rampage shootings

Texas A&M University, 11

"Thanatopolitics" (Murray), 214

Thompson, Jack, 217

Thoreau, Henry David, 90, 115, 235

Tiananmen Square, Beijing, China, 238–41

time, travel and, 235–36

time of nonbeing, 241

Unabomber, 41, 48, 246

United States: children in the, 248, 250; economy, 109, 113; equal opportunity myth, 210–11, 231, 233; hegemony, 224, 247; middle class, 231–32; post-WW II, 231–32; poverty in, 111, 241; professional/managerial class in, 230, 233; youth culture, 46, 232–33

United States culture: community and isolation in, 248–50; forms of attack against, 215; hatred of the rich in, 210–11; ideology of the individual in, 113–14, 144, 155, 248; of masculinity, 39, 43–44, 68, 72, 73, 98, 100–101; the Nacirema compared, 108–14; of social psychosis, 99–100, 103; spectacle in, 108–14, 249; the suburbs role in, 232; supernatural, belief in the, 110–11; of violent authoritarianism, 86–92; Virginia Tech massacre in the context of, 95–98

United States culture of violence: cause of, 44–45; causes of, 231, 232–33;

denial of (social amnesia), 98–103, 229–30; ending, 103; gun ownership statistics, 10–11, 110, 130; gun-related injury and deaths, 11, 111, 113; gun sales, economics of, 113; hegemony and, 224; historically, 9–10, 13, 14, 98, 101–2, 207–12; influences on, 247; pay-per-view-slaughter, 217; religious justification for, 102; on television, 11

university. *See* academia:

University of Denver, Basici Communications Course, 146–54

University of Texas, 7, 121, 208

University of Virginia, 9

The Unknown Citizen (Auden), 159

utopia, possibility of, 248, 250

Van Cleave, Philip, 43

"Victims Sought in Next Week's Shooting" (*Onion*), 80

video games: Cho's interest in, 46, 47, 53n39; reasons for, 248; violence and, 53n39, 66, 73, 142, 212, 216–17, 220–22, 244–45; in youth culture, 46

violence: Baudrillard on, 213; in China's history, 238–42; community created through, 160–68; media commodification of, 7–16, 23–24, 216, 245; media role in perpetuating, 36–38, 41, 63n5, 116, 213–14; normative, 160, 174–81, 224, 241; origins of, 68; payoffs of, 61–62; preventing, 145, 221–22; rage and, 222–24; slow-motion, 89; in Swif't's writing, 107–8; transformation through, 166–68, 174–81; video games and, 53n39, 66, 73, 142, 212, 216–17, 220–22, 244–45; *See also* United States culture of violence

Virginia, 13–17, 20–21

Virginia Commonwealth University, 9

Virginia High Schools, 17

Virginia Military Institute, 8, 11

Virginia State University, 8

Virginia Tech: about, 8–9, 17; communications policies, 164; Convocation,

37–38, 161; culture of Hokie Nationhood, 18, 21–23, 59, 73, 76, 95, 160–68, 249; gun policy, 42; guns on campus, 11, 130; practices for dealing with violence, prejudice, or injustice, 20–21, 75; violence at, 3, 9, 167
Virginia Tech, post-shooting: advantage to external funding and research opportunities, 18–20; attempts at healing, 21–23, 167; counseling services, 4–5, 169–70, 176–80; e-mail communications, 2–7, 160–61, 164–67, 169–72; emotion, permission to express, 168–74; enrollment, 24; guidelines for faculty, 59, 164–74, 181–82; gun control debate, 42–48, 94–95; investigative commission, 25–26, 42, 144; ontological fiction imposed, 160–68, 181–82; security measures, 25–27; survey of emotional effects, 176–80; "We Will Prevail", 160–68
Virginia Tech Corps of Cadets, 11, 130
Virginia Tech dead: forgetting the, 241; memorials to, 20–22, 189–90; monies distributed to families of, 22; posthumous degrees awarded to, 12, 21; unmoved, cell phones ring, 6–7
Virginia Tech faculty: administrative guidelines post-shooting, 59, 164–74, 181–82; emotion, permission to express, 170–71; promotion and tenure process, 171–73; responses to Cho's mental health issues, 36, 74, 145, 245–46; responses to the media, 56–61; student teaching evaluations, 170–71; *See also* academia, university faculty
the Virginia Tech Family, myth of, 161, 165–68
Virginia Tech massacre: blame assigned to, 43–46; chronology, 2–7; Columbine school shootings compared, 10; in context of U.S. culture, 95–98; gun control debate and the, 42–48, 94–95; heroism, 44, 137, 141–42; media exploitation of, 214; social and political elements of, 41, 73, 97, 243–50; strategies of response, 16–27
Virginia Tech students: Asian, hate crimes experienced post-shooting, 14; attacked for not fighting back, 43–44; described, 181–82
virtue, personal, 90–92

Waco government siege, 37
West Ambler Johnston Residence Hall, 6, 33
Westfield High School, Chantilly, Virginia, 17
"We Will Prevail", 160–68
"What's the Matter with College" (Perlstein), 156
Whitaker, Ruth, 217
Whitman, Charles, 7, 121, 208
Williams, Brian, 39
Williams, Patricia, 100–101
Woo, John, 39
Woodford, Joseph, 85–86
Woodford, Mrs., 85–86
Wrong, Dennis, 115

Yates, Charlie L., 20
Young, Richard, 146
youth: anger of, 124, 130, 231; homicide statistics, 82; levels of self-esteem, 222; responsibility toward, 90–92; social network lifestyle, 42, 95, 193, 222; suicide in, 74, 82, 119, 133–36; *See also* students
youth, incarcerated: in context, 86–92; Jeff's story, 83–86; statistics, 82, 83, 87
youth culture, 46, 222, 232–33
YouTube, 25, 34, 42, 77, 222

Zahn, Paula, 35
Zapruder, 247
Zimmerman, Sacha, 43